Researching Education from the Inside

Investigations from within

Pat Sikes and Anthony Potts

Routledge
Taylor & Francis Group

LONDON AND NEW YORK

First published 2008
by Routledge
2 Park Square, Milton Park, Abingdon, Oxon OX14 4RN

Simultaneously published in the USA and Canada
by Taylor and Francis Inc
270 Madison Ave, New York, NY 10016

*Routledge is an imprint of the Taylor & Francis Group, an informa
business.*

Typeset in Times New Roman by Keyword Group
Printed and bound in Great Britain by Antony Rowe Ltd,
Chippenham, Wilthire.

British Library Cataloguing in Publication Data
A catalogue record for this book is available from the British Library

Library of Congress Cataloging in Publication Data

Researching education for the inside : investigations from within /
[edited by] Pat Sikes and Anthony Potts.
    p. cm.
 ISBN 978-0-415-43593-2 (hardback) — ISBN 978-0-415-43594-9 (pbk.)
 1. Action research in education. I. Sikes, Patricia J. II. Potts,
Anthony, 1952-
    LB1028.24.R474 2008
    370.7′2—dc22

                                                    2007030649

ISBN10: 0-415-43593-5 (hbk)
ISBN10: 0-415-43594-3 (pbk)
ISBN13: 978-0-415-435932 (hbk)
ISBN13: 978-0-415-435949 (pbk)

Contents

Contributors

Peter Dickson, Education Officer, Sheffield.

Pat Drake, University of Sussex.

Linda Heath, University of Brighton.

Rosalie Holian, Royal Melbourne Institute of Technology, Melbourne.

Andrew Loxley, School of Education, Trinity College, Dublin.

Gary McCulloch, Brian Simon Professor of the History of Education, London Institute of Education.

John Portelli, Headmaster of a Sixth Form College in Malta and part-time lecturer in the Faculty of Education at the University of Malta.

Anthony Potts, Liverpool Hope University, Liverpool.

Ann Sherman, School of Education, University of Calgary.

Aidan Seery, School of Education, Trinity College, Dublin.

Pat Sikes, School of Education, University of Sheffield.

Anne Smyth, Royal Melbourne Institute of Technology, Melbourne.

Mark Vicars, teacher and ESRC researcher, North East Lincolnshire.

Charles F. Webber, School of Education, University of Calgary.

Section 1

General issues

Chapter 1

Introduction
What are we talking about? And why?

Pat Sikes and Anthony Potts

This book is about research that can be described as 'research from the inside', as 'insider research' or as 'member research'. Whilst we are aware that each of these descriptors could mean different things to different people, we are going to resist the temptation to offer a definitive definition. This is not because we condone academic sloppiness or because we are lazy, but rather because we are uncomfortable about creating categories which can lead to what one of us has called Cinderella's slipper syndrome (Sikes, 2006, p. 46) which occurs when writers and researchers end up behaving like Cinderella's sisters and resort to remorselessly cutting, slicing and distorting what they have to say in order to make it fit. Consequently, in the chapters that make up the volume, you will find that contributors use whatever term seems most appropriate at any particular time. This, we feel, is an approach in keeping with our stance of acknowledging multiple perspectives and respecting the ways in which researchers chose to define and describe their own work.

The focus of the book is research projects that are undertaken by people who, before they begin to research, already have an attachment to, or involvement with, the institutions or social groups in, or on, which their investigations are based. They can, therefore, be considered to be 'insiders'. In some cases, their insider positioning (their 'insiderness') is primarily important because it gets them access to the particular people (e.g. school boys) and/or the phenomena that they want to investigate (e.g. research assessment exercises). At other times, however, aspects of their own 'insidership' will, in themselves, come under scrutiny, when, for instance, they are studying topics such as the experience of institutional inspection, the maintenance of status hierarchies, or what it is like to be a gay man studying gay men.

In recent years, research from the inside has become increasingly common, particularly in the UK, North America, Australia and New Zealand, where its growing popularity can be seen to be associated with rising participation in professional higher degree programmes. As part of these courses, students are often required to undertake a substantial piece of research and complete a thesis related to their professional interests and concerns. Doing this research in their own workplace is often the easiest, if not the only, practical option, given that most of these people are studying at the same time as being in a fulltime job, such as teaching in a school, college or university, or working in educational administration, social care, health sciences, business and law (Scott, Brown, Lunt and Thorne, 2004). These are all fields where relationships are central, both in terms of relationships with colleagues and with regard to the 'clients' these institutions serve. When a teacher or social worker or nurse also becomes a researcher, existing relationships are, inevitably, in some ways altered as new (research related) concerns and understandings are brought into the frame. Often, too, relationship changes come about as a consequence of the researcher obtaining new information about the people they work with. In some cases the change may have 'positive' consequences, in others, it won't, but, regardless of outcomes, the introduction of a researcher identity has, at least, a potential impact upon the status quo, which needs to be anticipated and planned for, insofar as that is possible.

But it is not just with regard to obtaining personal qualifications that research from the inside is being more widely used. Institutional self-evaluations and peer reviews, whereby insiders investigate their colleagues', clients' and stakeholders' perceptions and experiences, is becoming commonplace, and is even, in some instances, taking the place of scrutiny and assessment by independent inspectorates (for UK education based examples, see http://www.ofsted.gov.uk/schools/dataandinformationsystems.cfm; Blanchard, 2002; McBeath, 1999). This type of inspectorial, evaluatory research can have significant consequences for people's work loads, their conditions of service, their career development, promotion prospects, pay, and even for their continued employment. Inevitably, given this degree of import, relationships between those conducting the 'research' and those being investigated can be affected. The situation can be complicated when, in an attempt to kill two birds with one stone, senior staff who are also enrolled on higher degree programmes, decide to use the evaluations or reviews they are required to do as part of their job, as the focus for a study. Obviously, taking such a decision requires very careful thought.

And then there is practitioner action research (see Carr and Kemmis, 1986; Elliott, 1991; Somekh, 2005). This, it could be argued, has moved from being the interest of a relatively small and committed number of individuals, concerned primarily to develop their practice and improve the experiences of their clients, into the mainstream repertoire of strategies for continuing professional development. Action research unequivocally sets out to make a difference and to effect change, change that can have consequences beyond the immediate focus on and at which the research was directed. In some cases too, action research which aims towards social justice ends can challenge orthodoxies, established hierarchies and long-held privileges. Redistribution to achieve greater equity may not be welcomed by those who may have to relinquish something that they value and have come to see as theirs. For example, action research which seeks to change beliefs, attitudes and practices related to gender and sex differentiation may not be universally welcomed if it 'threatens' traditional patterns of behaviour and achievement (e.g. as it did when girls begin to 'outperform' the boys, as seems to have happened in the

UK and elsewhere following implementation of strategies to increase female participation). Similarly, action research projects which result in changes to working practices which have traditionally placed minimal demands on staff, may face resistance. People who lead such research can find that their relationships with colleagues alter, and not always to the good.

From the 1980s onwards, there has been an auto/biographical turn within the social sciences and this is also significant when it comes to considering growing interest in, and use of, insider approaches. Nowadays, researchers almost routinely include a declaration of their positionality in their research writings. This is because it is generally accepted that biographical experiences arising from individual and social characteristics have (more or less) influence on, and import for, the research interests people have, the methodologies they adopt, the methods they use, how they interpret and analyse their data, and the ways in which they re-present and disseminate their 'findings'. Taking this concern with personal involvement a step further, autoethnographers (see Bochner, 2000; Ellis and Bochner, 2000; Ellis, 2004; Jones, 2005; Journal of Contemporary Ethnography: Thematic Edition, 2006) research their own lived experiences, relating these to broader contexts and understandings in much the same way as life historians analyse life stories in the light of historical, sociological and/or psychological theories and perspectives. Autoethnographers can be seen to be taking an insider stance, both personally, in terms of their introspective investigation, and with regard to the institutions and groups they belong to and in which the experiences they are researching are situated (see, for instance, Sikes and Clark, 2004). Once again, the practical and pragmatic benefits that autoethnography offers to a busy person, working full time whilst studying can, at first sight, seem to be obvious. However, autoethnography, like any other type of research from the inside, can raise issues for relationships, can give rise to ethical dilemmas and, what is more, can provoke personal questioning and uncertainties which may be uncomfortable and difficult to deal with. It is far from an easy option (see Ellis, 2004).

As even our brief consideration has suggested, people have different and complex motivations for embarking on inside, insider research. There are those who do it primarily in order to gain a further and higher qualification, perhaps for career progression purposes. Others do it out of a concern to change, develop and improve practice; some may get involved to prove or disprove a point, and so on. Whatever the reason, researchers need to be aware of what they may be letting themselves and those they study, in for. They need to give thought to the possible consequences that may follow from such investigations because this is research which can give rise to specific methodological and ethical issues.

Highlighting and discussing some of these concerns is the intention of this book, which we decided to put together on the basis of our respective experiences (a) of undertaking research from the inside and (b) of many years of working with graduate students doing this type of investigation. We have personal, informed knowledge of the sorts of things that can happen and so have all of the other contributors. We have all been involved in some form of research from the inside and all of us have lived to tell the tale (albeit sometimes only just). We write, therefore, from the basis of 'real', grounded experience – warts and all!

Groundings

Insider research has, traditionally, been a term associated with anthropologists and sociologists adopting an ethnographic approach within a specific social setting: namely – and variously – 'the field'. Key differences between the work of these people and the sort of research we are considering in this book are:

- that anthropologists and ethnographers primarily go into the field in order to do their research, whereas our contributors and, we anticipate, many of our readers will usually already be established in the setting where they intend to conduct their investigations. The intention is, usually, that they will be staying there and will continue to do whatever it was that they were doing before they began the research. These people are, in many cases, researching professionals, as opposed to professional researchers (Wellington and Sikes, 2006, p. 725) or to use Gregory's (1997) slightly different notion, 'scholarly professionals' as opposed to 'professional scholars';
- the researchers we have in mind will come from a variety of backgrounds and disciplines and will use a range of methodologies and methods; they won't all be sociologists and nor will they all be doing ethnography. Some may, for instance, be using formally administered closed questionnaires and interviews, whilst others might be conducting controlled experiments which will be analysed and interpreted using statistical tests.

Having said this, and reiterating our earlier point, we do not intend to imply that we believe that there are clear boundaries to, or, indeed, specific categories or types of insider research from the inside. For example, some ethnographers and anthropologists were already in what became their field and 'opportunistically' (Reimer, 1977) took advantage of their position to undertake research. David Hayano (1982), who studied professional poker players whilst being one himself, is a case in point.

Research from the inside can often be seen to have its roots in the work of Robert Park and other faculty and students of the department of Sociology at the University of Chicago. These sociologists, and those who followed in their stead, believed that understanding required immersion in the field and data, which provided insight into how and why people did what they did in the ways that they did it. This belief, particularly when manifest in the researcher adopting the role of a participant observer, posed a fundamental challenge to dominant notions of the researcher as necessarily occupying an objective, distanced observer, 'God's eye' type of position. In addition and for various reasons, the Chicago School type research was often focused on the marginalised and disadvantaged, with the emphasis being on redressing imbalances. Howard Becker's (1967) question 'whose side are we on?', with the answer being 'the underdog's', reflects this perspective, as it also underlies the work of those who adopt critical theory and research approaches (see Kinchloe and McLaren, 2005, for an overview).

A criticism often levelled at inside and insider research concerns the extent to which it can be considered to be 'objective' and hence 'reliable' and 'valid' according to the so-called scientific criteria. A further associated complication arises from the implications and consequences of researchers 'going native', that is, of 'over-identification with the culture and group under observation, getting too close ... or staying too long' (Stein, 2006, p. 72). 'Going native' means researchers adopt the same perspectives as those they are studying. Sara Delamont asserts that 'going native' is an 'objectionable term' (2002, p. 37) and we agree with her, for the phrase carries connotations both of distasteful colonial attitudes and of researcher superiority. Ethnographers are often exhorted to 'make the familiar strange' and 'the strange familiar'. This is good advice when seeking to gain a view of a situation which includes a number of participants of whom each may have their own personal perspective on matters. It is also worth bearing in mind that, as Susan Matoba Adler suggests, all researchers who investigate social situations are ambivalently positioned, simply because they themselves are social beings. They (and we) are always 'insiders in some contexts and outsiders in other situations' (Adler, 2004, p. 107).

For the inside researcher who is also a 'proper' member of the setting they are investigating, the problems associated with criticisms around failure to maintain a distance in order to be able to take a clear and an unbiased non-partisan approach are significant and complicated. This is because adopting a distanced approach may, in some cases, be inimical to doing one's job in the way in which one has been hired to do it. People are expected to be loyal and committed to their employer and employing organisation and, whilst loyalty and commitment do not preclude taking an objective stance in order to develop and improve, detachment can be problematic in institutional terms. Without wishing to appear to be flippant, our view on objectivity is similar to that of Lawrence Stenhouse's when he wrote, 'whilst I acknowledge the need to take up the issue of objectivity in social research, it is not an issue I am well equipped to handle, partly because I personally have been untroubled by the problem' (in Rudduck and Hopkins, 1985, p. 14). Our take on what Stenhouse is saying here is that he doesn't waste time worrying about the issue when there is research to be done and situations to be improved.

Indeed, and in general, it is as a result of people like Stenhouse popularising and championing insider research, along with what some commentators have referred to as paradigm shifting (e.g. Kuhn, 1962), others (e.g. Flyvbjerg, 2001) have talked about in terms of fashion, and which Norman Denzin and Yvonna Lincoln (e.g. 2005) refer to as 'moments', that we are in a position to be discussing research of this type as legitimate and 'proper' research that can be submitted for higher degrees and published in peer reviewed academic journals. As our contributors' chapters show, research from the inside can be both scholarly and rigorous.

That it may not be the same as some other forms of social science work is, on one level, neither here nor there. As Bill Tierney put it, we should:

> refrain from the temptation of either placing our work in relation to traditions or offering a defensive response. I increase my capacity neither for understanding nor originality by a defensive posture. To seek new epistemological and methodological avenues demands that we chart new paths rather than constantly return to well-worn roads and point out that they will not take us where we want to go.
>
> (1998, p. 68)

Nevertheless, regardless of the paths they take and the approaches that inside researchers chose to use, their work should be, at all times and in all respects, ethical. We have already emphasised the centrality of relationships when it comes to inside research and the need to be acutely sensitive cannot be stressed too highly. In the past, researchers working in the social sciences have often been guilty of negatively 'othering' the people who came within the gaze of their research by seeing and treating them as different to themselves. Such a stance, even if sustainable within a context in which, heretofore, the researcher was himself a colleague, is ethically questionable and is likely to cause relationship problems. Maggie MacLure suggests that othering is 'the pervasive concern in contemporary research' (2003, p. 3). For inside researchers, there is no doubt that alertness to the risks of othering, and of in any way doing harm to anyone, including the researcher himself, should be pervasive and paramount. Doing as you would be done by is a useful check here.

Organisation of the book

In seeking contributors, our primary concern was to find people who knew what they were talking about because they had personal experience of doing research from the inside. We wanted to represent work from a range of countries in order to demonstrate the universality of the issues and we were also particularly concerned that our writers should hold ethical considerations in as high regard as we ourselves do. Having been fortunate enough to locate researchers with the sorts of stories we wanted to tell, we offered them a framework consisting of five distinct stages that can lead to ethical dilemmas. These were:

> Entering the field – or starting out on the research,
> Being in the field – or doing the research,
> Leaving the field – or concluding the research,
> Writing,
> Disseminating the results.

However, these stages were not relevant for all of the writers so not every chapter follows the format.

We have chosen to group the chapters into sections. Thus chapters in Section 2, headed *Philosophical and theoretical issues*, deal with, not suprisingly, philosophical and theoretical issues, those in Section 3, *Insider research in action*, deal with insider research in schools, colleges and universities; and Section 4 contains one short chapter offering some concluding remarks.

In Section 2, Andrew Loxley and Aidan Seery examine philosophical issues associated with researching education from the inside. Their chapter argues that insider research is supposedly undertaken by members of the same group and/or the same institution. In contrast, the outsider researcher is undertaken by someone who is not a member of that group or institution. However, this simple definition obscures a plethora of tensions – philosophical, political and methodological – some of which are rehearsed here.

Drawing on their experience as inside researchers and supervisors of students undertaking insider projects, Anne Smyth and Rosalie Holian consider the sorts of issues that can result from dual role positioning as a researcher and as a worker. In particular, they look at the credibility issues which can arise at various points in the research process.

Section 3 commences with Gary McCulloch considering insider historical research that focuses on the researcher's own school, university, college or other institution. Such research tends to be of two types: that which seeks to be independent of the institution and that which is commissioned for anniversary and other celebratory purposes and which is often laudatory. The chapter examines the issues, problems and possibilities of both kinds of work.

Charles Webber and Anne Sherman examine researching school headship from the inside. They note that, while educational leadership programmes vary across the world, they are usually culturally or organizationally specific. In such programmes, potential and current principals undertake work designed to develop knowledge and skills necessary to function in a local context. Webber and Sherman examine the tensions and benefits that occur when studying how insiders from one context interact professionally with an insider group from another context.

John Portelli's chapter discusses his work, which looked at male students' understandings of masculinity and sexuality in a Maltese secondary school. John examines the issues of sexism, violence and unacceptable pedagogical practices that confronted him as both a researcher and a senior teacher at the school.

Mark Vicars considers his experiences of being a gay man doing research with gay men who were also his friends. He explores the various identities he occupied when engaged in his research and reflects on the implications it had for his PhD thesis.

Peter Dickinson tells the story of the conduct and aftermath of a problematic and contested Ofsted inspection of an Local Education Authority (LEA). As a senior LEA officer, Dickinson was very much an insider and, even though he was aware of the potential difficulties that could arise, he was not prepared for the ethical and other dilemmas he faced when conducting research into the inspection for his doctorate.

Pat Drake and Linda Heath draw on their research with students on professional doctorate courses to discuss the interpersonal tensions that can arise when casting a critical research gaze on one's colleagues.

Pat Sikes' chapter reflects on her experiences of an autoethnographic study of a critical action research strategy designed to contribute to the development of a research culture in a 'new' university. She considers what it is to be an insider/outsider at the same time as being an outsider/insider.

Anthony Potts takes a long-term view and reports on insider research in the same institution 21 years on. Seeking to study academics in the same institution, he confronted changed institutional and research climates and a heightened awareness of ethical issues, not to mention a much greater reluctance from his colleagues to participate in the research.

In a final brief section, the editors offer some closing thoughts.

References

Adler, S. M. (2004) 'Multiple Layers of a Researcher's Identity: Uncovering Asian American Voices', in Mutua, K. and Swadener, B. B. (eds), *Decolonizing Research in Cross-Cultural Contexts: Critical Personal Narratives*. New York, State of New York University Press, pp. 107–121.

Becker, H. (1967) 'Whose Side Are We On?' *Social Problems* 14, pp. 239–247.

Blanchard, J. (2002) *Teaching and Targets: Self Evaluation and School Improvement*. London, Routledge Falmer.

Bochner, A. (2000) Criteria Against Ourselves. *Qualitative Inquiry* 6, 2, pp. 266–272.

Carr, W. and Kemmis, S. (1986) *Becoming Critical: Education, Knowledge and Action Research*. Lewes, Falmer.

Delamont, S. (2002) *Fieldwork in Educational Settings: Pitfalls and Perspectives*, 2nd ed. London, Routledge Falmer.

Denzin, N. and Lincoln, Y. (2005) 'Introduction: The Discipline and Practice of Qualitative Research', in Denzin, N. and Lincoln, Y. (eds), *The Handbook of Qualitative Research*, 3rd ed. Thousand Oaks, Sage, pp. 1–32.

Elliott, J. (1991) *Action Research for Educational Change*. Buckingham, Open University Press.

Ellis, C. and Bochner, A. (2000) 'Autoethnography, Personal Narrative, Reflexivity', in Denzin, N. and Lincoln, Y. (eds), *The Handbook of Qualitative Research*, 2nd ed. Thousand Oaks, Sage, pp. 733–768.

Ellis, C. (2004) *The Ethnographic I: A Methodological Novel About Autoethnography* Walnut Creek, AltaMira.

Flyvbjerg, B. (2001) *Making Social Science Matter*. Cambridge, University of Cambridge Press.

Gregory, M. (1997) Professional scholars and scholarly professionals. *The New Academic*, pp. 19–22.

Hayano, D. (1982) *Poker Faces*. Berkeley, University of California Press.

Jones, S. (2005) 'Autoethnography: Making the Personal Political', in Denzin, N. and Lincoln, Y. (eds), *The Handbook of Qualitative Research*, 3rd ed. Thousand Oaks, Sage, pp. 763–792.

Journal of Contemporary Ethnography: Thematic Edition. 2006 *Defective Memory and Analytical Autoethnography*, 35, 4.

Kinchloe, J. and McLaren, P. (2005) 'Rethinking Critical Theory and Qualitative Research', in Denzin, N. and Lincoln, Y. (eds), *The Handbook of Qualitative Research*, 3rd ed. Thousand Oaks, Sage, pp. 303–342.

Kuhn, T. (1962) *The Structure of Scientific Revolutions*. Chicago, University of Chicago Press.

McBeath, J. (1999) *Schools Must Speak For Themselves: Arguments for School Self-Evaluation*. London, Routledge Falmer.

MacLure, M. (2003) *Discourse in Educational and Social Research*. Buckingham, Open University.

Reimer, J. (1977) 'Varieties of Opportunistic Research', *Urban Life* 5, pp. 467–477.

Rudduck, J. and Hopkins, D. (1985) *Research as a Basis for Teaching: Readings from work of Lawrence Stenhouse*. London, Heinemann.

Scott, D., Brown, A., Lunt, I. and Thorne, L. (2004) *Professional Doctorates: Integrating Professional and Academic Knowledge*. Maidenhead, SRHE/Open University Press.

Sikes, P. (2006) 'Towards Useful and Dangerous Theories'. *Discourse* 27, 1, pp. 43–51.

Sikes, P. and Clark, J. (2004) 'Nobody told me there were schools quite like this': Issues of Power, Discourse and Resistance in Writing About a School for Emotionally and Behaviourally Disturbed (EBD) Children, in Satterthwaite, J., Atkinson, E. & Martin, W. (eds), *The Disciplining of Education: New Languages of Power and Resistance*. Stoke on Trent, Trentham, pp. 89–102.

Somekh, B. (2005) *Action Research: A Method for Change and Development*. Maidenhead, Open University Press.

Stein, M. (2006) 'Your place or mine: the geography of social science', in Hobbs, D. and Wright, R. (eds), *The Sage Handbook of Fieldwork*. London, Sage, pp. 59–75.

Tierney, W. (1998) 'Life History's History: Subjects Foretold'. *Qualitative Inquiry* 4, 1, pp. 49–70.

Wellington, J. and Sikes, P. (2006) 'A Doctorate In A Tight Compartment: Why Students Choose to Do A Professional Doctorate and Its Impact on Their Personal & Professional Lives'. *Studies in Higher Education* 31, 6, 723–734.

Section 2

Philosophical and theoretical issues

Chapter 2

Some philosophical and other related issues of insider research

Andrew Loxley and Aidan Seery

Introduction

It would be safe to assume that most forms of social science and educational research are an intervention into the lifeworlds of other people and their communities. It would also be safe to further assume that research is a mode of cultural practice predicated on the adoption of certain roles and positions by the researcher vis-a-vis those people or phenomena which 'fall' within the ambit of what is to be explored. It can be argued that, traditionally, this demarcation has been built around what Giddens (1991) refers to as an expert system that not only possesses (and professes to have) a range of technical competences to undertake research, but also, more importantly, has a monopoly over the production and, to some degree, circulation and consumption of that knowledge. Issues around the subtle and not so subtle manipulation of the research process by funders or sponsors notwithstanding, this control over the political economy of knowledge sets the 'insider–outsider' distinction as one about a contest over the production and organisation of meaning. And, more significantly, the capacity to define what counts as legitimate and illegitimate forms of knowledge.

Central to this view is the notion that it is not so much the veracity of the 'truth claims' which are important, but who is making them and their ability to legitimise this privileged position. To a large extent, this line of reasoning is now part of our received wisdom in social science and educational research. The more traditional forms of sociology of knowledge (e.g. Manheim, 1997) and, more recently, the cacophony of poststructuralist and postmodernist deconstructions of the past 30 years, in conjunction with 40 years of various feminist critiques of, for want of a better phrase, 'normal' social science, have thrown up numerous challenges to the orthodox institutionalised forms of going about research. The corollary of all this is that we are confronted with a blurring of multiple boundaries which coalesce uneasily around issues such as power, epistemology, axiology and ontology. This emergent 'fuzziness' also brings into the debate questions around the purpose of social and educational research in terms of both process and product, as well as how that *process* is undertaken and the ends to which *products* are put. These are 'big' issues and at best our purpose in this chapter is to try and unpack some of these debates, whilst trying to set them in the context of the shifting rhythms of insider and outsider research. We have, for the sake of simplicity, split the chapter into two parts. The first part will explore some of the issues around 'outsider' research and the second part, predictably enough, the 'insider' dimension.

From the outside: or everything about us without us?

A slight problem with conceptual demarcation and questions of 'in-ness' and 'out-ness', values and objectivity

It would be reasonable to state that you cannot have an 'inside' without a corresponding 'outside'. This simple binary (post-structuralism and theoretical physics notwithstanding), has for generations of orthodox researchers helped them to quite literally 'know their place' in the social science scheme of things as it functioned as a line of demarcation which you did not cross.[1] The preservation of good methodological hygiene (i.e. the avoidance of data and analytical contamination and reactivity in the 'field'), which stems from this dictum, is further underpinned by that other old rallying cry of 'value freedom'. In traditional social science folklore, insider research is undertaken by members of the same group, who supposedly share one or a number of characteristics (cultural, biological, linguistic, political, occupational and so on). In contrast, outsider research is undertaken by someone who is not a member of that group and *de facto* is in 'possession' of a different set of characteristics. From this observation it is palpable that what or *who* counts as an insider or outsider can be seen as a simple matter of sociological bookkeeping. Social and psychological taxonomies are called into action and used as points of reference so as to determine who can be admitted into what group and, more importantly, be legitimately called an 'insider'. This notion of 'identity' or, more significantly, the cultural politics of identity, is critical and we will return to it later on in this chapter, as it is so embedded in contemporary forms of research. But, first, it is useful to briefly examine the genealogy of the 'researcher'.

Although making generalisations can be dangerous as well as disingenuous, there was a time, perhaps just before the 1970s, when there prevailed a fairly orthodox, almost hegemonic, view in the world of social sciences that there was a group of individuals, which we collectively refer to as the researchers, and then there was everyone else, or not-researchers. Within their institutionalised discursive formations, as Foucault described them, they would be socialised into adopting a distinctive position vis-à-vis their work as social scientists and the 'outside world'. Two random(ish) examples of this habitus at work from 1968 will suffice:

> In every generation of students raised in the Western tradition of rationality they optimistically call for the application of science to social problems …

[however] as a citizen the social scientist can fight wholeheartedly for the causes which he [sic] values, but he should not imply his position follows logically from his scientific work. As a scientist he may find the greatest utility of his work lies in his contribution to the richness of man's intellectual and cultural heritage, rather than the direct application of scientific knowledge to social problems.

(Waitzkin, 1968, p. 419)

I don't know much about what goes on in laboratories but in anthropological fieldwork detachment is neither a natural gift or a manufactured talent. It is a partial achievement laboriously earned and precariously maintained. What little disinterestedness one manages to attain comes not from failing to have emotions or neglecting to perceive them in others not yet sealing oneself into a moral vacuum. It comes from a personal subject to a vocational ethic ... to combine two fundamental orientations to reality the engaged and the analytic into a single attitude.

(Geertz, 1968, p. 156)

As part of this scientific habitus, Waitzkin and his fellow social scientists grapple with what he calls the necessity to make clear distinctions between 'positive statements' and 'normative statements' about the world. The former refers to the kind of statements or empirically verifiable propositions which social scientists produce as the outcome of their research. The latter are a different magnitude of 'talk', as normative statements go beyond cataloguing or explaining the world as 'it is', and proscribe 'how it should be'. It is from this edict that the division between the world of the researcher and her/his object of study is drawn. But this is much more than the setting of discursive boundaries around who can say what it is meant to be emblematic of a whole *dispotif*.[2] Although the above quotations provide convenient straw donkeys to knock over, it should be noted that the view from 1968 is not merely some historical curiosity, which in all our postmodern 'sophistication' we can smile at, but is a reminder that there is by no means an unequivocal consensus within research communities as to what the role of the researcher should be. For example (and we could draw on many others), Hammersley (2004) would see the role as being similar to that of Waitzkin or Geertz. You do not exist in a state of political naivety, but these values need to be held in check, otherwise they will dirty your research. There is no denial of values, as they guide what you do as a researcher (choice of topic, methods and so on)[3], but they do not pre-empt what you may find. In the social sciences there are a number of theories which can be defined as being teleological (i.e. specify an end-state), which can also be seen as normative. This can take a moral and political dimension, especially when the theory is concerned with explaining the structure and mechanisms around social oppression. Marxism is a good example, as the end point is the dismantling of (oppressive) capitalist forms of social organisation and its replacement with a (non-oppressive) communist system. However, theories, no matter how moral or well meaning, should not become personal crusades, but remain theories and open to modification or negation. This Popperian stance of either 'fix it or ditch it' (which of course is contingent upon empirical robustness) towards your favourite theoretical model is critical. The epithet of 'my theoretical position right or wrong' is not just an expression of rigid absolutism or even martyrdom, but a marker of risible social science. For example Hammersley and Gomm (1997), in their discussion of what they term 'positional research', are particularly critical of feminist modes of research for this entrenched stance.

Waitzkin is also arguing that the work of the social scientist is one requiring separation from the mundane day-to-day concerns of the world, although ironically it is these problems which become the focus of their work. This self-imposed state of moral and political exile from the profane, along with the quest for the positivist nirvana of value-freedom is paradoxically (or ironically?) seen as the social scientist's *moral* imperative. Only when we stop being a sociologist at the end of the working day can we engage in making the world a better (or worse) place as the non-researcher. Here we are confronted by a marker of 'insiderness' and 'outsiderness' across two dimensions: (1) institutional and (2) technical expertise. Our location in the 'academy' and the rights and responsibilities which stem from that, coupled with our knowledge of how to do research, does, whether we like it or not, place us in a powerful position vis-à-vis most of those social groups who form the focus of our work. Our potential to align ourselves in the course of our work with one group or another (and hide or not behind some presumed veil of neutrality) is something that needs to be guarded against. Hence, the reader's trustworthiness and credibility in the research which is undertaken, and the outcomes generated, is seen as a function of explicit 'outsiderness'.

Conversely, there is the genre of work typified by such writers as Henry Giroux (e.g. 1983, 1992), which shows commitment to some form of praxis.[4] The disinterested social scientist as the exotic tourist is expunged from Giroux's research world. Instead it is characterised by a form of co-habitation between researcher and research participants, joined together by a unity of purpose and action; the researcher is still an expert, but one who does not position him or herself as an authority over their participants. However, this notion of the researcher and educator joined together as proto-revolutionaries, building barricades out of school desks and plasticine and ushering in a new epoch of social justice, is easy to parody. But, in this critical theoretic take on research, the role of the researcher transcends that of someone who just makes descriptive and even normative – if they're feeling political – statements about the social world, but is an active participant in generating change, whatever that may be. For researchers to talk about the 'outside' is meaningless, as academic and participant, by virtue of their shared *value orientation*, are both insiders. So as the parody runs, regardless of whether one is a white middle-class, middle-aged, well-paid, tenured, male/female academic living in the suburbs, and the other a disenfranchised, unemployed, young male/female, working-class, person of colour living in relative abject poverty, what unites them is their common goal of the pursuit of social justice.

However, lurking beneath this distinction between value-free and value-orientated research is a more messy set of questions around the epistemological and theoretical principles and claims, which partially structure and temper these *weltanschauungen*.

And now for some philosophy: part I

The insider/outsider debate is, in philosophical terms, part of a much wider discussion rooted in the theory of knowledge about the nature of theory. As conceived, first of all by those clever Greeks,[5] theory is aimed at some kind of objective, deep description of things in the real world. Knowledge (*episteme*), the stuff of research and dissertations, was regarded as essentially different to opinion (*doxa*). The latter was a mere taking-for-granted of things as seen and heard, while the former had to do with rational accountability and justification and/or evidential warrantability. However, as clear as this differentiation might seem to be on the surface, it has given rise to centuries of complex and heated debate. Evidential warrant, for instance, in one interpretation, has been regarded as being based in empirical evidence, i.e. data which has come to us via our senses: taste, touch, smell, vision. This in turn has been understood as describing 'something' that is present in the real world which is independent of anyone's recognition of it. So there are states of affairs in the world that are not dependent on my knowing them (the ontology question), but nevertheless reveal themselves to me in inquiry and knowledge (the epistemology question). Thus, there are things out in the world such as 'dogs' (furry animals that bark), which exist whether or not I perceive them via my sensory faculties. These two elements (realist ontology and epistemology) constitute the basis of a naïve realism and the beginning of a further analysis of how exactly the world reveals itself in knowledge. John Locke (Locke, 1997), for instance, believed that the connection between knowledge and the world went through mental impressions in the mind that were structurally the same as the structure of the thing in the world under investigation. If I see a Dublin bus, a copy of the structure and shape of the bus (big, blue and yellow and covered in dirt and colourful metaphors) is copied to a mental image in my mind. Hence, there is a direct connection between knowledge and the world guaranteeing objectivity and truth. Significantly, from methodological considerations, what we know about the world is independent of any particular conceptual approach or theory.

Not unsurprisingly, the Lockean view has not survived very well. Kant argues against Locke that the mind is not just receptive of the outside world, but that the mental impressions are a result of conceptual processing. But, the Lockean view can still be seen as a first model of how objective outsider investigation works. A more sophisticated model of the connection between the mind and the world that holds to these two fundamental premises of realism is at the heart of both scientific realism and the ontology and epistemology of 'outsider' research. The idea that science, including the social sciences, was in a position to produce knowledge that was both theory-independent and thus researcher-independent, formed one of the core understandings of the discipline for much of its history.

This strong realism, with its robust notion of objectivity and theory-independence, has come under considerable attack from a number of quite distinct quarters. From within philosophy the assault begins, perhaps with Nietzsche, who, in a famous passage in *The Will to Power*, proclaimed: 'No, facts is what there is not, only interpretations. We cannot establish any fact "in itself"' (Nietzsche, 1968). This declaration is an epistemological claim about what we can know, but later in the same passage Nietzsche points to a (deeper?) ontological problem. Against the conclusion that then everything is relative, a matter or opinion and subjective, he states: '"Everything is subjective" you say, but even this is interpretation. The subject is not something given, it is something added and invented and projected behind what there is' (ibid. p. 481). Nietzsche foresees here one of the great debates of contemporary philosophy on the nature of subjectivity and the eroding of the clear distinction between subjectivity and objectivity.

Objections to a strongly realist view of science come also from inside the philosophy of science. Beginning with the work of Popper (Popper, 1959) and through the work of Thomas Kuhn (Kuhn, 1962) and beyond to the cultural relativism of Paul Feyerabend (1975), the claim that science describes a mind and theory-independent reality has been dismantled and few now hold that what science produces is neutral, value-free truth. Though the emergence of critical realism in the 1970s and 1980s in the work of Bhaskar (1975, 1979) and Harre (1986) and given more recent expression in, for example, the work of Pawson and Tilly (1997) and Sayer (2000) can be seen as an attempt to square the objectivist circle. That is, there is (1) a reality which exists independently from our consciousness of it and (2) our ever changing scientific (natural or social) theories of it are constructs we use to try and make sense of reality. What this implies is that we can never know this reality directly, and all we can ever hope for is to get more proficient at being able to describe what we think it 'looks like'. Here we can have our realist cake and relativistically eat it as well.

Objectivist theories in science have also come under attack from other quarters, cultural and political. Ernst Cassirer, in his work *The Philosophy of Symbolic Forms* (1923/1953), takes Kant and modernist philosophy to task for a view of reality that was constructed from scientific facts as building blocks and a narrow notion of scientific rationality as mortar. He argues that 'not only science, but language, myth, art and religion as well provide the building stones from which the world of "reality" is constructed for us'. The emergence and growth of the science of anthropology in the last century also provides a critique of the superiority of western positivist science as a model, not only for other sciences, but also for all of knowledge. The discovery and growing appreciation that there were other ways of both seeing and acting in the world provided previously unknown alternatives to living. Finally, and perhaps, the most critical event for modern, positivist science, is the nightmare of two world wars and the Holocaust of the last century. Under the irrationality and brutality of these events, the 'project of modernism'

(Habermas, 1987) collapses almost completely. Western rational thought and its science are seen by some to be not only the victims of these events but also responsible in some way. The search for new forms of knowledge begins in earnest.

This sense of epistemological and ontological discomfort with what was once seen as the guiding axiom of social science research, i.e. value freedom and realism, began to make significant inroads into the various social science disciplines from the 1970s onwards. For instance, George Marcus (1997) refers to the emergence of an awareness of the politics of fieldwork in anthropology in the 1980s and 1990s which has generated a sustained and growing critique of the political context, in which fieldwork was undertaken and the cultural presuppositions of the researcher. Though, generally speaking, anthropologists since the 1950s had always been more than a little sensitive to and uncomfortable with their discipline's role in colonial and neo-colonial escapades from the mid-nineteenth century onwards (see for example Clifford and Marcus, 1986). But, nonetheless, here was a reflexive engagement with how anthropological knowledge is produced[6] and once the mantle of the authority of the researcher is brought into question, it logically follows then that so too is the nature of the claims that is being made. As the metaphorical space left by the quickly retreating realists and their once dominant discursive regime (Lyotard, 1984) begins to be occupied by the relativists, then this opens up all sorts of new possibilities; in particular, this provides space for insiders to legitimately set out their epistemological and ontological stalls.

The reflective and reflexive accounts by researchers engaged in ethnographic approaches to research provide us with a fascinating insight into the strange choreography of being enmeshed in different cultures. The problematising of the researcher's 'self' and the way in which we define and construct the 'otherness' of those who participate in our work, generate a more fluid and less stable relationship. But this abandonment of older divisions between 'in' and 'out' is not something that is accepted lightly. For example, Brayboy and Dehyle (2000), in their discussion of undertaking ethnographic forms of educational research with Native Americans as members from that community, argue that they continually struggled with the conflict between being a 'good ethnographer' and 'being a good Indian'. They describe a process in which the usual methods of ethnographic data collection (formal and informal interviews, participant observation and so on) can be seen as disrespectful, hostile or just plain stupid to the community. In their discussion around conducting interviews they remark that:

> To ask questions is to be nosey, which means the individual asking questions is either 'shut out' from all further conversations or are given false or misleading information to keep them at bay … both of us [Brayboy and Dehyle] tried to keep out mouths shut and listen deeply. And both of us struggled to adapt 'traditional' methods to be less culturally offensive.
>
> (Brayboy and Dehyle, 2000, p. 176)

In short, Brayboy and Dehyle are making a case that in order to generate trust-worthy knowledge of a cultural group, it is both necessary and sufficient that the producers of such accounts are also members of that community. In addressing the same issue some 28 years before Brayboy and Dehyle, the sociologist Robert Merton (1972) is uncertain as to the methodological strength of such positions. He divides the 'insider doctrine' (as he calls it) into two groups: the 'strong' and 'weak'. In the case of the former he suggests that certain groups have 'monopo-listic access to knowledge', whereas, with the latter, there are some groups which have privileged access, but this too can be attained by other groups (sociolo-gists?), albeit with some difficulty. In either scenario Merton is uncomfortable with such propositions, as it implies that knowledge stems from and only from ascribed status. As the old cliché runs, only old people study old people, corrupt politicians study corrupt politicians, and one-eyed three-headed green gooey slimy monopeds can study one-eyed three-headed green gooey monopeds; the list is potentially infinite. As Merton points out:

> In all these applications the doctrine of Extreme insiderism represents a new creditionalism … in which understanding becomes accessible to only a for-tunate few or to many who are to the manner born … it moves to a doctrine of *group* methodological solipsism [where] in the end each group must have a monopoly of knowledge about itself.
>
> (Merton, 1972, p. 14).

Thus, any account of a group being studied (e.g. bald white middle-aged pipe smoking university professors), produced by either the insider or the outsider, will be different, as their frames of reference, as well as understandings, originate from dissimilar positions. As with the Brayboy and Deyhle (2000) example, this lack of 'sharedness' becomes a barrier to any genuine understanding. But, as Merton goes on to argue, this ethnocentrism is not just a game of attempting to control the public interpretation of a group's identity, but also needs to be seen in the con-text of the structural (historical, political, economic) location of different groups; which brings us back to the issue of power. The emergence of the civil rights movement in the US during the late 1950s and through the 1960s, provided a cat-alyst to challenge the hegemonic bases of power (political, economic, cultural, military, legal, etc.) for groups other than black people. As such, social groups mobilise themselves in opposition to these sources of power as a way of asserting their own right to exist equitably alongside others (Thomas and Loxley, 2007). The slogan 'nothing about us without us' is commonly used as a rejoinder to forms of research which treat the participants as objects in the same vein as bacteria in a Petri dish, or patronisingly purport to 'speak for' them. The emergence of col-laborative forms of research, which attempts to break down the barriers between researchers and participants, could be seen as trying to find a 'negotiated' solu-tion between the extreme outsiders as well as insiders (see McGettrick, 1994 as an interesting example of this approach) which we discuss below. Richardson and

Le Grand (2002) provide an example of researchers engaged in a reflexive discussion with a group of people over their (Richardson and Le Grand's) conceptual schema around social exclusion. The group was drawn from communities which fell into the category of being 'disadvantaged' and they found some critical differences between the academics' view and understanding of social inclusion and their 'participants'. The outcome of this was that they argued that academics should be more sensitive to contextually mediated interpretations of their concepts and ideas about the world. This may seem like a fairly trivial assertion, but for ortho-dox researchers working in the area of social policy, it represents a significant admission that they might not always be right.

In shifting the terrain slightly into the area of *what* is said, the pioneering anthropologist Franz Boas (1943) argued that 'if it is our serious purpose to understand the thoughts of other people then the whole analysis of experience must be based on their concepts not ours' (cited in Feleppa, 1986). This move towards more phenomenological modes of inquiry, by privileging the 'emic', does, if not completely displace the outside researcher, at least begins to place limits on an overly hierarchical order of interpretations and starts to reference the legitimacy of the community's cultural resources rather than the university trained researchers' expert rendition. However, merely allowing one's participants to speak with their own 'voice' does not deal adequately with the process of gener-ating accounts which end up in the public domain (e.g. journal articles, confer-ence presentations, etc.). As Harris (1976) argues in the case of the emic, the 'ethnographer discovers principles that represent and account for the way in which a [knowledge] domain is organised or structured in the mental life of the informant'. Whereas, for the etic, it is the 'discovery of the principles that exist outside of the minds of the actors' (p. 331). But, as Felappa points out, we are still confronted with the problem of translation in the development of the emic. For anthropologists this is a major concern, particularly so if the medium through which representation occurs is not the indigenous language of their participants. Thus we are still left with a double-hermeneutic – an interpretation of an inter-pretation – which implies that where an outsider is involved, there will never be any uncontaminated communication, even if the intention is to try and be as authentic as possible. But, this is a problem which plagues all forms of outsider researcher and not just the anthropologists.

From the inside: or nothing about us without us?

Tripe and politics: action research and the revolt against revolting expert systems

By far the most obvious and well-known example of insider research is the action or practitioner variety. But (and it's an important 'but') it would be somewhat of a misnomer to categorise all forms of action research as being undertaken by 'insiders'. As Reason and Bradbury (2001) argue, the archetypal (or even stereotypical) image of the lone practitioner engaged in some sort of research endeavour aimed at 'improving' some dimension of their professional life is but one of three possible models.[7] Since its early beginnings as a form of quasi-experimental design to explore the dynamics of changing patterns of meat consumption during World War 2 (Lewin, 1948), Hammersley (2004) has argued that the scope (theoretically and methodologically) and substantive focus of what constitutes action research has grown to become very broad.[8] However, what seems to unify this disparate collection of ideas and communities is the explicit axiom of generating some kind of change through some form of intervention in the world. Like Giroux's metaphorical raising of the barricades, the various flavours of action research take as their starting point the old Marxist adage that the purpose of philosophy is not simply to describe the world, but to change it. In his critique of action research Hammersley (2004) identifies three main modern (i.e. 1980s onwards) clusters: (1) instrumentalism, focusing on the resolution of practical classroom problems; (2) social change, with the emphasis on political engagement in issues around social justice and inequality; (3) personal professional development. But whatever particular orientation it has, action research as both a methodological and political (with a big or small 'p') endeavour is a direct challenge to more orthodox modes of inquiry.

The emergence of practitioner research (albeit on a small scale) in the late 1960s in the UK, symbolised for John Elliot (1991) the beginning of a radical break with the hegemony of university research. Explicit within the creation myth of action research are two currents. The first is seen as a way of dealing with what was seen to be an asymmetrical relationship between the university research community (which existed both physically, culturally and politically outside of the school) and the school itself. The second current is more of a focus upon the content of the research agenda. But, nonetheless, central to both is the locus of power and control over not only *who* can 'do' research but also *what* counts as research. As Elliot (1991) argues in relation to the process of curriculum development through what he characterises as reflective practice:

> Teaching and research become posited as two separate activities ... whereas from the standpoint of the practitioner, reflection and action are two aspects of a single process ... the academic is in danger of interpreting methodology [teaching and learning] as a set of mechanical procedures and standardized techniques rather than a cluster of dynamic ideas. The separation of 'research' and 'teaching' implies a separation between teaching and curriculum development.
>
> (Elliot, 1991, p. 14)

However, for Elliot the liberation of practitioners from the oppressive yoke of the academics was short-lived. Once the idea of 'reflective practice' had crossed the boundaries from vivacious staff room dialogue and innovative classroom practice, and into the university as a form of institutionalised discourse, the line of demarcation had become somewhat blurred.[9] For Elliot, this was not seen as the academy and school joining together to construct a new mode of engagement around research and teaching or theory and practice, but outright 'academic imperialism'. The colonisation and commodification of action research by the university and the re-selling of it back to practitioners (mostly by ex-practitioners), in the form of accredited programmes, have sanitised, routinised and homogenised its critical orientation. In short, it allows the university to assert control over the production and consumption of knowledge through steering at a distance. As such, concepts like 'democracy', 'collaboration' and 'criticality' become part of a set of competencies to be demonstrated and 'ticked off', rather than struggled for and debated over in the localised context of the school. This is a debate which Elliot (2001) takes up with David Hargreaves (1997, 1999) over the contested terrain of evidence-based practice and the proffering of outcomes based on research undertaken in different contexts and by the so-called experts and used as models of 'good' or 'best' practice elsewhere. However, as Oakley (2001) has pointedly remarked, for all Elliot's (2001) posturing around professional autonomy in the realms of undertaking and applying research, he runs the risk of merely replacing one expert system (academics) with another which is based on the privileging of teacher knowledge over that of any other group such as 'parents or students'. From Oakley's position Elliot is tied to a view of schooling in which the insiders (teachers) are able to exert their own power over other insiders (parents, students, cleaners, support staff) in determining who can play the research game. This is probably a little harsh, as not all action researchers would either recognise or see themselves as some form of Praetorian Guard of the teaching profession.

Allied to the problem of methodological *anschluss* is that of the theory-practice debate, which again floats around the epicentre of old chestnuts such as 'whose theory are we talking about' and 'what is theory for anyway?' Again, the owner-ship and, for some writers such as Whitehead (1989, 1998) and Whitehead and McNiff (2006), the origin of theory is seen as being critical. Theory which is constructed dialogically and within a localised context, is more appropriate than that which is built far far away and a long time ago in a distant university. Whitehead (1998) talks about what he calls 'living educational theory', which is in its simplest form a variant of dialectical thinking; though in this context there is a strong current of praxis within it. For Whitehead the starting point is with the 'I' acting in the world:

> The creation of living theories begins in practice. The creation begins in the kind of enquiries which I think you will have engaged in of the kind, 'How do I do this better?', or 'How can I help you to improve your learning?', or 'How can I live my values more fully in what I am doing?'
>
> (Whitehead, 1998, p. 2)

Here the position of the insider is not so much of ethnocentrism, but egocentrism. But, for Whitehead, this is not an egocentrism wrapped in the comfort blanket of solipsism, but an emergent reflexivity which demands that the practitioner-researcher confronts and questions their own value system. Living educational theory is not intended to be an exercise in instrumental logic (i.e. just fixing a problem such as poor classroom management), but the 'end product' of a practitioner trying to deal with the contradictions between their values and their practice. For example a teacher may fully *believe* in participatory classroom democracy, but unfortunately *behaves* in a fascistic manner. As poetically expressed by Whitehead (1998): 'In my educational enquiry, "How do I improve what I am doing?", I exist as a value-laden centre of consciousness where my "I" has no experiential beginning and no end for me'. But this 'I' is not socially disconnected, as, like for Elliot (1992) or Kemmis and Wilkinson (1986), action research is not the sole preserve of heroic individualism, but needs to be set within that great euphemism of a critical 'community of practice', whose role is to support, critique and legitimise the emerging living theory.

In shifting the debate away from issues of ownership and control, Hammersley (2004) offers a more fundamental (but not unique) critique, which centres on the apparent contradiction between *action* and *research*. Although, as Hammersley recognises, the intention of action research is to enlist the use of research to transform practice, it falls short of this promise as it is unable to 'transcend the difference between … the component parts'. The crux of his argument rests on the proposition that research and action are two very different forms of social behaviour, which articulate different foci, processes and goals. They may overlap at certain points, but do not form a neat and tidy alliance of equal partners. Put simply, research, in Hammersley's scheme of things, is about the generation of knowledge. Action, or activities (in the realm of action research) is about finding 'solutions to practical problems or improving strategies for dealing with them' (p. 171). For Hammersley, this pragmatism does not sit easily with the more esoteric aims of research in a number of ways. First, research may not generate anything which is easily utilisable. Second, the lack of certainty as to when a conclusion is reached at the end of a study. Though it should be added that in most 'how to do action research' texts (e.g. Whitehead and McNiff, 2006) the process is conceptualised as being open-ended and that an optimum solution is never reached, only strived for; this also connects to Elliot's (2001) critique of Hargreaves (1999). Lastly, the opportunity costs involved may lead to questionable decisions, in that undertaking a form of intervention may bring about deleterious effects which may not occur with a different set of actions not tied to a research process. The solution to these kind of problems would necessitate either subordinating research to activity or prioritising it and detaching it completely from activity. Although Hammersley is a bit thin on details of the first option, it seems that his view of research as an open-ended mode of inquiry becomes circumscribed by the aims and objectives of the activity. Whilst Hammersley argues that this may generate 'useable information … this is achieved at the risk of overlooking the falsity of key assumptions built into the activity' (p. 174). The solution to this problem is simple; all you need to do is 'separate them institutionally'. Thus, in three small words, the teacher researcher movement is not just set back 40 years, it is removed like some Orwellian erasure of history. The practitioner, Hammersley goes on to argue, even when 'temporally suspend[ed] from other activities' cannot generate a sufficient enough distance, or in Geertz's (1968) terms, detachment from those activities. In short, the primary role and identity of the teacher cannot be bracketed off, as their occupational socialisation runs too deep for this and they have an unconscious attachment to the activity under inquiry. All of this can only lead to poor quality research which generates dubious outcomes. But what we have here is essentially ersatz psychology dressed up as methodological critique. There is no *a priori* reason to presume that 'professional' researchers will be any less inclined toward biasing tendencies than will 'amateurs'. What is more pivotal is the researcher's capacity for critical thinking and technical ability to do research.

However, another variant is the model referred to as participatory action research (PAR) (see Hall, 1984, or Kemmis and Wilkinson, 1998). This is another attempt to blur the distinction between the researcher and their participants, which is underpinned by the kind of value system commonly referred to by Elliot (1991) or Whitehead (1998). The principles on which this is based are, according to Hall (1984):

1. Research should involve people (researchers and non-researchers) in the complete process: from initial questions to final analysis and reporting;
2. Research should result in a direct benefit to the community involved;
3. Research is the systematic creation of knowledge which may involve people who are not professionally trained researchers;
4. Knowledge is deepened, enriched and more socially useful when it is produced collectively;
5. Research involves a combination of methods to facilitate co-operation and collaboration; and
6. Research, learning and knowledge production are often aspects of the same process in the context of action.

The domain of participatory action research traverses the spectrum of experimental studies, organisational studies, professional development to empowerment approaches. However, as Hart and Bond (1995) point out, one of the most important features of PAR is the possibility that the focus of research projects very often changes over the time of engagement and thus classifying action research projects using a field topology such as the above is limited in its usefulness. This flexibility, while popular with researchers of complex situations in which they are collaborators and promoters of change, also brings with it the difficulty of deciding whether an intervention for change is 'research' if it is not either theory-driven or theory-generating. The blurring of knowledge, interpretation and empowering action also raises a set of ethical issues in PAR. For instance, change resulting from this form of research affects people emotionally and socially and sometimes even physically, calling for careful and sensitive examination.

And now for some philosophy: part 2

The aim of all research is to gain knowledge of a state of affairs in the world. Knowledge, since the critique of the natural science model, is regarded not as a collection of facts (a disputed concept) but of an engagement with the world that produces meanings and understandings that are culturally, historically and temporally bound, but nonetheless allows human beings to orientate themselves in the world. Knowledge comes about in an interaction between a knower and 'the world', demanding a theory or understanding of how human beings, or their minds, or their brains and experiences, 'hook onto' the world. Theories that suggest how this interaction takes place have a privileged and extensive space in the work and works of philosophers. Central to many of these theories is the idea that 'experience' (and in particular sensory experience) provides this bridge between a knower and the world. In most empirical research, for instance, the object of analysis is a sensory experience; the sounds of an interviewee's words, the drawings of a child and so on.

The two sides of the 'bridge' (if the metaphor is valid) are worth a little attention. On the one hand, it would seem necessary that experience (in order to stand up to the critique of scepticism) has to be constructed or at least constrained by an external reality. If this is not the case, then we are left with the condition of pure idealism, in which all knowledge is a matter of the mind alone. In this case, research findings and interpretations are a matter of the mind of the researcher alone and, to use another metaphor of a nutshell, what fits in the mind of a researcher (alone) probably should stay there. On the other side of the bridge lies the complete landscape of the insider researcher. The second condition that research experience must be able to fulfil is that it can enter a relationship with belief. Belief in this case is construed as the possibility of a human being making meaningful (linguistic) assertions about the world. This demands of experience that it is already in some way conceptual. Here debate has ranged from whether the conceptual instruments that human beings possess are universal in character or whether they too, like other elements of experience, are culturally, ethnically, historically or politically shaped and tooled.

The tradition of 'insider' research' is at home in the tradition of socially shaped experience. Within this understanding there are a number of different ways in which this shaping or determining of experience and, ultimately, knowledge can affect research. (1) The conceptual framework that a researcher brings to a situation and that shapes the investigative experience is shared by all members of a particular culture, society and history and little translation or interpretation is necessary provided discourse remains within certain cultural boundaries. (2) While conceptual frameworks are culturally shaped, they are not so dissimilar to frameworks invoked by other groups that translation and interpretation are impossible. It might be difficult to do but there may, at least, not be a theoretical problem. As Biro has pointed out using Nagel's famous question, there is a difference perhaps between the question of what it is to be *a* bat (a type) and what it is to be *this* bat (an index) (Biro, 2006). (3) It could be that some experiences and resulting points of view are really available only to a single individual. In this case, the question must be asked whether these experiences are theorisable or, even if they are, whether they are theoretically interesting. There is no doubt that there are private and individual aspects to a researcher's work and interactions. However, the question is whether these aspects are substantially significant in the generation of knowledge. They are present but perhaps as an epi-phenomenon of the process of engaging with people and the world. My experiences are my own but may not be substantially significant. As Vendler has put it 'indexicality is not a source of qualitative difference' (Vendler, 1988), and points of view are individuated by their *content* and not by their *ownership*. Thus, there is an onus on strict 'privileged perspective' theorists to show that the perspective is, apart from being of purely idiosyncratic interest, also in some kind of dialectical connection with the 'other side of the bridge' in the world of external reality.

Viewing points of view in a little more detail, it is clear that these can be categorised depending on whether the view is from a spatial, ideological or temporal standpoint. In the first case, the claim is made that only those inhabiting a certain space share certain experiences and thus knowledge. The experiences and knowledge of the classroom, for instance, is reserved for those who occupy this space. Less concretely perhaps, there are points of view that are determined not by position in time and space but in the space of sets of beliefs, ideas and aspirations. Thus, it is sometimes claimed that gay and lesbian studies can be carried out only by those who hold and share certain common convictions and aspirations characteristic of this sexual orientation. Among the difficulties that seem immediately apparent is, first, the claim that there exists any such set of common beliefs, desires and aspirations within the group, or whether it is much more the case that people's convictions have nothing to do with their sexual orientation. The second difficulty is to show convincingly that shared beliefs and aspirations necessarily imply a shared perspective on experience and knowledge.

A third possibility that is brought forward is that a perspective is tied to a particular time so that those who share perspectives must also share the same time. While this argument has an intuitive appeal, there are obvious consequences for historical research here, depending on the limits that are set to assuming the perspective of historical figures. While no historian would claim that one can take up the perspective of a historical figure completely, the equally extreme claim that, because historian and figure do not share the same time, there is no possibility of shared perspective would undermine historical research completely. Finally, if perspectivalism is pushed to its limits and since all experience has a sensory and physical element, the claim might also be made that those who share perspectives also share the same perceptual apparatus, but this leads perhaps too far here.

A few concluding comments

Research approaches in the social sciences, whether 'inside' or 'outside', cannot but reflect the richness, depth and complexity of the life-worlds they wish to understand or control or change. For this reason alone, all approaches are complicated and sometimes tangled. The seeming simplicity of a realist scientistic view is possible only if the object of investigation has been reduced to its constitutive parts with all elements but one controlled. This situation is rarely, if ever, achieved in social systems. Neither would it seem possible to achieve even conceptual clarity about the nature of the research object. Conceptual frameworks, whether perspectival or purportively objective ('inside' or 'outside'), reveal ontological, epistemological and political commitments that researchers need to understand and uncover. Only in this way can research avoid being misused and made to speak by a network of discursive devices suggesting (but not showing) certain truths about modern subjects (Pechoux, 1994), that can become 'naturalised' (Barthes, 1957) and ultimately (and dangerously) self-evident.

Notes

1. This is to a large extent a product of traditional Anglo-American models of social science practice, which have historically taken its prompt from the natural sciences. There are of course historically different models which stress a more radical, i.e. political, role for social science in which this demarcation is, if not irrelevant, then downright absurd.
2. It should be noted that this way of thinking about and doing research was not merely the preserve of those mythical creatures and *bête noir* of qualitative researchers called the 'positivists', but held by those held up to be the doyen of interactionism, the 'Chicago School'.
3. Max Weber (1921/1968) referred to this influence of context on research as 'wertbeziehung'.
4. Praxis, in Aristotle's scheme, was relegated to the realm of practice, but in its more recent, i.e. twentieth-century form, it tends to be used in Marxist and critical theory contexts as referring to the relationship between action and theory how it is jointly mobilised as a way for generating social change.
5. The distinction between episteme and doxa is perhaps most clearly discussed for the first time by Plato in Theaetetus.
6. There are of course parallels with this in the growing critiques of mainstream sociological empirical research from the early 1970s onwards by those sociologists informed by feminist thinking (see, for example, Oakley, 2000).
7. **First person** – this mode of AR is characterized by research which has as its focus some dimension or aspect of the researcher's own life or practice. It is centred on what effect and impact the researcher-practitioner has upon the world whilst they are *acting in it* and not as a detached observer. Far from being an isolated and insulated mode of inquiry, it is undertaken in the context of a community of critical and supportive friends.
   Second person – the focus here is upon AR as a collaborative activity. It is undertaken with friends and colleagues who have a mutual concern and interest in particular aspects of their practice. Reason and Bradbury are of the view that this can and should lead to the development of 'communities of inquiry' and 'learning organisations'.
   Third Person – this is an attempt to go beyond face-to-face modes of inquiry as implied by first and second person research and construct much broader communities of inquiry. In this mode there is a strong emphasis on developing inquiry through different mediums (textual, visual, audio) of communication to foster critical dialogue.
8. The history of action research is an interesting one, as, parallel to its absorption into the world of educational research, it was used in industrial contexts during the 1950s to foster some variant of workplace democracy as a means of managing conflict and generating trust. The techniques commonly associated with Japanese car production in the 1980s had their origins in the Swedish car industry and were developed via the use of Lewin's action research cycle.

9. To be fair to Elliot, he sees himself as being partially responsible for this commodification of reflective practice through his own shift from being teacher to a university based teacher educator.

References

Bhaskar, R. (1975) *A Realist Theory of Science*. Leeds, Leeds Books Ltd.

Bhaskar, R. (1979) *A Philosophical Critique of the Contemporary Human Sciences: 1 – The Possibility of Naturalism*. Brighton, Harvester Press.

Barthes, R. (1957/1972) *Mythologies*. Paris, Seuil.

Biro, J. (2006) 'A Point of View on Points of View'. *Philosophical Psychology*, 19, 1, pp. 3–12.

Boas, F. (1943) 'Recent Anthropology'. *Science* 98, 3, pp. 334–337.

Brayboy B. and Dehyle D. (2000) 'Insider-Outsiders: Researchers in an American-Indian Community'. *Theory into Practice,* 39, 3, pp. 163–169.

Cassirer, E. (1923/1953) *The Philosophy of Symbolic Forms,* trans. Ralph Manheim. New Haven, Yale University Press.

Clifford, J. and Marcus, G. (1986) *Writing Culture: The Poetics and Politics of Ethnography*. Berkeley, University of California Press.

Elliot, J. (1991) *Action Research for Educational Change*. Milton Keynes, OUP.

Elliot, J. (2001) 'Making Evidence Based Practice'. *British Journal of Educational Research,* 27, 5, pp. 555–574.

Feleppa, R. (1986) 'Emics, Ethics and Social Objectivity'. *Current Anthropology,* 27, 3, pp. 243–255.

Feyerabend, P. (1975) *Against Method*. London, NLB.

Geertz, C. (1968) 'Thinking as a Moral Act: Ethical Dimensions of Fieldwork in New States'. *Atioch Review*, 28, 2, pp. 139–158.

Giddens, A. (1991) *Modernity and Self Identity: Self and Society in the Late Modern Age*. London Polity Press.

Giroux, H. (1983) *Theory and Resistance in Education: A Pedagogy for the Opposition*. London, Heinemann.

Giroux, H. (1992) *Border Crossings: Cultural Workers and the Politics of Education*. London, Routledge.

Habermas. J. (1987) *The Philosophical Discourse of Modernity*. Cambridge, Polity.

Hall, B. (1984) 'Research, Commitment and Action: The Role of Participatory Research'. *International Review of Education*, 30, 3, pp. 289–299.

Hammersley M. and Gomm R. (1997) 'Bias in Social Research' *Sociological Research Online,* <http://www.socresonline.org.uk/socresonline/2/1/2.html>.

Hammersley, M. (2004) 'Action Research: A Contradiction in Terms?'. *Oxford Review of Education*, 30, 2, pp. 165–181.

Hargreaves, D. (1999) 'The Knowledge Creating School'. *British Journal of Educational Studies*, 47(2) pp. 122–144.

Hargreaves, D. (1997) 'In Defence of Evidence Based Teaching: A Rejoinder to Martyn Hammersley'. *British Educational Research Journal*, 23, pp. 405–419.

Harfe, R. (1986) Varieties of Realism: A Rationale for the Physical Sciences Oxford, Blackwell.

Harris, M. (1974) 'Why a Perfect Knowledge of all the Rules One Must Know to Act Like a Native Cannot Lead to Knowledge of How a Native Acts'. *Journal of Anthropological Research*, 30, 4, pp. 242–251.

Hart, E. and Bond, M. (1995) *Action Research for Health and Social Care: A Guide to Practice.* Buckingham, Open University Press.

Kemmis, S. and Wilkinson, M. (1998) 'Participatory Action Research and the Study of Practice', in B. Atweh, S. Kemmis and P. Weeks (eds) *Action Research in Practice: Partnerships for Social Justice in Education.* London, Routledge, pp. 21–36.

Kuhn, T. (1962) *The Structure of Scientific Revolutions.* Chicago, Chicago University Press.

Lewin, K. (1948) *Resolving Social Conflicts; and Field Theory in Social Science.* New York, Harper Row.

Locke, J. (1997) *An Essay Concerning Human Understanding,* ed. R. Woolhouse. London, Penguin.

Lyotard, J-F. (1984) *The Postmodern Condition: A Report on Knowledge* [translation from the French by Geoff Bennington and Brian Massumi]. Manchester, Manchester University Press.

Manheim, K. (1997) *Ideology and Utopia.* Routledge, London.

Marcus, G. E. (1997) 'The Uses of Complicity in the Changing Mise-en-Scene of Anthropological Fieldwork'. *Representations,* 59, pp. 85–108.

McGettrick, G. (1994) *Nothing About Us Without Us: Evaluation of the INCARE Professional Assistant Service Programme.* Dublin, Centre for Independent Living.

Merton, R. K. (1972) 'Insiders Outsides: A Chapter in the Sociology of Knowledge'. *American Journal of Sociology,* 78, 1, pp. 9–47.

Nietzsche, (1968) *The Will to Power* [trans. W. Kaufmann and R.J. Hollingdale]. New York, Vintage Books.

Oakley, A. (2000) *Experiments in Knowing: Gender and Method in the Social Sciences.* Cambridge, Polity Press.

Oakley, A. (2001) 'Making Evidence Based Practice Educational: A rejoinder to John Elliot'. *British Educational Research Journal,* 27, 5, pp. 575–576.

Pawson, R. and Tilly, N. (1997) *Realistic Evaluation.* Sage, London.

Pechoux, M. (1994) 'The Mechanism of Ideological (Mis) recognition in Slavoj Žužek (ed.) Mapping Ideology London, Verso pp. 141–151.

Popper, K. (1959) *The Logic of Scientific Discovery.* London, Hutchinson.

Reason, P. and Bradbury, H. (2001) *Handbook of Action Research: Participative Inquiry and Practice.* London, Sage.

Richardson, L. and Le Grand, J. (2002) *Outsider and Insider: The Response of Residents of Deprived Neighbourhoods to an Academic Definition of Social Exclusion (CASE paper 57).* London, LSE.

Sayer, A. (2000) *Realism and Social Science.* Sage, London.

Thomas, G. and Loxley, A. (2007) *Deconstructing Special Education and Constructing Inclusion.* 2nd ed, Open University Press, Maidenhead.

Vendler, Z. (1988). 'Changing places', in D. Seanor and N. Fotion (eds), *Hare and his Critics.* Oxford, Oxford University Press, pp. 171–183.

Waitzkin, H. (1968) 'Truths Search for Power'. *Social Problems,* 15, 4, pp. 408–419

Weber, M. (1921/1968) *Economy and Society* [translated and edited by Guenther Roth and Claus Wittich.] New York, Bedminster Press.

Whitehead, J. (1989) 'Creating a Living Educational Theory from Questions of the kind. How do I Improve my Practice? *Cambridge Journal of Education,* 19, 1, pp. 41–52.

Whitehead, J. (1998) Educational Action Researchers Creating their Own Living Educational Theories. A paper for presentation to the Action Research SIG, Session 9.45 at AERA, San Diego, 13–17 April, 1998.

Whitehead, J. and McNiff, J. (2006) *All You Need to Know About Action Research.* Sage, London.

Chapter 3

Credibility issues in research from within organisations

Anne Smyth and Rosalie Holian

Introduction and overview

Research from within (insider research) that is done by members of the organisation under study is, and feels very different from, research that is conducted by and provided to organisations by outsiders. On the one hand, taking up the *research role* as an 'insider' confronts the researcher with many dilemmas, questions and decisions to weigh up, not the least of which is that it is in addition to their usual *organisational role*. On the other hand, these dual roles open up enormous opportunities to do work that can have a valuable and significant impact on organisations and individuals involved, as well as contributing to the growth of shared knowledge.

Research from within is different to, not better or worse than, other forms of research. It is concerned with questions that cannot be tackled as effectively by more traditional approaches. This chapter explores and grapples with a number of critical issues that arise out of this type of research, with the primary intention being to investigate the core question of credibility, what this means and how it can be achieved and assessed. It raises the issue of objectivity and its relationship with credibility and considers the unique perspective that research done from within can offer. It discusses the often difficult and complex choices and dilemmas researchers who research their own setting face, and it looks at the issues involved in reporting the findings of the research within and beyond the organisation.

We draw on our own experiences over many years of conducting research from within and also of supervising many practitioners who have undertaken substantial research projects from within, usually from an action research perspective. We want to share what we have learned from working with managers/students who have done these projects and our collective experiences and reflections about the rewards, difficulties and risks inherent in them. Most of these projects have had dual objectives; to gain a higher degree for the individuals involved and to contribute to organisational and personal change and improvement.

In particular, we wish to offer a practitioner's guide to the realities of research that are conducted by members of organisations and the contribution this can make to knowledge, meaning, understanding and practice. Those who try to solve practical problems with others in real situations can effect change to improve things and at the same time learn how to enhance their own practice.

What needs to be attended to when researching from within?

When the researcher has a shared history with research participants and plans to continue in their work role after the completion of the project, extra care needs to be taken to manage interdependence in working relationships and boundary issues during the research process. When reporting research findings to an external audience, issues of validity, such as bias and subjectivity and ethical issues, including anonymity and coercion, need to be addressed. Both internal and external credibility issues need to be considered during the initial planning phases and there is a need to address impact on the organisation, quality of the research and demands on the researcher.

We believe that research conducted from within is worthwhile and special because it can help solve practical problems. It forces us to ground our work in everyday issues as those involved experience them, it confronts us and others with our assumptions, perceptions and their consequences, it enables us to learn, reflect and act and it insists that we engage with what and who we are curious about. Above all, it is about learning and making a difference.

Eikeland's (2006) concept of othering-effects highlights the tendency for insider researchers to be evaluated from the perspective of an inappropriate ontological stance. Unlike approaches where the researched are 'othered' as research subjects, researchers from within, particularly those undertaking action/practitioner research, are immersed, embedded and strongly connected with the researched in a shared setting, where they operate together on an ongoing basis. In this way, knowledge is co-created in organisational settings which are characterised by complex role and inter-dependent relationships. At the same time these characteristics present a range of challenges and risks to rigour and credibility.

Research from within occurs on a daily basis in organisations and we believe that it is important to identify the factors that contribute to and detract from its effective practice. This is a different approach from discounting the contribution that insider research can make by labelling it subjective or anecdotal, and there-fore, not 'real' research, or by trying to rationalise and sanitise it by collecting and analysing data that makes it appear to fit into a 'scientific' quantitative paradigm or an accepted qualitative framework. The latter is still a contentious issue for some researchers, some who fund or authorise research and particularly those who judge the validity of the research within and outside organisations. So let us briefly consider some of these concerns and how they impact the question of credibility.

Can or should research from within an organisation be objective?

What does this mean?

Research within organisations can be done by members attempting to include an objective aspect to their work and acting as if they were external, almost as if they were joining or entering an organisation in order to study aspects of it, as ethnographers or participant observers would do. Research within organisations can also be done by members who are deliberately trying to understand, change and influence the purpose, direction and behaviour of others – hardly an objective position. Action research is a well established approach to organisational research which undertakes this pathway, often in active, conscious conjunction with teams of 'co-researchers' who are other members or stakeholders from the same organisation (Reason and Bradbury 2006).

While the notion of objectivity is a key element in some research paradigms, others not only permit but also acknowledge and celebrate a subjective perspective as a valid research stance. Positivism can be seen to have an objectivist ontology and epistemology, with hermeneutic and post-modern approaches having a subjectivist ontology and epistemology, Critical realism and action research can be regarded as having an objectivist ontology and a subjectivist epistemology (Coghlan and Brannick 2005). A constructivist perspective is that we learn and know things through interaction with the world. In action research, in particular participatory action research, the researcher is not and cannot be seen as separate from their research (Wadsworth 1998). In the editorial for the first issue of the journal *Action Research*, Brydon-Miller, Greenwood and Maguire (2003) state that:

> Action research challenges the claims of a positivistic view of knowledge whichholds that, in order to be credible, research must remain objective and value-free. Instead, we embrace the notion of knowledge as socially constructed and, recognizing that all research is embedded within a system of values and promotes some model of human interaction, we commit ourselves to a form of research which challenges unjust and undemocratic economic, social and political systems and practices (p. 11).

They go on to describe how Russell Ackoff's (1999) term 'messes' 'sums up one of the ways a great many action researchers differ from their conventional social science colleagues ... most action researchers have disciplined themselves to believe that messes can be attractive and even exciting' (p. 21). The messy nature of action research, particularly when undertaken by researchers from within, can be a great source of rich data. Insider status enables researchers to engage with and report events and issues as they occur, allowing understandings to unfold naturalistically. Their accounts are less inclined to present an ordered and sanitised picture of either the phenomenon under study or the research process itself, and unexpected data is consequently more readily recognised and captured. Like all good qualitative research, systematic and transparent data gathering and analysis and reflective journaling are very important in enabling this (Progoff 1975; Schon 1987; Daudelin 1996). In contrast, external researchers and those maintaining a more distanced stance risk not noticing or throwing out some of the most interesting and useful data because of a lack of understanding of history and context.

In applied research in business it is useful to consider objectivist and subjectivist positions as two poles of a continuum, with most research projects having a proportion of each. Objective and subjective points of view can be complementary, as can quantitative and qualitative research methodologies and methods. Insider research very often utilises qualitative, quantitative or mixed methods (Cresswell 2003).

It is our view that it is necessary to surrender the idea that researching the meanings and interpretations we make of people in social situations can be objective. Researchers who undertake research from within their own organisation can offer a unique perspective because of their knowledge of the culture, history and actors involved. The tests of good research from this perspective are in important ways quite different from traditional approaches and yet, in other ways, similar. Organisational researchers/members are concerned with relevance, usefulness, resonance and data that support informed, evidence-based decision making. They are not typically focused on outcomes that can predict future behaviour and results, be generalised to broader populations, or need to be proven, validated or replicated. However, like all credible researchers, those who research from within should regard as essential: rigour, robustness, transparency of process and method, systematic and internally consistent approaches to data gathering and analysis, a clear chain of evidence and ethical practices.

Validity and the problem of bias

Approaches to establishing validity in qualitative research can be defined in different ways to those used in quantitative research, and these have been summarised as including cumulative, communicative, argumentative and ecological forms of validation (Sarantakos 1998). Miles and Huberman (1994) discuss ways to demonstrate credibility, trustworthiness and authenticity, and suggest tactics which may be employed to test and confirm findings from qualitative research.

Participant observation has roots in anthropology, where 'going native' has been seen as a threat to 'good' research. However, research from within organisations can be seen as involving the position of an observing participant (Alvesson 2003), rather than the more traditional notion of a participant observer. Thus, concerns about 'going native' are inappropriate.

Researchers who undertake research from within often feel that they are targets of criticism about being biased and may be vulnerable to attacks launched from the point of view that the inherent subjectivity associated with their role and existing knowledge about the organization and its members is perceived as contaminating and as a potential source of error. We challenge this perspective and take a different view. There is really no such thing as pure objective observation of much human behaviour in real work situations, regardless of whether the research is conducted by either external researchers or researchers from within. All observation is theory or value laden, and dependent on past experience of the observer. The lack of a researcher's knowledge of the history and culture of a particular organisation under study should probably more often be part of the critique of external organisational research. Why this has not been the case to date is not entirely clear. Researchers from within normally include details about themselves and their role in the story of the research, including how they may have influenced the process, and what they have learned. Researchers from without often do not describe themselves, or how they interacted with members of the organisation in their accounts of research. Not including this information, and writing the report in the third person does not mean that their work has been objective, however, it does make it impossible for readers to know where their account may have been influenced by personal factors and biases.

The issue of engagement is at the core of action research and participant observation within a researcher's own organisation. It is obviously not possible, or desirable, to develop the same sort of relationships that an outside researcher could make, nor can scientific definitions of validity, reliability or generalisability be meaningfully applied. The tests of good research here are rather around reflections on links between theory and practice, understanding meaning and the significance and impact of constructions of meaning, making knowledge shareable and useful and relevant to practice. The learning, insights and contribution to shared knowledge and improved practice comes from immersion in the everyday workings of the organisation and the iterative cycles of interaction between data gathering, reflection, analysis, theory and action (Altrichter et al. 2002; Kemmis and McTaggart 2000).

This enables observations and learnings to be grounded in the very often messy and difficult to access multiple realities of organisational life, rather than filtered through a research approach concerned with only admitting data that is regarded as objective, measurable and triangulated.

A unique perspective

As we have noted, research from within offers a unique perspective because of the researchers' knowledge of the history and culture of people and institutions involved.

Robson (1993) outlines his view of both the practical advantages, and the disadvantages of 'insider' research as:

> You don't have to travel far. Generally you will have an intimate knowledge of the context of the study, not only as it is at present, but in a historical or developmental perspective. You should know the politics of the institution,

not only of the formal hierarchy but also how it 'really works' (or, at least, an unexamined commonsense view of this). You will know how best to approach people. You should have 'street credibility' as someone who will understand what the job entails, and what its stresses and strains are. In general, you will already have in your head a great deal of information which it takes an outsider a long time to acquire. (pp. 297–298)

He goes on to say that he considers the disadvantages to also be substantial, for reasons related to power and status, working relationships, confidentiality, and having to live with the consequences of mistakes, and 'more fundamentally, how are you going to maintain objectivity, given your previous and present close contact with the institution and your colleagues?' (p. 300).

An alternative view is argued by Brannick and Coghlan (2007), who recognise that there are some disadvantages to being 'close to the data', but see the advantages as far outweighing any of these, concluding that:

> It is argued that insider researchers are native to the setting and, therefore, they are perceived to be prone to charges of being too close and thereby not attaining the distance and objectivity necessary for valid research. We have challenged this viewpoint and shown how insider research, in whatever research tradition it is undertaken, is not only valid and useful but also provides important information about what organizations are really like, which traditional approaches may not be able to uncover. In our view, insider research is not problematic in itself and is respectable research in whatever paradigm it is undertaken. (p. 72)

The trick is to work out how to try to derive maximum benefits whilst minimising the negative side effects on the researcher, the researched and the research outcomes. This way research from within can offer a truly different perspective to that obtained from a more distanced position. Together, these different perspectives may contribute to a form of information triangulation, to describe aspects that lead to a richer understanding of organisational behaviour and experiences.

Risks and tensions when researching from within

Whilst doing research in your own organisation can potentially deliver enormous benefits in terms of learning and improvement of organisational (and researchers') practices, there are also some real risks to researcher and research. Researchers from within are often in roles and positions of formal and informal power, that place both constraints on, and opportunities for, access to people, processes and information (Holian 1999; Coghlan and Brannick 2002, 2005; Boucher and Smyth 2004). Recognising and managing these risks and tensions are important if researchers are to demonstrate sound research practices and strengthen the credibility of the work.

Researchers from within have past, current and expected future roles in the organisation which bring aspects of organisational history, working relationships and personal alliances into play. These considerations and influences shape the perception and behaviour of the researcher and those involved in the research. They impact the nature and extent of the content of data and its interpretation. The problem is not just that the researcher may not receive or see important information because of the nature of their organisational membership and the relationships she/he has developed, but that she/he will see more.

The greater risk may be that the researcher from within gains access to organisationally sensitive information and risks exposing previously undiscussable issues, disturbing arrangements that serve particular people or purposes, confronting others with less than welcome observations regarding organisational practice and surfacing and naming dilemmas. The ability to conduct credible research-from-within involves an explicit awareness of the possible effects of perceived bias on data collection and analysis, as well as ethical issues related to the anonymity of the organisation and individual participants. It also involves the influence of the researcher's organisational role on coercion, compliance and access to privileged information. These issues need to be considered and addressed at each and every stage of the research.

Coghlan and Brannick (2002, 2005) tackle these tensions as they discuss the role of the insider researcher and highlight three issues in particular that require active attention. These are role duality, pre-understanding and access.

Role duality

In research when the researcher is an outsider, their role is often a discreet one, with activities confined to the life of the project. There are, however, inherent tensions between the role of researcher and the organisational role (colleague, subordinate, research partner and friend) that the researcher occupies as an organisational member. This is especially true when the researcher is a manager. Power and authority issues can become especially significant in that case. It is sometimes difficult for co-workers or staff or the researcher to distinguish between the roles, which may constrain information, behaviour and relationships in each. Ethical dilemmas may arise if data gained from acting out of one role has negative or risky implications for another one. Conflicts may occur as unexpected or unwanted information arises. Researchers need to be aware of the influence of their organisational role on coercion, compliance and access to privileged information. Equally, much learning, new insights and creativity and the strengthening of relationships may also be released as a result of engaging with and working through these tensions.

Pre-understanding

'Pre-understanding refers to such things as people's knowledge, insights and experience before they engage in a research programme' (Gummesson 2000, cited in Coghlan and Brannick 2002, p. 54). The researcher can approach the task with a detailed and rich understanding of the issue being investigated and the people and organisational dynamics contained within it. This potentially enables a deeper and more insightful investigation and exploration of the issue and especially the often unspoken aspects that may elude an outsider or take a very long time to discover.

This does not come without some risks, however. Too many assumptions can be made or the research brought to a premature conclusion when preconceptions appear to be confirmed. Coghlan and Brannick (2002, 2005) suggest that the insider researcher must work to stay in touch with their feelings to ensure that they are not caught in familiar patterns and experiences of organisational life, becoming too close to the processes and unable to rigorously interpret the data. Qualitative research practices, such as the keeping of a reflective journal and seeking external supervision to provide a reflective and challenging other voice, are valuable tools to realise the benefits of pre-understanding and minimise the potential pitfalls.

Access

Researchers require both primary access (entry) and secondary access (within) to the organisation during the life of the project. Coghlan and Brannick (2002, 2005) argue that insider researchers may have difficulty accessing areas within the organisation due to their prior membership of the organisation. For example, access to information at various levels within the organisation may be limited due to the researcher's hierarchical role, or because of a prior history of conflict between parts of the organisation. On the other hand, researchers may have pre-existing relationships that enable them to move freely around the organisation and to access a wider range of information. Difficulties can arise when organisational members fear that they may be exposed if they share information or be at risk if they raise problems that may be very relevant to the issue.

What it's like – the complexities and stresses involved

When all this has to be managed while continuing to operate in their organisational role, there can be some stress involved in maintaining working relationships and considerable tension may build from continuing to address the issues, do the research, and keep on top of job requirements and role expectations.

When organisational research is also part of the work for an academic programme it is likely to involve academic supervisors, who provide advice and support as well as guarding the gates to the academy. They decide if the balance of theory and practice is right, if there is enough independent support from the literature and, finally, if the thesis is ready for submission. In turn, the wider academic community guards its gates against those academics (and academic supervisors) they may see as subversive, or overly permissive. Demands for tests of rigour drawn from conventional, externally driven research approaches, can be used as an excuse to maintain a perceived or desired status quo which separates University research from Industry research, and academic from vocational education.

Researchers from within are sometimes in relatively junior or marginal organisational roles, and where this is the case their research opportunities and experience may be quite different from that of others who are senior executive managers, who have considerable influence to make decisions and initiate and lead change. Work based research projects conducted as a proportion of a coursework Masters differ from those associated with a research Doctorate. If nothing else, Doctoral research is likely to take much longer and involve the collection of more in-depth data and information. A short-term special project may be able to be set up for a single subject, and involve a temporary assignment outside or in addition to a normal work role. Doctoral research, particularly by senior managers, is more likely to involve critical aspects of core business and impact on the researcher's role and career. Senior members of an organisation may manage or lead longer term research projects, often in close partnership with external consultants. Junior members may have a quite different perspective and experience of both the organisational and research process and outcomes.

There is still a view by some that good research is only done by external, objective researchers. When organisational research is seen as best done by academics or other external consultants, then academics researching practice within educational institutions seem to find themselves in a curious position (Davies 2005). They should be seen to be qualified and able to research organisations, but what if the research is about their own organisation? Suddenly their skills may be regarded as having been neutralised by their subjective position, by having values and feelings, work experience and working relationships. Yet they had values and feelings, experience and relationships which influenced their decisions when researching other organisations. External researchers accept that members within an organisation may have an understanding of what is going on, why it is happening and what is likely to be the outcome under the given circumstances. Why should members of academic organisations be made to feel that they need to call in external researchers for the outcome to be accepted as credible research?

In addressing practical problems and real issues in their own organisation, an insider researcher can experience both external pressures and internal dilemmas. They may be the target of personal abuse or general organisational defensiveness and anger, which sometimes has a negative impact on their work and career. The perceived risk of becoming Joan of Arc or a sacrificial lamb can be real. In some cases the justified fear of such outcomes can result in a temptation and, sometimes, the need to beat a tactical retreat and, occasionally, the decision to separate from the situation or the organisation. (Holian 1999; Coghlan and Brannick 2002, 2005; Brannick and Coghlan 2007).

One of our suggestions is to be aware of the disturbance that may arise and have a contingency plan for where to stand when it hits the fan. This does not mean that no real issues can ever be confronted. Initial resistance to facing challenges to the status-quo may be converted to working out ways to overcome the barriers to improving organisational and individual practice. Indeed, it is at points of disturbance that some of the most valuable organisational and personal learning and change can potentially take place. Yet a keen, anticipatory awareness of potential risks is crucial for researchers-from-within and an essential characteristic of the reflective practitioner (Schon 1983).

If you have been abseiling you would know that feeling when you defy gravity, lean back into empty space parallel to the ground far below and step off down a cliff-face. Researching from within can also be a little like abseiling, which is why we advise careful thought before starting out, going with others experienced in the process and having both a main line and a safety line. As part of your safety plan we advise having a co-researcher, advisor, consultant or supervisor who is interested in, but not directly involved in, your organisation or your research project, who you meet with regularly and can also contact in case of emergencies. This contact can assist your decision making and learning by enquiring about your choices and reflections, perceived risks and observations and challenge you to explore blind-spots, assumptions and new ways of approaching or interpreting events. It is difficult to assess risk, to know when you are taking a gamble, because of the potential for a significant breakthrough, when it may be a suicidal mission and/or is just tilting at windmills. The researcher must be able to alternate between immersing themselves in the situation and withdrawing to reflect and analyse what is going on and the next steps they may take; an external advisor can assist with this (Boucher and Smyth 2004).

Not only is this advice relevant to managing the inherent tensions and risks of researching from within, it is highly relevant to the issue of credibility. Demonstrating an awareness of these risks and developing strategies for managing them, especially in the planning phases of the research, systematically reflecting on how these issues emerge and play out as the research proceeds, taking action to deal with them and tracking how they impact on the research project itself, any outcomes, the researcher and all participants, provide evidence of rigour, robustness and attention to ethical practices. This is at the cornerstone of credible research practices.

Strategies for ensuring credible research from within

Researchers from within need to be aware of the indicators of good research practice and skilled in the use of those practices (see Yates 2004). If they are new to research they need access to more experienced staff who are aware of what contributes to rigorous research and credible outcomes. Internal and external supervision are tools that encourage reflective practice and can assist with such requirements. Supervision is built into organisational research conducted as part of an academic award, but is not confined to such settings. However, not all academic supervisors have appropriate experience in external organisations to be well placed to understand and help students manage the range of complex issues that can arise when undertaking research from within, or the impact they can have on issues of credibility as well as achieving a successful outcome.

Ongoing, transparent monitoring and review, built into the research design, are essential. The systematic keeping of a reflective journal is an acknowledged device to enable all aspects of the research to be examined and reviewed. The cycles of planning, action, evaluation and review embedded in action research and reflective practice approaches used by ourselves and our students have offered a strong framework for surfacing and tracking problematic issues inherent in research from within. The failure to notice or attend to these can seriously undermine the credibility of the research (Dick 2002; Reason and Bradbury, 2006). For example, the early and ongoing identification and management of ethical issues can be assisted by such strategies.

Ethical issues when researching from within

Where the research is part of an academic programme it is likely to be subject to rigorous ethics processes before, during and as it is undertaken. These processes prompt the researcher from within to anticipate the dilemmas, tensions and risks involved in this approach to research and, most importantly, to develop strategies for managing so that they do not cause harm and so that the research is credible. Increasingly, many organisations where staff are engaged in research are also requiring them to go through an organisationally based ethics process.

When ethics committees consider applications for ethics approval featuring research undertaken from within, they may face many of the contentious issues outlined in this chapter and attempt to apply processes developed for experimental or scientific research paradigms. Practice based research conducted from within raises different practical issues and needs to be managed accordingly. One approach to dealing with these situations is to advise researchers from within to go off line or take on a special project where they may be able to act as if they are more like an external researcher. Attempting to act as if they are an external researcher can be appropriate in some circumstances. However, it is not always appropriate or the best option available.

Indeed, as Holian and Brooks (2004) argue, it may introduce additional ethical issues that could increase the perceived risk to participants, since it may not accurately describe what is really occurring. In addition to this ethical drawback, recommending the 'as if' option also fails to recognise the benefits of using existing avenues for research that arise from being part of, rather than separated from, the researcher's normal work role. The ethical issues involved in doing research from within that is part of one's normal work can be more complex than doing external research or research as if it were external. It can be particularly challenging to find ways to explain how this can be done ethically as part of a standard written proforma that is to be assessed by members of an ethics committee. The key to addressing this difficulty is to work from first principles, to be clear about how the purpose of the research, the information provided to participants, the methods of data collection and analysis as well as the proposed means of dissemination of findings are all based on ethical principles.

It is crucial to have clear strategies to minimise the risks involved and show how those that cannot be eliminated can be managed. These generally include: widely advertising the project in the organisation, obtaining consent from the organisation and participating individuals, providing genuine choice to opt in/out of the research, developing ways of ensuring confidentiality and anonymity where this is possible and being honest when this is not. However, as noted earlier, research from within is characterised in organisational settings by possible role conflict and confusion, power and authority issues and many sensitivities around revealing unwanted information about the organisation and those who work within it. So decisions around consent, voluntary participation, what is normal work and what is research, anonymity and confidentiality may not always be quite clear cut.

The ethics of publishing research findings based on information collected from human subjects can involve making a distinction between the purpose of sharing suggestions for quality improvement and 'research'. However this distinction can be superficial, if not spurious, if the main distinction is to do with your initial purpose rather than the practices actually involved in data collection and analysis. Publishing research findings under your real name which are about your own organisation can have both ethical and political implications. While you may be able to preserve anonymity in one sense, even if you do not name the organisation or key members, the details are hardly confidential when your affiliation allows the focus to be easily identified.

Credibility issues when reporting findings

While research may be conducted within organisations as part of business as usual, most in-house research projects would not normally be submitted for publication in refereed academic journals or books, either due to being commercial–in–confidence, or because there is no perceived benefit to the individuals or organisation from doing so. Research conducted within organisations primarily for organisational purposes (whether or not some of those involved are also writing it up for credit in an academic programme) is not normally sought for publication unless it is also considered to be of academic interest.

The quality of research may be judged differently for a dissertation, a journal article or a conference paper. The structure of a thesis may be theory driven or data driven, done to a recipe by an apprentice, or it can be a performing art, with learning through questioning enquiry involving examination of assumptions about the nature of knowledge and of methodologies (Dick 2002, pp. 161–162). Individuals undertaking part-time postgraduate study while working full time may choose their own organisation as the field site for research for a number of practical reasons, including familiarity and access, only to later encounter diffi-culties in getting this accepted by academic journals as real research rather than a company project (Brannick and Coghlan 2007).

Why publish, who wants to read about it? In answering the so what or who cares question, we may come to the core of one of the issues of contention. Practitioners may not read research published in what is, in their view, obscure tier one academic journals which take a high stance that can appear to be conde-scending at best, sneering at worst, about the seemingly impossible situations within some organisations. Rather than expounding on the historical, philosoph-ical, social and political reasons why problems appear to exist, it can also be use-ful to publish descriptions of some practical ways that have been found to move organisations in a positive direction.

We have encouraged our practitioner/researcher students to disseminate their work in a number of ways. With coursework action research masters students, we structure their final piece of work in their portfolios as a journal article and work with them to shape it to an appropriate audience. In the case of Masters and Doctoral/PhD research candidates, we encourage and support the submission of papers for conference presentations and publications during their candidature. This rarely includes tier one academic journals but focuses on respected journals in their field, usually peer reviewed. A number have followed this through. They are also encouraged to present their research to significant and well-regarded conferences in their professional fields and many of them do this successfully.

In conjunction with other colleagues, we have also challenged practitioner/researchers to investigate ways to conduct their research and represent their find-ings using alternative forms that are different to conventional text based methods and conference presentations (Boucher and Holian 2001). This has resulted in a range of outputs from research and coursework Masters and Doctoral programmes, including forms of a written exegesis accompanied by multi-media material (poetry, music and visual images), a suitcase fitted with many compart-ments, a box of artefacts and a quilt. In each of these cases the research was done a researcher from within a perspective where the nature of the topic being inves-tigated, and the data as it emerged, required alternative forms of representation; the usual methods were simply not adequate to the task. The criteria for assessing the standard and credibility of the research emphasised relevance, robust, trans-parent, rigorous and consistent research processes, fitness for purpose, usefulness and resonance. While examiners do need to be carefully chosen and suitably briefed, all the higher degree students we have supervised who have chosen these alternatives passed, often with special commendations.

Our students have also presented their findings in a variety of research and management forums within their organisations, their professional associations and to other organisations interested in what they can learn from what they have done. We emphasise the importance of framing the work as research, clearly artic-ulating their research approach and explaining specifically how they ensured a rigorous and robust processes. Part of our task was to make sure their ontology, epistemology and method were appropriate, internally consistent and well argued. Specifically we stress how important it is that the claims they make about their findings and conclusions are appropriate to the research questions that guided the work, the nature of the issue being researched and the methodology used.

Above all we encourage them not to take a defensive stance in relation to more conventional approaches to research. Rather we encourage them to go onto the front foot so to speak. We do this by providing them with the information, tools and support to enable them to design, implement and evaluate their projects in such a way that they can confidently explain the appropriateness, relevance and robustness of what they are doing, how they are doing it and why. Demonstrating both their understanding of these issues and showing how they addressed them in their research practices provides clear evidence of credible research.

References

Ackoff, R. (1999). *Ackoff's best.* New York, John Wiley and Sons.

Altrichter, H., Kemmis, S., McTaggart, R. and Zuber-Skerritt, O. (2002) 'The concept of action research'. *The Learning Organisation,* 9, 3, pp. 125–31.

Alvesson, M. (2003) 'Methodology for close up studies–Struggling with closeness and closure'. *Higher Education,* 46, pp. 167–193.

Boucher, C. and Holian, R. (2001) *Emerging Forms of Representing Qualitative Data.* Qualitative Research Methods Series, Melbourne, RMIT University Press.

Boucher, C. and Smyth, A. (2004) 'Up close and personal: Our experience of supervising research candidates who are using personal reflective techniques'. *Reflective Practice,* 5, 3, pp. 345–355.

Brannick, T. and Coghlan, D. (2007) 'In defense of being "native" the case for insider academic research.' *Organizational Research Methods,* 10, 1, pp. 59–74.

Brydon-Miller, M., Greenwood, D. and Maguire, P. (2003) 'Why action research?'. *Action Research,* 1, 1, pp. 9–28.

Coghlan, D. and Brannick, T. (2002) *Doing Action Research in Your Own Organization.* London, Sage.

Coghlan, D. and Brannick, T. (2005) *Doing Action Research in Your Own Organization.* 2nd ed, London, Sage.

Cresswell, J. (2003) *Research Design Qualitative, Quantitative and Mixed Methods Approaches.* 2nd ed, Thousand Oaks, Sage.

Daudelin, M. (1996) 'Learning from experience through reflection'. *Organizational Dynamics,* Winter, pp. 36–49.

Davies, P. (2005) 'Insider research: From a position of privilege'. *TASA Conference 2005.* University of Tasmania, 6–8 December 2005, TASA 2005 Conference Proceedings.

Dick, B. (2002) 'Postgraduate programs using action research'. *The Learning Organization,* 9, 4, pp. 159–170.

Eikeland, O. (2006) 'Condescending ethics and action research'. *Action Research,* 4, 1, pp. 37–47.

Holian, R. (1999) 'Doing action research in my own organization: ethical dilemmas, hopes and triumphs'. *Action Research International, Paper 3,* <http://www.scu.edu.au/schools/gcm/ar/ari/p-rholian99.html>.

Holian, R. and Brooks, R. (2004) 'The Australian National Statement on Ethical Conduct in Research: Application and implementation for "insider" applied research in business'. *Action Research International, Paper 7,* <http://www.scu.edu.au/schools/gcm/ar/ari/p-rholian04.html>.

Kemmis, S. and McTaggart, R. (2000) 'Participatory action research', in Denzin, N and Lincoln, Y. (eds). *The Handbook of Qualitative Research,* Thousand Oaks, Sage.

Miles, M. B. and Huberman, A. M. (1994). *Qualitative Data Analysis.* 2nd ed, Thousand Oaks, Sage.

Progoff, I. (1975) *At a Journal Workshop: The Basic Guide and Text for Using the Intensive Journal Process.* New York, Dialogue House Library.

Reason, P. and Bradbury, H. (2006) *The Handbook of Action Research.* London, Sage.

Robson, C. (1993). *Real World Research.* Oxford, Blackwell.

Sarantakos, S. (1998) *Social Research.* 2nd ed, South Yarra, Macmillan.

Schon, D. (1983) *The Reflective Practitioner: How Professionals Think in Action.* Aldershot, Avebury.

Schon, D. (1987) *Educating the Reflective Practitioner: Towards a New Design for Teaching and Learning in the Professions.* San Francisco, Jossey-Bass.

Wadsworth, Y. (1998) 'What is participatory action research?'. *Action Research International, Paper 2,* <http://www.scu.edu.au/schools/gcm/ar/ari/p-ywadsworth98.html>.

Yates, L. (2004) *What Does Good Research Look Like?* Maidenhead, Open University Press.

Insider research in schools

Chapter 4

Historical insider research in education

Gary McCulloch

Insider research in education is not confined to contemporary practices or to the study of institutions as they exist in the present day. It also extends to historical research that focuses on the researcher's own school, university or other institutional base. Much of this work is commissioned for the purposes of the institution itself, whether to commemorate a specific anniversary or, more generally, to celebrate its growth and successes. Such 'house-history' has a poor reputation, owing to its lack of independence and its tendency to develop uncritical accounts devoid of candour. In many cases, this reputation is well deserved. Yet the complexity and ambiguity of 'insider' and 'outsider' research that some discussions have recently observed in relation to research on contemporary education may also be found in historical insider research. This chapter reviews the problems that commonly attach to this kind of research, and then goes on to examine more interesting examples which may challenge the usual insider/outsider dichotomy.

A number of recent discussions of educational research have shown how a rigid typology of 'insider research' and 'outsider research' may not be helpful in all cases. For example, David Bridges points out that it is not always obvious who is inside and who is outside a given group, and that a particular individual may have personal characteristics that make them partly an insider and partly an outsider to the group. In addition, as he is aware, the insider researcher may become an outsider in his or her own community through the act or process of researching it. However, Bridges himself persists with the dichotomy of insider and outsider research, in order to defend the potential value that, he argues, 'outsiders' can offer to the understanding of an institution (Bridges 2002). Justine Mercer goes further to propose that the insider/outsider dichotomy is a continuum with multiple dimensions, in which the researcher constantly moves backwards and forwards, depending on the time, location, participants and topic involved. She suggests, indeed, that there are varying levels of 'insiderness', and that the boundaries between insider and outsider research should be regarded as permeable, involving potentially multiple identities (Mercer 2007).

The history of education literature, by contrast, exhibits no such subtlety, stressing a rigid dichotomy between insider and outsider research, generally to the detriment of insiders. A classic example of this is Marjorie Theobald's pungent critique of school histories, published thirty years ago. Theobald described school histories as 'a blight upon the landscape of historical research'. Indeed, she continued, 'Of all the institutions which can claim the distinction of longevity, schools are undoubtedly the most prolific in the production of histories, and the most narcissistic in approach' (Theobald 1977, p. 22). Whether they were concerned to reassure ex-pupils that their *alma mater* continued to survive, or to celebrate the traditions cultivated in the past, Theobald concluded, 'there are any number of "scissors and paste" school histories available, including several from the government schools, ranging in format from a bumper edition of the school magazine to a coffee table glossy designed to catch the Christmas market'. Either way, she insisted, most had little interest beyond their nostalgic appeal to former pupils. Those principally to blame for this parlous state of affairs, according to Theobald, were the 'enthusiastic amateurs' entrusted by the schools to write such works, whereas 'skilled historians' with 'integrity' would give closer scrutiny to them. In future, therefore, such historians, the inheritors of 'an appalling tradition of scholarship', would have to formulate 'alternative methods of attack' (Theobald 1977, p. 22).

Theobald's piece illustrates well the rigid divide that historians have habitually perceived between insider and outsider researchers. The insiders were 'enthusiastic amateurs', while skilled historians engaging with the school from the outside would be able to examine its record without fear or favour in an objective and dispassionate way. It is not difficult to find a wide range of examples to support this basic dichotomy. Nevertheless, this division is not always as clear cut as such a view would suggest.

Amateurs and professionals?

Many undistinguished school histories have been produced by members of a school commissioned to mark a centenary or some other major event with a published record of the growth of the institution. These have tended to conform to Theobald's basic stereotype of Prize Day history – flattering stories of growth and progress designed for staff and former pupils.

One typical example of this approach is Heather Northey's book on the first hundred years of Auckland Girls' Grammar School in Auckland, New Zealand, published under the auspices of the school's Old Girls' Association. Northey, a former pupil and prefect at AGGS, approaches this task by means of explaining the ideals of the successive headmistresses of the school. Most of the chapters are named after the headmistresses themselves, complete with full page photographs of each of them in turn. Thus, for example, chapter three is entitled 'Miss Whitelaw', after the first head, Anne Whitelaw. Northey's account views the development of the school through Whitelaw's eyes: 'Her heart must have sunk when she arrived in Auckland in January 1907 and realized clearly for the first time the conditions under which she would be working'. (Northey 1988, p. 46). The discussion emphasizes Whitelaw's high-minded principles and her innovations.

This pattern is repeated in subsequent chapters for all of the later headmistresses up to the centenary of the school in 1988. Chapter nine, sub-titled 'Trials and triumphs', focuses on Miss Louise Gardner, headmistress from 1962 to 1978, and details the administration of the school's expansion. It emphasizes her high academic values and the school's achievements in examinations and scholarships. It discusses the finer points of the orchestra and drama presentations at the school under Miss Gardner. It also notes the changing social configurations of the school zone at this time, which threatened the school's academic tradition, in a highly sympathetic treatment of Miss Gardner's stance.

The underlying message of this 'insider' approach to school history, in the case of Northey's work, is the maintenance of the school's tradition, forged in the early years and cultivated and renewed over the years despite challenges and the changing educational and social context. This is identified as a distinctive grammar school tradition, more or less on English lines, surviving the perils of the post-primary education developed in other schools during the twentieth century. Northey's sanctification of the school tradition is difficult to sustain when she reaches the headship of Charmaine Pountney in the 1980s, as Pountney was much more sympathetic to changing social and educational values than her predecessors had been. However, Northey proves to be flexible and praises Pountney's more inclusive approach to educational change, giving her a due place on the pantheon reserved to the headmistresses of the school. The book concludes with a forty-page Appendix providing full details of the teaching and office staff of the school since its origins, all prefects and games captains in the school's history, and all university scholars and graduates.

Another insider school history is R.H.S. Randles' work on the history of the Friends' House in Lancaster, north-west England. Randles had been the deputy headteacher of the school from 1948 until his retirement in 1973, and was entrusted with the task of recording its history by the school authorities. As Charles Carter, vice-chancellor of Lancaster University, observed in his preface to the book, Randles' 'own service to the school was outstanding', and he was now 'ready to use his qualities of patience and scholarship to unravel the complexities of the story' (Randles 1982, p. v). The school allowed Randles full access to the records of the Meeting House. The Old Boys Association loaned him useful material for the project, while a number of Old Boys gave him their recollections of their own schooldays. Randles brought the school's history to a close when it reached 1969, partly because of a change in its name to the George Fox school which took place at that time, but mainly because he was unwilling to chart recent developments, on the grounds that 'it is almost impossible to take a "birds eye view" of recent events and place them in a true historical context' (Randles 1982, p. viii). These were all classic features of the insider school history. The author's trusted position within the school community ensured that he gained access to the necessary records, and his loyalty meant that he focused on the cultivation of the school's tradition rather than on criticisms or broader issues. The reticence about the recent past might well have been partly due to a wish to maintain a detached historical perspective, as he suggested, but because of his own position he was not well placed to provide this anyway. In many such works, a reluctance to discuss contemporary changes is due to being averse to becoming involved in current controversial or sensitive issues affecting the school.

As for Randles' work itself, it followed a familiar path of emphasizing the early struggles of the school to become established from its foundation to the disinterested and heroic efforts of the early masters. George Aldridge, master of the school from 1863 until 1883, is celebrated for his success in recruiting students and improving academic standards. Aldridge himself went bankrupt in 1883 after failing to keep accounts of his receipts from parents or any other sources. This was a particularly serious matter for a private Quaker school, but Randles remains sympathetic and understanding towards what he describes as 'a fine headmaster cut down by financial mismanagement at the height of a successful career' (Randles 1982, p. 78). In the twentieth century, James Dodd Drummond, under whom Randles himself served as a deputy headteacher for many years, is accorded heroic status for his 'truly magnificent' role in a major expansion of the school, as well as for his personal qualities as 'a man of character with great determination and self-discipline' (Randles 1982, p. 162). A twenty-eight page Appendix with full details of pupil numbers, headteachers and staff members, school secretaries, caretakers, presidents of the Old Boys' Association, school captains and winners of school sports competitions brings the book to a close.

A further instance of such work relates to an independent school, Canford, in Dorset, England. Founded in 1923, this school has already been the subject of two 'insider' school histories. The first, celebrating the sixtieth anniversary of the school, was by Michael Rathbone, who had taught history at Canford from 1946 until his retirement in 1974 (Rathbone 1983). Rathbone's wife had also served as a member of staff, and both of their sons had been educated at Canford. The second, for the school's seventy-fifth anniversary, was produced by Henry Baynham and Robin Whicker (Baynham and Whicker 1998). Almost the whole of Baynham's teaching career had been spent at Canford, from 1958 to 1993, where he had taught mathematics, history and politics, served as a house tutor and housemaster, and was also involved with rugby, rowing and adventure training at the school. His co-author, Whicker, had also taught at Canford for nearly all of his career, was on the staff from 1961 until 1996, and had been head of the English department, second master, a house master and house tutor, besides being involved in rugby, hockey, sailing and drama. In his foreword to this latter work, the headmaster of the school refers approvingly to its authors as 'experienced water rats' who 'guide us well' (Baynham and Whicker 1998, p. 7). Rathbone's work arranges the school's history in conventional style according to the tenures of its headmasters. Baynham and Whicker offer an alternative perspective by focusing on topics such as the buildings and grounds, the chapel, sports and games, drama and music. Both are short and colourful productions, drawing on full and privileged access to records, photographs and former pupils and staff at the school, and designed to cultivate and sustain the school's traditions.

By way of contrast, it is not at all difficult to point to examples of school histories produced by outsiders to the school which have very different characteristics. These question and challenge the traditions cultivated by the school, discuss aspects of the school other than the view from the principal's office and examine the relationship that has developed between the school and its broader social, political and economic surroundings. It is tempting indeed to categorize these outsider histories as being professional in nature as opposed to the amateurish work of the insider tradition.

One highly notable instance of this is the historical study by the leading historian of education, W.E. Marsden, on Fleet Road Board School in Hampstead, London, in the late nineteenth century. Marsden approaches this work as a case study of an elite elementary school catering for the 'respectable' that 'expanding social cohort between the rich and the tough'. The main purpose of this school, according to Marsden, was 'in defining and meeting the requirements of economically comfortable and socially respectable lower middle and upper-working class children who, prior to the 1870 Education Act, had been badly provided for' (Marsden 1991, p. xii). In order to do so, Marsden makes use of a range of historical source materials that more than compensate for a lack of records within the school. He also sets out to demonstrate features of the social milieu of the school, the 'cross-currents impinging on society and schooling in the late nineteenth century' (Marsden 1991, p. xiii). Third, he employs an inter-disciplinary methodology to highlight the position of the school in its historical context.

All three of these features are evident in Marsden's investigation of Fleet Road Board School in its geographical context. He demonstrates the nature of the school's social position through close and detailed reference to maps of the local area. The senior school catchment area for 1916, for example, is drawn from admission register detail, and compared with the catchment of scholarship winners in the period 1894–1903. Detailed studies of streets within the school's catchment zone are used to show the complexities of socio-economic status within the broad range of respectable urban society. Census enumerators' returns are matched up with photographs of surviving houses to give a 'detailed sense of place' (Marsden 1991, p. 91). Railway timetables for the period illustrate the time spent by pupils travelling to and from school. Marsden also gives close attention to the successive headteachers of the school, but in a very different way from the general run of insider school histories. He brings out the significance of the heads' family backgrounds and histories. This is particularly intriguing when the author traces the remarkable teaching dynasty of the Adams family, and also the social background of the headmistress of the school's infant department, Louisa Walker. The construction of the school's image and tradition is another aspect that Marsden scrutinizes with care, as he shows how the school hall, the school choir, and its prize days and concerts helped to elevate the status of Fleet Road Board School in its local community.

A further and no less fascinating example of this kind of outsider approach to school histories is David Labaree's work on the Central High School of

Philadelphia between 1838 and 1939. Like Marsden, he approaches this as a historical case study to relate it to a larger pattern of issues. As he explains, 'My approach is to focus on the point of articulation between the life history of a particular school (Central High) and the social history of the institution it helped to shape (the American high school)'. (Labaree 1988, p. 2). In order to achieve this, he organizes his treatment of the school, not in chronological fashion, but in terms of themes and topics that illustrate key aspects of the historical growth of the American high school. Indeed, he suggests that this is not a history of a school, but rather 'an essay on the historical sociology of the American high school', with the aim of preserving a balance between historical detail and social theory, 'maintaining a healthy respect for the complex contingencies surrounding historical events and a strong sense of the need for developing theoretical generalizations about these events' (Labaree 1988, p. 3).

Labaree's particular concern is to demonstrate the struggle between politics and markets in the history of the American public high school. He argues that although the high school was founded to produce citizens for the new republic, it soon became a vehicle for attainment of individual status due to the role of the market. Demand for high school credentials led to the rapid expansion of high school enrolment. The Central High School of Philadelphia is investigated for the light it sheds on these trends, with the help of a wide range of sources, including annual reports, faculty meeting minutes and individual records on every student who attended the school during this period.

Such works as Marsden's and Labaree's delineate the differences between the conventional insider school histories produced for the benefit of staff and students of the institution by well established teachers, and the outsider research of professional historians seeking to make a contribution to literature in the history of education. Nevertheless, there are a number of cases that are by no means as clear cut in terms of an insider–outsider divide. The possibilities of transcending or undermining this divide also raise significant ethical and strategic issues for the would-be insider historical researcher, as well as for the institution itself.

Subverting the tradition

How far is it possible to challenge or subvert the established stereotype of historical insider research in education? The responsibility of being loyal to one's own institution and fear of the consequences of criticizing it are powerful inducements to maintain the standard line. Nevertheless, there are cases where the usual approach may be at least modified, with interesting results. Moving into open challenge against one's own colleagues and employers requires further reflection about the issues involved.

In some cases, it is not entirely clear how far the author is an 'insider' or to what extent an 'outsider' to the institution being examined. Roy Shuker's history of the Workers' Educational Association in New Zealand is an instructive example of this kind of ambiguity. Shuker, a historian of education at Massey University, was commissioned by the New Zealand WEA to research and write its history, and his independence was limited as a result. The chairman of the History Committee of the WEA, in his foreword to the book, appears satisfied that Shuker has prepared an insider-type work that emphasizes 'the concern and commitment of so many of the men and women who have given their services to the WEA as an independent voluntary association concerned entirely with the further education of adults' (Shuker 1984, p. 6). Shuker's writing, he notes admiringly, exhibits not only 'his scholarship as an educational historian', but also 'the human qualities that enable him to appreciate the enthusiasm and dedication inspiring so many of those who have worked to establish and further the work of the Workers' Educational Association in this country' (Shuker 1984, p. 6). A photograph of the author signing the publication contract for the book reinforces the image of him becoming at least an honorary insider through the process of its writing.

At the same time, Shuker attempts to develop in his work a theorized and critical discussion of the social class dimensions of the New Zealand WEA. This may not be wholly clear in the text, but the author clarifies his purpose in an 'afterword' tucked away at the end. In this, he characterizes the WEA as 'a site of struggle, where various factions compete for ideological dominance of the Association' (Shuker 1984, p. 162). He insists on the need for historians to become more conscious users of social theory, pointing as an example of this to the WEA's ambiguous role as both a force for social change and an agency for middle-class cultural hegemony. The working class origins of the WEA, he argues, were at odds with the middle-class clientele that increasingly dominated the Association's courses. This conflict is related to struggles between liberals and radicals within the Association, and also to the arguments between the WEA and outside forces. In this way, Shuker concludes his work on a note that reminds us of his position as an outsider, legitimizing a critique of the WEA even as he is taken to its bosom.

A recent major history of Harrow School is also fascinating for its success in fashioning a detailed insider account that has elements of an outsider history. This work, by Christopher Tyerman, surveys the historical development of this leading public school since its foundation in 1615. Tyerman himself has clear credentials as an insider to the institution, in that he is a senior tutor at Harrow School, but he is also a lecturer in medieval history at Hertford College, Oxford. It is this combination that allows him to be relatively detached and critical of some aspects of the school's history, even while he takes advantage of privileged access to its archive and records. He suggests himself that he had tried in writing the book to 'tread a path between sociology and sentimentality' (Tyerman 1999, p. 3). It is striking that the book eschews the usual detailed Appendices of staff and students, and also that the chapters are not organized in homage to the school's headmasters.

Tyerman's book is also unusually candid in its appraisal of the failings and difficulties of Harrow. It discusses the excesses of corporal punishment, fagging and bullying, and the incidence of sexual relationships among both pupils and staff, in frank and engaging fashion. Sex and violence, he makes plain, were 'intrinsic parts of school experience' (Tyerman 1999, p. 475). This also extended to the marriages of masters as, for example, all new wives, at least until the Second World War, were expected to wear their wedding dresses when first entertained at the school, 'as if they were marrying the school, which, in many cases, it may have seemed to them they were' (Tyerman 1999, p. 476). Initiation rites for the boys, such as mock executions and physical torture, are also acknowledged, as is the school's general indulgence of homosexual behaviour. Moreover, Tyerman examines the social class characteristics of this elite and avowedly elitist establishment, together with the problems arising from changes in twentieth-century society.

Tyerman's open and frank approach even extends to what might appear as the ultimate apostasy in an insider school history, a vigorous critique of some of Harrow's headmasters. For example, the Harrow of Joseph Drury between 1785 and 1805 is criticized for a 'glamour and self-satisfaction' that 'concealed a transience and an inertia that were soon exposed' (Tyerman 1999, p. 140). Drury himself is painted as an 'elusive personality' (Tyerman 1999, p. 148), driven by a search for personal security and concerned with maximizing profits despite his popularity with pupils and parents. The election of Charles Longley, a student of Christ Church, Oxford, in 1829, is described as 'the consequence of a Christ Church conspiracy' (Tyerman 1999, p. 205) and, according to Tyerman, he was 'not cut out to be a schoolmaster' (Tyerman 1999, p. 218). Tyerman is particularly scathing about the role of Cyril Norwood as a headmaster between 1926 and 1934: 'Many believed he never took to Harrow; some said the feeling was mutual' (Tyerman 1999, p. 505). He rightly identifies the influence on Norwood of his family origins and especially of his father, 'an obscure drunken clergyman and failed headmaster', arguing that 'to his youthful experiences he probably owed his often chilling reserve and social awkwardness as much as his ambition' (Tyerman 1999, p. 505). He depicts Norwood as a theorist who indulged in 'fads' and who tried to mould the school in his own image, severely concluding that:

> Typical of self-confident and not unsuccessful self-publicists, Norwood was honoured less by those working closest to him than the outside world ... Privately affectionate and concerned, he was viewed by snobbish boys and masters as common, dictatorial, insensitive, a poor listener, and, in his views on education, faintly absurd, judgments that his admirers were forced to acknowledge if not support
>
> (Tyerman 1999, p. 512).

This kind of analysis certainly cuts against the grain of insider school histories. In another sense, though, Tyerman's approach still fits within the established tradition of insider historical research in education. In general his discussions of sexual improprieties, of physical and psychological torture, of social privilege and of the peculiarities of headmasters are couched in terms that are affectionate and tolerant, suggesting overall a robust school tradition that could withstand and survive such problems. In the end, he emphasizes the resilience of the school and its ability to respond to changing requirements imposed by the world outside. His harsh judgment of Norwood might well be regarded as the exception that proves the rule, as Norwood came from outside and never came to terms with the school's values and traditions. Norwood, therefore, is cast as an outsider, an intruder, who challenged the ideals of Harrow and was ultimately disappointed and rejected. This interpretation is based on an insider approach, whereas verdicts on Norwood's position from an outside perspective might well be more sympathetic to his social background and his attempts to reinvigorate the public school tradition of England as a whole (see McCulloch 2006, 2007).

Thus, there are definite limits on Tyerman's challenge to the established conventions of insider school histories. Nevertheless, his book demonstrates the potential scope for subverting the usual stereotype of such works. Candour and honesty might well be potent antidotes for their worst traits, the anodyne and pious image of the past that they habitually create as an example to imitate for the future. A more realistic approach could also be considered to be of more value to the institution itself, when considering the lessons of its history, than the flattery and praise that are most common. In opening up such possibilities, however, there are also likely risks for the insider researcher, as well as for the school, that need to be acknowledged and negotiated.

Ethical issues loom large for the insider historian who wishes to develop a critical interpretation of their educational institution. Especially in the context of the usual expectations of insider research, such an approach might well be considered by colleagues as a betrayal of trust, a breach of loyalty. School authorities might deem it to be a form of whistle-blowing, posing a danger to the reputation of the institution. There may be implications for the researcher's future employment and progress at the school, depending on their position and vulnerability. Access to institutional records and individuals, normally taken for granted in insider research, might begin to be limited and subject to increased surveillance.

In mitigating these risks, the insider researcher should be as clear as possible from the outset about the nature and aims of their proposed project, negotiating agreement on access to records and individuals and the use of such sources in the same way that would be expected of outsiders to the institution. The potential effects of the discovery of damaging or embarrassing episodes in the school's past should also be carefully considered and assessed, both in terms of the reputation of the school itself and with respect to named individuals and their relatives. It is an established norm of historical research, unlike the social sciences, that institutions and individuals should generally be identified rather than given anonymity or false names, and this should also be clarified to avoid misunderstandings (see also McCulloch 2004).

University challenge

Thus far, we have been concerned mainly with school histories, but there are similar issues relating to histories of universities. It is certainly the case that university histories have been beset by the same kinds of tendencies as school histories.

The institution is viewed from the top down as a symbol of growth and progress, finally dissolving into a mass of lists and statistics. Such work has commonly been the preserve of the university registrar. The history of the University of Newcastle upon Tyne, published to mark the centenary of the establishment of the College of Physical Sciences at Newcastle upon Tyne, provides an instance of this familiar approach. Its author, E.M. Bettensen, the university's registrar, charts the emergence and rise of the university, before leaving it to a thirty-page set of Appendices to list its principal officers, professors, student numbers and accounts (Bettensen 1971).

It is also true that there are many constraints on insider historical research in universities. According to one recent account, the official history of the University of Southampton was censored before its publication, and similar tensions arose at Liverpool and Keele (North 2003). Yet there are intriguing possibilities for such research. In part, these arise from the greater freedom enjoyed by university academics, at least when compared with school teachers. In many cases, too, the authors of university histories may themselves be experienced educational and social historians, well used to negotiations with reserved and suspicious educational institutions. How far is such work able in practice to cross the boundaries between insider and outsider research?

One interesting case in point is the centenary history of the University of Auckland in New Zealand, written by Keith Sinclair, a professor of history at the university and, indeed, the most widely known historian of New Zealand. Sinclair reflected frankly on the challenge posed by this commissioned work. He noted in particular the difficulty of discussing recent events, which he explained as a problem of perspective on contemporary change, leading him to confine his final chapter on the years preceding the centenary to an 'interim account' (Sinclair 1983, preface and chapter 16). His work was also embellished with an extensive Appendix covering administrators, teachers and librarians in the university's first century. Nevertheless, he was able, within the confines of the genre, to explain how the members of the university had progressively adapted their institution to a new environment, and how the urban and national community around it had reacted to its presence.

The published histories of the University of Sheffield provide further grounds for caution on the possibilities for subverting the traditions of insider research, although again there may be some basis for a mild optimism. The first history of the university, published in 1955 to celebrate its half-century, was a work in the classic style. Produced by the university's registrar, Arthur W. Chapman, it provided a lengthy, worthy and somewhat ponderous account of civic progress. It charted constitutional changes and the development of new buildings alongside some of the leading personalities of the university, concluding with Appendices of over seventy pages in length detailing particular aspects, such as key reports and heads of academic departments (Chapman 1955). For the centenary in 2005, another approach was adopted through the commissioning of a specialist historian, Helen Mathers, who was also a graduate and an associate lecturer at the university. Mathers succeeds in addressing a number of issues that had been absent in Chapman's work, notably the daily life of students and staff and the university's changing position in the city of Sheffield. Hers is a nicely judged account that is sympathetic and affectionate but not uncritical or boastful, nor yet overly sentimental. She is clearly aware of the limitations of the genre of university histories, but strives still to create a historical study of some value. There is a risk of retreating into reticence when discussing the student unrest of the 1960s and 1970s, but generally this is traced and its implications examined with the necessary frankness (Mathers 2005).

The difficulty with the Sheffield history comes at the end with a postscript by the Registrar and Secretary of the university, David Fletcher, who is also the chairman of the editorial board of this centenary study. The postscript purports to look forward to the challenges of the twenty-first century, but constitutes an uncritical celebration of the university's position at the end of its first century that somewhat jars with what has gone before. In many ways this is a reversion to the tone set by Chapman, with a boastful quality that reflects the image sought by the institution:

> As it reaches its centenary the standing and strength of the University has never been greater ... The challenge in 2005 is to build on this position of strength, particularly in the areas of research excellence, which now encompass every faculty .... Visionary leadership, sound strategic direction and academic excellence remain the keys to continued future success
>
> (Mathers 2005, p. 394).

Even in the most sensitive and well researched university history, it appears, that the heavy hand of the administrators and marketing department is never far behind.

For all these constraints and difficulties, however, a useful literature is slowly emerging, based on insider histories of universities, often produced to mark a suitable anniversary. An oral history of the University of Strathclyde, researched by a team of historians based at the university, develops an interesting and detailed account of the 'university experience' of the 1960s and 1970s, based on the testimonies of the students themselves. This constitutes 'determinedly a history of people's experiences, not an institutional history of the university' (Brown et al. 2004, p. 1). A centenary history of the Institute of Education at the University of London, by the professor of the history of education at the Institute, Richard Aldrich, has given a full and fair assessment of its institutional growth, together with its impact on teaching and research (Aldrich 2002).

Conclusions

Overall, in both schools and universities, there continues to be some clear tensions evident between insider and outsider histories. The limitations of insider history have become well recognized, and in many cases they can be very difficult to avoid. Nevertheless, in recent years, some research has begun to play creatively with the established traditions of Prize Day history, with promising outcomes in a number of cases. There are potential dangers that may emerge as a result, of which the researcher must perforce be aware. Yet there are substantial benefits to be found in steering a careful path around the imperatives of the institution, while seeking to develop a useful historical account. Experienced water rats may after all be able to combine sociology with sentiment in the interests of insiders and outsiders alike.

References

Aldrich, R. (2002) *The Institute of Education 1902–2002: A Centenary History*. London, Institute of Education, University of London.

Baynham, H. and Whicker, R. (1998) *A Portrait of Canford 1923–1998*. Wimborne, Canford School.

Bettensen, E.M. (1971) *The University of Newcastle upon Tyne: An Historical Introduction*. Newcastle, University of Newcastle upon Tyne.

Bridges, D. (2002) The ethics of outsider research. In M. McManee, D. Bridges (eds), *The Ethics of Educational Research*. Oxford, Blackwell, pp. 71–88.

Brown, C.G., McIvor, A.J., Rafeek, N. (2004) *The University Experience 1945–1975: An Oral History of the University of Strathclyde*. Edinburgh, Edinburgh University Press.

Chapman, A.W. (1955) *The Story of a Modern University: A History of the University of Sheffield*. Oxford, Oxford University Press.

Labaree, D. (1988) *The Making of an American High School: The Credentials Market at the Central High School of Philadelphia 1838–1939*. New Haven, Yale University Press.

McCulloch, G. (2004) *Documentary Research in Education, History and the Social Sciences*. London, Routledge.

McCulloch, G. (2006) 'Cyril Norwood and the English tradition of education'. In *Oxford Review of Education, 32/1*, pp. 55–69.

McCulloch, G. (2007) *Cyril Norwood and the Ideal of Secondary Education*. New York, Palgrave Macmillan.

Marsden, W.E. (1991) *Educating the Respectable: A Study of Fleet Road Board School. Hampstead 1879–1903*. London, Woburn Press.

Mathers, H. (2005) *Steel City Scholars: The Centenary History of the University of Sheffield*. London, James and James.

Mercer, J. (2007) 'The challenges of insider research in educational institutions: wielding a double-edged sword and resolving delicate dilemmas'. *Oxford Review of Education, 33/1*, pp. 1–17.

Northey, H. (1998) *Auckland Girls' Grammar school. The First Hundred Years 1888–1988*. Auckland, Auckland Grammar Old Girls' Association.

North, M. (2003) 'A hairy tale of how plum jobs can go sour'. *Times Higher Education Supplement*, 15 August, pp. 16–17.

Randles, R.H.S. (1982) *History of the Friends' School, Lancaster*. Lancaster, Allan Sharpe Limited.

Rathbone, M. (1983) *Canford School 1923–1983*. Wimborne, Canford School.

Shuker, R. (1984) *Educating the Workers? A History of the Workers' Education Association in New Zealand*. Palmerston North, Dunmore Press.

Sinclair, K. (1983) *A History of the University of Auckland 1883–1983*. Auckland, Auckland University Press.

Theobald, M. (1977) 'Problems in writing school histories'. In *ANZHES Journal*, 6/1, pp. 22–28.

Tyerman, C. (1999) *A History of Harrow School 1224–1991*. Oxford, Oxford University Press.

Chapter 5

Researching leadership preparation from the inside

A Canadian perspective

Charles F. Webber and Ann Sherman

Introduction

Educational leadership preparation initiatives vary internationally, but are almost always culturally or even organizationally specific. Thus, aspiring and current principals follow programmes designed to enhance the knowledge and skills necessary to function as administrators in their local context. As a result, most school leaders get on by subscribing to a set of assumptions and beliefs shared by most other members of their specific educational communities. This chapter looks at the tensions, cognitive dissonance and potential benefits that ensue when examining the effects leadership programmes have on the success achieved by their participants.

Contextual statement

There is no doubt that the role of the school leader is changing. Expectations placed on school principals have expanded over the recent years to accommodate new demands placed on schools (Robertson and Webber, 2002). The role of the school leader has grown and intensified (Alberta Teachers' Association, 1999; Fullan and Hargreaves, 1991) to meet the changing needs of students, teachers and members of the community.

Pressures for change in leadership preparation are similarly intensifying. Murphy (2006) suggested that there is a need to reshape leadership to meet the demand for leaders to be educators, moral stewards and community builders (Murphy, 2002), which leadership preparation programmes are currently not meeting. Leadership in schools must also adapt to meet the challenges of society, technology and the economic market (Dimmock and O'Donoghue, 1997; Dimmock and Chi-Kin Lee, 2000). As we face new political challenges, economic struggles and social dilemmas, we must consider how we can best change our approach to leadership and leadership preparation. This is particularly important when we think about the influence the principal has on a school's culture (Deal and Peterson, 1999). 'Tomorrow's principals will both shape the organization and overhaul the system to meet the demands of a new social structure' (Murphy, 1998, p. 14) with regards to teaching practices, moral and ethical issues and significant economic change. Successful leadership mentoring programmes can help aspiring leaders get off to a solid start when entering a school as a leader for the first time (Walker, 1994). However, evaluation of such programmes is essential and careful consideration of the approach to research used during such an evaluation is required.

Across Canada, the challenge of hiring new administrators is compounded by lack of qualified people to fill vacancies. An aging leadership force is retiring in large numbers, but teachers seem reluctant to seek leadership positions because of perceived low pay and complex and difficult work situations (Glasman, Cibulka and Ashby, 2002) resulting in shortages, as witnessed in media headlines, e.g. *Principal Shortage* (CBC Television, 1999). Academics too are beginning to address the issues (Grimmett and Echols, 2002; Normore, 2006). So there exists a situation where demands on principals are increasing, critiques of leadership preparation programmes are beginning to occur and school boards are unable to recruit. Attempts to change educational leadership programmes have, in the past, frequently been thwarted by powerful cultural norms and societal rules that preserve the status quo (Bjork and Richardson, 1997). Leadership preparation programmes within universities are often limited by internal institutional barriers. Demands from stakeholders rub against these institutional norms and can instigate examination of the quality of the programmes offered. However, other barriers can also prevent change for 'professional, policy, institutional and market factors push in many directions but traditionally have tended to reinforce the status quo' (Glasman, Cibulka and Ashby, 2002, p. 259).

Leadership preparation programmes operate within markets where universities compete for potential students. Universities face competition from for-profit groups that provide courses, as well as from school boards who offer 'home-grown' leadership and leadership mentoring programmes. This competition has been exacerbated by the traditional lack of collaboration between school board practitioners and university academics. This lack of collaboration may also be responsible for the theoretical nature of many university programmes and the corollary is that many of the school board-based programmes focus largely on practical skills.

The introduction of leadership standards in a number of countries has also encouraged examination of leadership preparation programmes. For example, American universities now aim to provide programmes for school and district leaders that meet a set of standards articulated by the Council of Chief State School Officers (1996) in a document titled *Interstate School Leaders Licensure Consortium: Standards for School Leaders* (ISLCC). The ISLLC standards were intended to promote dialogue about quality educational leadership and to improve leadership practices throughout the United States. These standards are based on principles that assume the centrality of student learning, recognize the changing role of educational leaders, emphasize the need for collaborative school leadership, highlight the importance of high quality leadership, call for performance-based evaluations of educational leaders, and strive to achieve educational access, opportunity and empowerment for all.

A similar effort to promote high quality leadership in the United Kingdom was the formation of the National College for School Leadership (NCSL) in 2000, designed to provide a national focus on the preparation and ongoing professional development of school leaders. Applicants for leadership posts are required to hold the National Professional Qualification for Headship, an NCSL certificate, which may have led to a decrease in the attractiveness of university-based courses. The NCSL has had a major influence in the UK and beyond by focusing on practice-based leadership development and by involving practitioners in the design of leadership education (Bush, 2006).

In Alberta, Canada, the recent development of principal quality standards drew in part upon the ISLLC Standards in the United States and stated clearly the goal of guiding principal preparation and ongoing professional growth (Alberta Education, 2006). The Alberta initiative includes a focus on seven leadership dimensions: effective relationships, visionary leadership, creation of learning communities, instructional leadership, shared leadership, effective management and relating to the larger societal context.

Conceptual framework

Insider research is rooted in anthropological research and 'anthropologists seek in their research and their work to preserve wholeness of culture' (Williams, 1967, p. 60). Within an insider research framework, examination of principal effectiveness and the thoroughness of leadership preparation programmes should involve the holistic description of the context and culture of the organization. Anthropological approaches to insider research can provide a rigour and structure to enable research of high standards.

Action research is another 'active' approach which draws on the perspectives of those embedded within a particular situation to examine their own context (Altricher, Posch and Somekh, 1993). Many benefits are accrued from striving to articulate the beliefs and opinions of persons from within an institution or organization by an insider in the role of researcher. The idea is that insiders provide a level of understanding unavailable to outsider researchers. Insiders approach particular research questions with knowledge of the language and culture of the organization they are examining. Agar (1980) suggested that this knowledge of the language of the culture is essential in the analysis of the research.

When examining institutional policies and practices from an insider perspective, it might seem useful to assume the eyes of a stranger. Yet, how does one who is deeply embedded in a specific site develop the ability to observe a situation as being new (Delamont, 2002)? Hennigh (1981) suggested that acting as an insider and informant within your own culture is not simply a matter of transferring research skills developed as an outsider researcher. While Wolcott (1975) suggested that previous experience with outsider researcher is an asset in preparing to complete insider research, Hennigh (1981) said that this is not enough. He suggested that becoming a stranger to those familiar to you is an artificial situation that is not helpful in researching your institution. Insiders researching their own institution should remain familiar, while outsiders can provide the needed perspective of a stranger. Nonetheless, you keep your distance at the risk of failing to understand the complexities of a human situation (Agar, 1980).

The purpose of the research will also determine whether insider research can provide the necessary evidence for careful examination of a situation and thoughtful planning of potential changes or improvements. Altricher, Posch and Somekh (1993) suggested that research on an organization or institution with the intent of evaluating and working towards positive changes is likely to be more successful if the research is conducted by insiders, with the cooperation of everyone involved in the process. Similarly, 'covert observation would be incompatible with supporting openness and trust' (p. 77) between school leaders and teachers. Powdermaker (1966) claimed that, in insider research, respondents talk about each other as well as themselves and it is therefore possible to see a subject through their own eyes and also through the eyes of their friends, acquaintances, co-workers and supervisors. Thus, familiar perspectives result in deep understandings of a context, something not always available to the outsider.

However, it is important to note that insider perspectives may not provide complete understandings of educational organizations. That is, although insider perspectives are advantaged by a greater degree of cultural literacy specific to an organization, outsider perspectives can add to what insiders believe they already know about their institution. As well, outsiders can challenge taken-for-granted beliefs that insiders may not examine adequately.

Current examples in Canada

In response to an increasing need to hire new principals across Canada, leadership/mentorship programmes are being developed to help prepare and mould potential school leaders. These leadership programmes can include opportunities for candidates to shadow administrators, enrol in university Master of Education programmes and participate in practical sessions which focus on school policies and practices. Some of these programmes are created and offered by individual school boards; however, in certain provinces, leadership preparation is offered by groups outside of school boards and are meant to supplement the Master of Education (M.Ed.) programmes offered by many universities.

Local leadership programmes are designed to introduce potential school leaders to issues and concepts which help them fit into a school principalship and also to develop a fuller understanding of issues particular to the board or institution offering the leadership preparation. The leadership programmes that are selected or created by individual school boards can help those boards meet an implicit promise or commitment to employees that there exists the opportunity to 'get ahead' in your own school district and that it is possible that principals will be hired from within a board, not from other school boards. This strategy of enrolling potential leadership candidates in local programmes risks perpetuating the like-mindedness of those individuals who provide leadership within a school board. While a common mission and vision amongst leaders of a single school board is understood to help provide consistency and stability within schools and the board, it can also create a limitation in perspective which hinders development and blinkers understanding.

Across Canada a variety of leadership preparation programmes currently exist outside of university settings. What follows is a brief description of a selection of these.

Nova Scotia Educational Leadership Consortium

Leadership preparation programmes are sometimes offered through consortia which create programmes that can be purchased by school boards. In Nova Scotia, for example, the Nova Scotia Educational Leadership Consortium (NSELC) has a membership which includes all provincial school boards, the provincial school board association, all universities that offer leadership M.Ed. programmes, the Nova Scotia Teachers Union and the provincial ministry of education. The goal of the consortium is to provide practicing and potential school administrators with the skills development they need to ensure they become more effective educational leaders (NSELC, 2007). The programmes NSELC offer include a series of units covering topics ranging from supervision to school law, and local school boards determine which units to buy and run for their people. Some boards select cohorts of potential leaders to participate in a series of the NSELC modules which are taught by educators, some retired, who are trained by NSELC.

The Saskatchewan Educational Leadership Unit

The Saskatchewan Educational Leadership Unit (SELU) is a non-profit agency which serves as a coordinator, developer and administrator of leadership development activities within the province of Saskatchewan. This is a collaborative agency designed to utilize the entire pool of experts and expertise in the province of Saskatchewan and is governed by an inter-agency management advisory board, consisting of representatives from a variety of stakeholders, including the Saskatchewan Teachers' Federation, the Dean of the College of Education at the University of Saskatchewan, the Head of the Educational Administration Department at the University of Saskatchewan and the League of Educational Administrators, Directors and Superintendents (SELU, 2007).

SELU presents its material to potential participants by suggesting that the ability to practically apply current research is essential to enhancing staff and system performance. It seeks support from those who have access to such information and competencies, recognizing that, in a rapidly changing educational world, such specialization is critical to maintaining appropriate educational programmes (SELU, 2007). Many SELU clients are from school divisions which lack sufficient staff to develop, implement and evaluate leadership development programmes.

Ontario Principal's Qualification Program

The Ontario Principal's Qualification Program (2001) is offered through the Ontario College of Teachers, which is an organization, governed jointly by representatives of teachers and members of the public, which regulates the teaching profession in the province of Ontario. Successful completion of the two-part Ontario Principal's Qualification Program is required if a teacher wishes to become a principal or vice principal in elementary and secondary schools in Ontario. Participants in part one of the programme study a range of topics such as human resources, interpersonal skills, decision making, students with special needs, legal issues, school operations and communication strategies. In part two, participants learn about similar topics, plus leadership theory, community-school relations, assessment, school planning and resource management. As well, educators in this leadership development programme participate in practices in which they observe school administrators and complete an associated inquiry project.

The Centre for Leadership in Learning (Alberta)

The Centre for Leadership in Learning (CLL) (2007a) is an educational consortium, whose members include the public and Catholic school districts in south-central Alberta, the Faculty of Education at the University of Calgary, the Alberta Teachers' Association, the Alberta School Boards' Association and the Alberta College of School Superintendents. The CLL was established in 1991 and since then has offered large numbers of educators opportunities to participate in annual seminar series, summer institutes, research forums and workshops in both face-to-face and online delivery formats. The CLL also co-sponsors an online academic journal, with the intent of promoting study and dialogue related to significant leadership issues. CLL programmes are intended primarily to fulfil ongoing professional development needs of educational leaders and not to license principals or provide graduate credit. It also provides a unique opportunity for educational leaders in many roles – teachers, principals, superintendents, elected school trustees, university faculty members, parents, teachers, education students and graduate students – to participate in cross-role dialogue about education.

Canadian connections to the larger context

Work on leadership preparation is also underway worldwide, supported by Canadian organizations and institutions. One of these programmes has supported the development of a Master of Education in Leadership in the newly formed

Royal University of Bhutan. A five-year project, funded by the Canadian International Development Agency, saw St. Francis Xavier University (StFX) in Nova Scotia work alongside new professors to offer leadership courses to 100 M.Ed. candidates. At the same time, a set of nine Bhutanese Leadership modules were prepared by Bhutanese masters' students enrolled at StFX. These modules were offered to 200 school principals, who were not able to be enrolled in M.Ed. due to the lack of B.Ed. qualifications. At the time of this project, Bhutan had fewer than 500 principals and so the effect of a leadership project of this nature is far reaching. Similar projects are under development with leadership groups in Africa, China, Lebanon, Kosovo and East Africa through the University of Calgary.

Evaluations and opinions of leadership preparation programmes

A number of international principal preparation programmes have been evaluated for their effectiveness in preparing school administrators for the demands of leadership. Many of these programmes are run with a cohort of individuals and this has been found to enhance the experience for the participants (Browne-Ferrigno and Muth, 2003; Herbert and Reynolds, 1998). In the United States, there is a growing discussion about the usefulness and applicability of leadership preparation programmes. While the Council of Chief State School Officers (1996) developed standards for school leaders, there has been little systematic review of the application of these standards (Barnett, 2004).

Murphy (2006) claimed that current leadership preparation programmes are of questionable value and Glasman, Cibulka and Ashby (2002) reported what they saw as insufficient self-assessment of preparation programmes. Writing as an insider and member of a faculty that provides such programmes, Murphy conversed with hundreds of practicing school leaders about the preparation they engaged in within schools of education. Overall, their perspective is somewhat negative and unflattering. Levine (2005) also suggested that leadership programmes need substantial overhauling if they are to effectively educate school leaders. In the *SREB Report on Principal Internship* (Southern Regional Education Board, 2005), findings and recommendations suggested that many of the preparatory internship programmes for school leaders failed to provide authentic leadership opportunities for the participants to demonstrate that they had mastered the skills and knowledge necessary for enabling change within school settings. Individual participants also rate the success and effectiveness of leadership preparation programmes with great variation (Tucker, Henig and Salmonowicz, 2005). In an earlier report, Tucker and Codding (2002) suggested that participants of educational leadership programmes within universities report that 'there is typically very little connection between curriculum as taught and the actual demands, conditions, and problems of everyday practice' (p. 13). Only 4% of school principals cite their university-based training as the most valuable source of preparation for their leadership positions (Farkas, Johnson and Duffett, 2003). Clearly, there is a need for rigorous study of leadership preparation programmes in North America and internationally.

Conducting studies of leadership preparation

Individuals who study leadership preparations, such as those described above, may do so from several 'insider' perspectives. For instance, they may be members of organizations that develop and deliver leadership development programmes, or they may be members of educational organizations that rely on outside agencies and consultants for leadership development services. Whichever insider perspective researchers may hold, there are key considerations, discussed below, that are specific to the examination of educational leadership preparation programmes. The critical nature of the considerations emerges in part from the growing importance placed by governments and the general public upon educational leadership in both Western and developing nations. Key considerations will be outlined in the context of the following stages of research: entering the field, being in the field, leaving the field, writing and disseminating the results.

Entering the field

Understanding the political nature of educational leadership is the key to researchers gaining permission to study leadership preparation programmes. Virtually everything about the principalship is political. Principals' actions are sensitive in terms of their impact on students, teachers, parents and community members. Moreover, most principals' professional practices are public in nature and subject to ongoing scrutiny by everyone in an educational community. Therefore, researching how principals are prepared is potentially controversial.

Principal selection procedures can be contentious because sometimes competing priorities are held by different members of educational communities, and who is selected to be principal determines at least in part whose agendas will be furthered. Although school districts across Canada normally require principals to have completed a Master of Education degree successfully, principals' degrees typically span the areas of educational leadership, curriculum, special education, educational foundations and more, so the relevant value of each area of study for principals is subject to ongoing debate. The institutions where principals studied have reputations of varying types, with some holding more prestige and credibility than others. In addition, any school district-specific leadership development programmes in which principals may have been required to participate were designed, approved and delivered by particular district employees who, therefore, have vested interests in who might study which programme components and how the components are examined. Even the motivation for providing district leadership development programmes is political in that internal programmes are offered to cover perceived gaps in leadership preparation programmes offered by universities. The political dimension of studying leadership preparation may be exacerbated when the work of outside consultants, whose livelihoods depend upon how well their work in leadership development is perceived, is included in proposed studies.

Researchers' roles and professional backgrounds will help determine if and when they will be permitted to study leadership preparation initiatives. For example, researchers who employ participant–observer methodologies, from the perspectives of either participant in leadership preparation programmes or providers of the same, may be perceived to be shaped by particular political agendas or self-interests. The roles that researchers hold may influence studies' ethical approvals from both universities if research is conducted as part of graduate degree programmes and school districts if researchers are employees or paid consultants. Further complexities may arise when researchers are both graduate students completing degree requirements and employees of the organizations involved in studies.

In short, the political aspects of studying educational leadership require researchers seeking entry to attend to participants' need for reassurance that research will be conducted fairly, ethically and respectfully. The possibility of satisfactory levels of trust between researchers and study participants must be evident in research proposals. Careful attention to meeting institutional and district ethics requirements is absolutely necessary if site entry is to be gained. Finally, the proliferation of educational leadership graduate programmes at universities means that senior administrators in many schools and school districts, particularly large urban districts located in proximity to universities, may perceive themselves as inundated by requests to study schools and the people in them. It is up to researchers to convince site gatekeepers that their proposed studies are worth conducting and that they will be well conducted.

Being in the field

Once researchers gain access to a leadership preparation programme, they will do well to develop the level of cultural literacy that will allow them to navigate the research environment. Cultural literacy in this context includes an understanding of why educators participate in leadership preparation programming, the formats for programme delivery and the risks and benefits associated with involvement, both as a participant and as someone who facilitates leadership development.

Educators participate in leadership preparation initiatives for a variety of reasons. Motives may range from a genuine interest in learning to a strong sense of altruism that leads to seeking a principalship or school superintendency, to a desire for the extra remuneration that accompanies leadership positions, to a perception that leadership positions come with some level of power over others, to outright coercion from superordinates who want to place certain individuals in principalships. The motives that led particular participants to access leadership preparation will shape how the researcher is perceived and influence the levels of authenticity in researcher-study participant communication.

In addition to understanding motives for participation, researchers will need to recognize the forms of leadership development they may encounter. They range from highly collaborative cohort-based models through to individualized studies. Leadership preparation may be focused more on practical application than on evidence-based theory, or vice versa. Programming may reflect the perception that academic knowledge is more valid than the knowledge accumulated by practitioners over many years of experience in schools. Large school districts may operate several leadership preparation programmes, each designed for different leadership roles: vice principal, assistant principal, principal and superintendent. Large school boards may also offer leadership preparation for staff in service roles such as facilities management, purchasing, capital projects and maintenance. Smaller school districts or groups of independent (private and charter) schools, usually restricted from participation in programming offered by larger school boards, are less likely to have enough resources to offer their own programmes and, therefore, may collaborate on the delivery of leadership preparation programmes. Some leadership preparation programmes, both district-based and those offered by universities or professional organizations, may place a strong value on 'elder knowledge' and seek facilitation by senior or retired educational administrators. Other programmes may reflect a classical approach to leadership development, such as those offered by the more traditional universities found in the United Kingdom and throughout Europe. Others may include face-to-face and online learning in various permutations. Most leadership preparation is directed towards specific leadership roles such as principals or school directors and superintendents, but some are designed to promote cross-role dialogue and learning among teachers, principals, elected school trustees and parent council members. Many leadership preparation programmes in the Western world will reflect the common conceptual components and mutual influence of initiatives such as the ISLLC standards, the Ontario principal's qualification programme and the Alberta principal quality standards.

Risks for participants that researchers encounter typically fall into three categories. First, leadership programmes may suffer from some level of incompatibility of the cultures in which leadership preparation programmes were developed and the cultures in which they are offered. An example of this might be the adoption of a leadership development model developed in a classical university setting by educators in a developing country. The societal affluence that permits extended periods of on-site study in some European nations is likely to be absent in most of the developing world. Attempts to implement a multi-year leadership preparation programme that demands total absence of participants from their workplaces is unlikely to build the same levels of leadership capacity as a more flexible programme that is designed to support part-time study while continuing to live and work in students' home communities. Nonetheless, there are numerous examples of educational systems throughout Eastern Europe and Africa, for example, which continue to import leadership programmes that were developed for implementation in very different social, cultural, linguistic and financial settings. Closer to home, leadership preparation programmes targeting educators in large urban settings may be less appropriate for rural school districts but are implemented there without sufficient site adaptation. In its worst form, inappropriately imported leadership preparation may constitute cultural imperialism or merely be reflective of unexamined beliefs about what constitutes good leadership in specific contexts.

A second risk area that researchers may need to include in their studies is that of reinforcement of biases and even discrimination. Examples of biases include leadership preparation programmes that fail to include instructional leadership as a major responsibility of educational leaders. Examples of discrimination, intentional or not, include instructional designs that do not reflect the perspectives of women and minorities and serve to perpetuate stereotypes of who can be educational leaders. Even the unexamined use of particular forms of language can lead to incomplete understandings, e.g. an absence of inclusive terminology or assumptions that terms such as 'leadership' or 'school culture' mean the same things to all participants.

A third area of risk that researchers may need to report is that of insincere communication among participants. Certainly, researchers will interact with participants in leadership development initiatives who feel they are part of a safe environment, where they can count on the support of their colleagues and programme facilitators, and others who are strong enough individuals to not feel a need to restrict what they say in case they challenge peers or superordinates. However, there will still be others who understand the career-limiting potential of expressing dissent or critiquing district practices while participating in leadership preparation activities. There is a real possibility that some programme participants will communicate what they believe will be rewarded by promotions.

To summarize, researchers who gain entry to sites where they can study leadership preparation programmes will benefit from a clear understanding of the possible programme formats they may encounter and the range of motivations for programme participants. Similarly, they should be prepared to analyze leadership preparation programmes that may be culturally inappropriate and/or perpetuate biases and cultural stereotypes. Finally, they may need to examine how and why participants communicate in particular ways within leadership preparation programmes.

Leaving the field

Studying leadership preparation from within organizations that receive or deliver programmes means that researchers never really do leave the field. Perhaps the best that they can hope for is sufficient time and space away from their normal work environments to review, analyze, and report their findings in a fair and balanced manner. Researchers may also need to stay in close enough touch with the leadership programmes they study to be able to seek clarification and pose additional questions.

For example, researchers may need to consider, while transitioning from active information gathering to analyzing data, the possibility that they may over-identify with particular leadership programmes because of the status and reputation of the organizations delivering the programmes. Similarly, programme participants, particularly those in developing nations or in rural communities, may be too accepting of leadership concepts and paradigms from more powerful settings or, alternatively, resentful of the wealth and experiences of outside agencies, causing them to reject potentially beneficial information. Researchers may need to engage in an iterative process of self-reflection, information analysis, and returns to the 'field' to probe for clarification and gather more data.

Another consideration for researchers in this stage of their studies is that of competing values from within the field of educational leadership. That is, the concepts and activities that are included in leadership preparation programmes reflect the relative importance ascribed to, for example, school-community relations, professional development, school law, educational finance, planning, team build-ing, instructional leadership and shared decision making. Researchers should ask themselves which components of educational leadership are viewed as more important by participants and programme providers and, as important, ask if those perceptions are consistent with the actual needs of the members of the educational community being studied.

A sometimes difficult perspective for researchers-from-within to analyze is the degree to which the settings they are studying are consistent with the view that leadership preparation should contribute to growth in human and social capacity. That is, how well do leadership development activities satisfy the learning needs of educational leaders and their communities and how much do they satisfy the needs of the organization itself? Further, can these two goals co-exist or can they become mutually exclusive? The significance of these questions becomes clear when researchers ponder if school districts, particularly large urban districts which can become almost like city states in their own right, seek to enculturate leaders who, consciously or otherwise, place the needs of the larger organization (and their professional advancement within that organization) above the needs of individual learners in schools.

Perhaps 'leaving the field' can be thought of as 'transitioning' from seeking information to determining if enough information has been gathered. The latter perspective encompasses a more fluid and iterative process in which researchers shift from information gatherer to information reporter. Viewing this stage as a transition gives researchers permission to contemplate various influences on the information they have in hand, identify gaps in their knowledge and analyze perspectives they may not have considered previously.

Writing

Researchers might want to consider the possibility that 'writing' is not a separate part of studying leadership preparation from within. Rather, it is part of the entire process of making sense of what is to be studied, how it will be examined, what ethical considerations must guide inquiry, what is learned and how it is to be reported. Self-preservation alone suggests that researching one's own organization be based on a written record of what was agreed to by whom, when and under what conditions. Furthermore, the writing ought to have begun while 'in the field' so researchers can check their perceptions with study participants, analyze their cumulative findings and identify patterns and inconsistencies that must be included in final reports. Throughout the research process, writing should be guided by the following principles that protect the credibility of researchers and the work they do.

First, researchers studying leadership preparation within their organizations must grapple with the reality that their research will highlight practices and beliefs that some would prefer ignored, while others will delight in the discomfort that the writing will elicit. Members of the group being studied will almost certainly recall for a very long time at least some of what researchers say in their research reports. Given that participants in researchers' studies are current and future leaders in the organizations that employ the researchers, it is reasonable to assume that researchers' careers and credibility will be affected by what they write. If the perceived dangers are too daunting or if researchers are not willing to face the impact of their work, then perhaps others need to undertake the research. On the other hand, researchers might think about why they would wish to work for organizations in which it is too risky to study what the organizations seek to accomplish, particularly public institutions that are accountable to their larger societies.

If researchers have resolved to conduct their studies and to report their findings, they must ask themselves a very practical question as they gather information. That is, 'have they got it right'? Answering this question means researchers have determined that they have spoken to enough people, asked appropriate questions and compiled a pool of information that has sufficient breadth and depth to make an informed report possible.

Once researchers can say that they think they have it at least partially right, they can begin the process of 'writing up' their findings (Wolcott, 2001, p. 4). This part of the writing process includes articulating clearly the purposes for writing the report. That is, do researchers plan to inform, educate or shape leadership preparation programmes in their organization? Whatever their answers, researchers have a responsibility to make their writing purposes clear. Researchers who plan to have their reports taken seriously by study participants and by decision makers within their organizations must also ensure that they present what is perceived to be a balanced, articulate report. They must demonstrate an intellectual distance and capacity to analyze and report in ways that lead study participants and colleagues to trust what is written. One aspect of building trust is knowing when to write assertively based on solid evidence and when to write tentatively because questions remain unanswered and answers are ambiguous. Very important, what is written must adhere to the ethical frameworks that were agreed to prior to the start of studies. For example, if anonymity was promised then anonymity must not be compromised.

In general, writing ought to be seen as a process that pervades the entire research process. It is a task that calls upon researchers to write with courage and integrity, to articulate their purposes for engaging in the research and to report findings so that the research and the researcher are trusted and can continue to participate in inquiry within their educational institutions.

Disseminating the results

Potential recipients of research reports about leadership preparation programmes include study participants, their employers, programme planners and facilitators, and department of education personnel. However, who receives reports of specific studies of leadership programmes will depend upon who was involved in giving researchers a mandate to proceed with research. That is, study sponsors and the individuals and groups they identify are legitimate recipients of study reports. Negotiation of data ownership prior to the commencement of research will determine if researchers may disseminate findings more widely without seeking permission from study sponsors.

Researchers are obligated to recognize study contributions made by others and to recognize intellectual ownership in accordance with international research standards, such as the Ethical Standards of the American Educational Research Association (1992). Researchers are also advised to follow internationally accepted standards for reporting research, such as those articulated by the American Educational Research Association (2006).

Conclusion

Leadership preparation programmes are intended to create stronger, more effective and more compassionate educational leaders, primarily not only for schools and school districts, but also for departments of education, colleges and universities. Studies of the degree to which leadership preparation achieves its purposes are necessary if the best leaders are to serve educational communities. Frameworks for considering principal effectiveness proposed by Leithwood and Montgomery (1986) offer researchers a set of lenses for reviewing principal preparation initiatives. However, more research is required if current leadership needs are to be met satisfactorily. Important questions need to be asked, such as can school boards enhance their abilities to facilitate growth in human and social capacity without input from outsiders and how can educational organizations avoid perpetuating already established visions and missions if they rely heavily on studies conducted by their own personnel? The procedures outlined above for conducting insider studies of leadership preparation programmes will assist in the ongoing improvement of educational leadership in schools and school districts.

References

Agar, M.H. (1980) *The Professional Stranger: An Informal Introduction to Ethnography.* New York, Academic Press.

Alberta Education (2006) *Principal Quality Practice Standard: Successful School Leadership in Alberta.* Edmonton, Alberta, Canada, Alberta Education.

Alberta Teachers' Association (1999) *Trying to Teach.* Edmonton, Alberta Teachers' Association.

Altricher, H., Posch, P. and Somekh, B. (1993) *Teachers Investigate Their Work.* London, Routledge.

American Educational Research Association (1992) *The Ethical Standards of the American Educational Research Association.* Washington DC: Author. [online] available from <http://aera.net/uploadedFiles/About_AERA/Ethical_Standards/EthicalStandards.pdf> [1 April 2007].

American Educational Research Association (2006) *Standards for Reporting on Empirical Social Science Research in AERA Publications.* Washington DC: Author. [Online]. Available <http://www.aera.net/uploadedFiles/Opportunities/StandardsforReportingEmpiricalSocialScience_PDF.pdf> [1 April 2007].

Barnett, D. (2004) 'School Leaderships Preparation Programs: Are They Preparing Tomorrow's Leaders?' *Education,* 125, 1, pp. 121–129.

Bjork, L.G. and Richardson, M.D. (1997) 'Institutional Barriers to Educational Leadership Training: A Case Study'. *The Educational Forum,* 62, pp. 74–81.

Browne-Ferrigno, I. and Muth, R. (2003) 'Effects of cohorts on learners'. *Journal of School Leadership,* 13, pp. 621–643.

Bush, T. (2006) 'The National College for School Leadership: A Successful English Innovation?' *Phi Delta Kappan,* 87, 7, pp. 508–511.

CBC Television (1999) *Principal Shortage,* 13 June, 2005.

Centre for Leadership in Learning. (2007a) *Seminars and Special Events* [online]. Available from <http://www.ucalgary.ca/~cll/semevnt.html> [28 March 2007].

—— (2007b) *International Electronic Journal for Leadership in Learning* [online], Calgary, Canada, University of Calgary Press. Retrieved 28 March, 2007, Available from <http://www.acs.ucalgary.ca/~iejll/> [28 March 2007].

Council of Chief State School Officers. (1996) *Interstate School Leaders Licensure Consortium.* Washington DC: Council of Chief State School Officers.

Deal, T.E. and Peterson, K.D. (1999) *Shaping School Culture.* San Francisco, Jossey-Bass.

Delamont, S. (2002) *Fieldwork in Educational Settings: Methods, Pitfalls and Perspectives.* 2nd ed, London, Routledge.

Dimmock, C. and Chi-Kin Lee, J. (2000) 'Redesigning School-Based Curriculum Leadership: A Cross-Cultural Perspective'. *Journal of Curriculum and Supervision,* 15, 4, pp. 332–358.

Dimmock, C.A.J. and O'Donoghue T.T. (1997) *Innovative School Principals and Restructuring: Life History Portraits of Successful Managers of Change.* New York, Routledge.

Farkas, S., Johnson, J. and Duffett, A. (with Syat, B. and Vine, J.) (2003) *Rolling Up Their Sleeves: Superintendents and Principals Talk About What's Needed to Fix Public School.* New York, Public Agenda.

Fullan, M.G. and Hargreaves, A. (1991) *What's Worth Fighting For? Working Together in Your School.* Toronto, Ontario Public School Teachers' Federation.

Glasman, N., Cibulka, J. and Ashby, D. (2002) 'Program Self-Evaluation For Continuous Improvement'. *Educational Administration Quarterly,* 38, 2, pp. 257–288.

Grimmett, P.P. and Echols, F.H. (2002) 'Teacher and Administrator Shortages in Changing Times'. *Canadian Journal of Education,* 25, 4, pp. 328–343.

Hennigh, K. (1981) 'The anthropologist as key informant: Inside a rural Oregon town'. In Messerschmidt, D. (Ed.) (2005) *Anthropologists at home in North America: Methods and Issues in the Study of One's Own Society.* Cambridge, Cambridge University Press, pp. 121–132.

Leithwood, K.A. and Montgomery, D.J. (1986) *Improving Principal Effectiveness: The Principal Profile.* Toronto, OISE Press.

Levine, A. (2005, April 15) 'Change in the Principal's Office: The Role of Universities'. *The Chronicle of Higher Education,* 15 April, 2005, B16.

Murphy, J. (1998) 'The Changing Face of Leadership Preparation'. *School Administrator,* 58, 10, pp. 14–17.

Murphy, J. (2006) 'A New View of Leadership'. *Journal of Staff Development,* 27, 3, pp. 51–52.

Murphy, J. (2002) 'Reculturing the Profession of Educational Leadership'. *Educational Administration Quarterly,* 38, 2, pp. 176–191.

Normore, A. (2006) 'Leadership Recruitment and Selection in School Districts: Trends and Issues'. *Journal of Educational Thought,* 40, 1, pp. 41–73.

Nova Scotia Educational Leadership Consortium (2007) *University Credit Information* [online] available from <http://www.nselc.ednet.ns.ca/> [3 April 2007].

Ontario College of Teachers (2001) *Principal's qualification program* [online] available from <http://www.oct.ca/teacher_education/additional_qualifications/principals_qualification/pdf/principals_qualification_program_e.pdf> [28 March 2007].

Powdermaker, H. (1966) *Stranger and Friend.* London, W.W. Norton & Company.

Robertson, J.M. and Webber, C.F. (2002) 'Boundary-Breaking Leadership: A Must for Tomorrow's Learning Communities'. In Leithwood, K. and Hallinger, P. (eds.) *Second International Handbook of Educational Leadership and Administration.* Dordrecht, The Netherlands, Kluwer, pp. 519–556.

Saskatchewan Educational Leadership Unit (2007) *What is the Saskatchewan Educational Leadership Unit?* [online] available from <http://www.usask.ca/education/selu/whatis.html> [28 March 2007].

Southern Regional Education Board (2005) 'SREB Report on Principal Internships'. *Techniques (Association for Career and Technical Education),* 80, 8, p. 10.

Tucker, P.D., Henig, C.B. and Salmonowicz, M.J. (2005). 'Learning Outcomes of an Educational Leadership Cohort Program'. *Educational Considerations,* 32, 2, pp. 27–35.

Tucker, M.S. and Codding, J.B. (2002) 'Preparing Principals in the Age of Accountability'. In Tucker, M.S. and Codding, J.B. (eds.) *The Principal Challenge: Leading and Managing Schools in an Era of Accountability.* San Francisco, Jossey-Bass, pp. 1–40.

Walker, A. and Stott. (1994). 'Mentoring Programs for Aspiring Principals: Getting a Solid Start'. *NASSP Bulletin,* 78, 558, pp. 72–77.

Williams, T.R. (1967) *Field Methods in the Study of Culture.* New York, Holt, Rinehart and Winston.

Wolcott, H.F. (2001) *Writing up Qualitative Research.* 2nd ed, Thousand Oaks, CA, Sage.

Wolcott, H.F. (1975) 'Criteria for an Ethnographic Approach to Research in Schools'. *Human Organization,* 34, pp. 111–127.

Chapter 6

Researching a secondary school in Malta

John Portelli

Introduction

This chapter concerns the research I carried out in 2002 as part of a Doctorate in Education undertaken at the University of Sheffield. My thesis, '*Boys will not be Boys' Understanding Masculinities: A Must in the Management of a Boys' School*, considers the social practices of masculinity impacting on boys' lives in the school I worked in then and work in now, namely a Catholic Comprehensive Boys' Secondary School in Malta. My findings enabled me to illustrate the ways in which Maltese boys, both similar to as well as differently from, their British or Australian counterparts featured in published studies, learn the ideals and parameters for being male from the school's masculinising practices, including the curriculum, the management system, relations and discipline among others.

Entering the field

Research method

By actively engaging with pro-feminist perspectives, methodologies and epistemologies, I initially intended to carry out empirical studies in a number of boys' secondary schools in Malta, to explore critically the extent to which the social structures of Maltese secondary schools exert pressure on boys to conform to the masculine role that Maltese society expects of them. However, the approach I eventually adopted was due to two factors: (i) the practical considerations that I shall discuss later and, more importantly, (ii) the fact that, as I worked within a pro-feminist methodological framework that is acknowledged to be practical as well as scholarly and which prides itself on contributing to social change (Reinharz 1992), I felt the need to explore the construction of masculinities in my own school so that I could use my findings to raise awareness there and, possibly, develop contextualised strategies to challenge problematic norms of masculinity. My intention was not to generalise findings to all schools in Malta. The aim, rather, was to examine gender issues in the education of Maltese boys in one specific setting.

Choice of site

Having identified the focus for investigation and the research method, the next question concerned where to locate my study. To address this, I turned to the literature on educational research.

Hitchcock and Hughes (1989, p. 12) suggest that 'research and its products should facilitate reflection, criticism and a more informed view of the educational process which will, in turn, help to improve educational practice'. Hammersley (2000, 2002) offers a spirited defence of what is termed the 'enlightenment model' of social research rather than the 'engineering model'. Research, he claims, should be treated as providing resources that practitioners can use to make sense both of the situations they face and of their own behaviour, rather than telling them what it is best to do.

This stance is very much linked to the pro-feminist educational research perspective which often seeks to bring about some kind of change, sometimes in a very specific location or specific purpose (Reinharz 1992; Deem 1996).

There is widespread agreement that educational research should be concerned with improvement (Bassey 1992; Griffiths 1998; Mortimore 1999) and this impacted significantly upon my decision to undertake the study in my own college, where I had also spent eleven years as a student. However, along with the hope that my findings would be useful within the institution, there were other considerations which informed my choice.

First among these was a professional concern. A study carried out in my school would enable me to make, implement and evaluate strategies to improve gender matters, if findings indicated the need. In addition, I aspired to becoming Assistant Head or Head in the institution and, if successful, the research would be of great relevance to me professionally. As Drysdale (1985) quite rightly claims, administrators find themselves in a position where they desperately need readily available intelligence of a kind which can be provided inter alia, by research.

My decision to study the institution from within was also made for practical reasons. One key preoccupation was time. Since I work full-time daily (from 08.00 – 14.30), travelling to different sites to carry out research during school hours would have been difficult, if not practically impossible. A further practical advantage of studying the school from the inside, which Johnson (1994) singles out, is that I was aware of management issues. At the same time, I considered that being seen on the premises by the students, some of whom would be participants in my research, would be beneficial for my rapport with them once the study got underway. I was well aware, however, that behind such a positive picture there were some significant concerns and that it would be foolish on my part to believe that undertaking research in my own institution would be entirely unproblematic.

I needed to take account of the fact that the sensitivity of the topic could have far-reaching consequences on the research process, on me personally and professionally, as well as on the participants themselves. What concerned me particularly was the reaction I would get from colleagues once I informed them that my subject area was 'Masculinities in School'. Would the study be misinterpreted as a perverse interest in boys and would my own masculinity and sexual orientation be questioned as a result? Sikes (2006, p. 109) does comment that such a topic could be 'dodgy' if 'someone, regardless of their sexuality, does not want to be the subject of such identity speculation or attribution'. Would my questions about this topic in my school affect my colleagues' and superiors' perception of me? Would a possible 'stigma' affect me professionally in the form of career disadvantage? Disheartening indeed is Lee's (1993, p. 10) remark that 'jobs or promotion may be closed … because administrators fear difficulty or controversy'. Haywood and Mac an Ghaill (2002) and Sikes (2006) comment on similar threats to the researcher.

Of equal concern was the way the school administration would react once the research began. Lee (1993) warns that research which might bring to light that which was formerly hidden can be unwelcome. In the likelihood of my research revealing deviant activities, would my position as a researcher be undermined? Considering the nature of the investigation, would I be charged with subverting or casting doubt on traditional values?

Another concern was the willingness or otherwise of my colleagues to openly comment on the school system or their peers even though confidentiality would be assured. I also had to consider the fact that my relationship with many members of staff, both on a personal and on a professional level, would have to continue after the research. As a consequence, one major concern was whether my enquiries would cast a long-term blight on my day-to-day interaction with my colleagues.

These constraints could not be overlooked. However, in view of the potential that conducting research from within had both on a personal and on a professional level, I concluded that this was still the most feasible option.

Bias

Initially, I was somewhat preoccupied by an issue which runs through the literature on educational research–that of bias. Wellington (1996) warns that to some extent prejudices and preconceptions on the part of the researcher, as well as problems of familiarity that might exist between researcher and staff members, can be an obstacle to objectivity. Carr and Kemmis (1986), remark that the charge is often made that research involving researchers analysing their own practices is always biased. However, they contend that this way of construing the problem of 'bias' suggests that there is some 'value-free' or 'neutral' medium in which praxis could be described and analysed in ways which are unrelated to the values and interests of those conducting the research. They maintain that this is an illusion created by the image of a value-free 'objective' social science. They hold that any science of human praxis must embody values and interests, both as objects of enquiry and as knowledge-constitutive interests for the science itself. Jones (2001) reminds us that educational research is concerned with human beings and their behaviour, involving a great number of players, each of whom brings to the research process a wide range of perspectives and 'truths', including the researcher's own. In her judgment, this can produce a more balanced and in this sense a more 'objective' account of the gradual development and modification of 'truths' as they emerge from the interplay of action and reflection. As a result, the researchers' experiences and values are not something to be bracketed away as if they are ashamed of their entry into the process. On the contrary, an examination of the basis of these values and their relationship to decisions and stages in research is required for the foundations of good social research (May 1993).

Such accounts of researcher positionality highlighted the need to carefully consider questions about clarity of roles, responsibilities and activities throughout the study. I had to recognise that the views and understandings which I had been striving to achieve as a researcher could be influenced or distorted by the 'individual/ personal me' as well as by the 'professional me'. In consequence, I carried out my research with a keen awareness, not only of the advisability of addressing professional ambiguities, but also of searching within myself and of being 'meaningfully attentive' (Peshkin 1988, p. 17) to my subjectivity and of keeping constantly in mind the assumptions embedded in my own positioning. After all, my project indirectly stemmed from my own life as a student in the school where I work and where my research was conducted.

In view of the above, it was useful to remember that this aspect of my subjectivity, which was rooted beyond visibility (Popkewitz 1988, p. 379), would continue to influence my perception since: '… history and social structures impinge upon us in ways of which we can never be fully conscious' (Thomson 1998, p. 3). I knew that, rather than exorcise my subjectivity, I had to manage it to prevent it from being unwittingly burdensome as I collected, analysed and wrote up my data. I understood all along that working in my own personal and professional backyard would make it impossible for me to achieve the strangeness of distance. However, it did not preclude cautious investigation, awareness and understanding.

The school in question

The study was conducted in the Secondary Section of St John's College,[1] a single-sex Church Comprehensive School comprising Junior, Secondary and Sixth Form sections.

It is worth noting that I occupied a unique position as a researcher from the inside, in that I am a member of the Sixth Form section of the college, whilst I carried out my fieldwork in the Secondary section. Although I maintained close social contact with many members of staff, considering that I had spent the first four years of my teaching career in the secondary school, I did not have much professional contact with them except with the nine members of the English Department, of which I was the Head. Therefore, I carried out research from within in the sense that I was on site, yet professionally was not very much part of that institution.

Following Bell (1997, p. 52) who insists that 'permission to carry out an investigation must always be sought at an early stage' and that 'no researcher can demand access to an institution', I was aware that I was a member of the organisation, I could not expect access as of right. Hence, before finalising my plans I approached the Head of the Secondary School. I explained what I planned to investigate and how I would go about it, and permission was immediately granted.

Since October 2005, all research done by staff and students at The University of Sheffield has to be ethically cleared by an ethics review procedure, yet this was not the case in my time. Thus, when I conducted my research I did not have to go through any formal ethics review.

In the field

The next stage was the search for adequate methods of data collection.

Methods of data collection

In attempting to operationalise the case study approach, I considered one consistent message from the literature, i.e. that 'good' case studies incorporate multiple sources of data (Anderson 1990; Johnson 1994). At the start, I was convinced that a single method for the investigation of the complex social reality I intended to investigate would be insufficient. Indeed, my decision was influenced by critical perspectives that advise the need to employ a multi-method approach (Fielding and Fielding 1986; Finch 1986; Brown and Dowling 1998; Ralph 1999; Holtzhausen 2001).

As I contemplated a multi-method approach, two over-riding concerns were: (i) Which methods to select? (ii) How were they to be combined?

In order to strengthen research design, I felt that it was appropriate to employ a 'between-methods data triangulation' approach and 'respondent triangulation' (Burgess 1985). The rationale behind this was that through careful and purposeful combination of different methods, breadth and depth are added to the analysis (Fielding and Fielding 1986), a more complete, holistic and contextual portrayal can be captured (Finch 1986; Holtzhausen 2001) and the trustworthiness of results is enhanced (Ralph 1999).

This entailed combining quantitative and qualitative approaches, as well as accommodating the perspectives of all participants – teachers, students and my own. Deciding how to combine methods involved analysing which ones, complementing each other, would build up as a detailed picture of the areas I was investigating as time and facilities permitted.

The research process

As I have previously stressed, the main intention of my study was to examine the extent of the impact of secondary schooling on the way boys experience being male.

I therefore placed the students themselves at the centre of the research and focused on their perceptions. The key aim was to plumb their beliefs and feelings and, in so doing, examine if, and in what ways, the ethos of the school influenced their attitudes and their personal identities as boys. I felt that, apart from capturing students' perspectives, I should also consider multiple and different perspectives and hence decided to regard the teachers' views too. In order to do this, I utilised a questionnaire and an interview as my chief instruments of data collection. Considerations of time, as well as previous experience of these research tools (Portelli, 1998), were behind this decision.

Questionnaires were chosen because they can provide a rapid and relatively inexpensive way of discovering the characteristics and beliefs of the population at large (Walker 1985; May 1993). They also tend to be reliable and, because they are anonymous, can encourage greater honesty. I constructed two questionnaires, one for a cross section of the student population and another for members of staff.

I opted to focus on three separate age groups of students: Form[2] 1 students (12-year-olds in their first year of secondary school), Form 3 students (14-year-olds midway through secondary schooling) and Form 5 boys (16-year-olds who had reached the end of their secondary education). I was particularly interested in investigating if there were any notable changes in the students' perceptions and attitudes towards gender as they grew older and experienced more of the social practices, routines and human interaction in the school. In order to obtain data about teachers' views on practices within the institution, I distributed the teacher questionnaire to all the teachers in the Secondary Section of the school.

I decided to conduct semi-structured interviews with a sub-sample of students to enhance understanding of findings emerging from the survey. I should add, however, that I did not interview members of staff. There were two reasons for this. Since the intention was primarily to capture students' perceptions, I felt that it would be better for the purposes of my study to focus more on them. Secondly, I did not believe that interviews would be advisable in the light of the sensitivity of the information I sought and, given the climate prevalent in the school at the time, to which I have already alluded.

Before I go on to discuss the research process in greater depth, I feel it is important to point out that although for many boys school is one of the few sites through which they learn about sexuality (Gilbert and Gilbert 1998) and that sex education plays a critical role in school curricula, I could not address this area of the curriculum in my research. Sex education is a particularly sensitive topic in Church schools in the light of the Catholic Church's views on a number of issues related to sex and sexuality. Hence, this area of the curriculum is closely scrutinised by local Church authorities. Because I was working from the inside, I felt uncomfortable placing Personal and Social Education (PSE) teachers (in whose lessons sex education takes place) in an awkward situation by asking them to openly discuss how they tackle such issues in their lessons.

The questionnaires

Mindful of the need to try out 'the research techniques' (Blaxter et al. 1996, p. 121) I piloted the questionnaires within the school: the student questionnaire with a sample (15) of the various age groups and the teacher questionnaire with three close colleagues. After this, the student questionnaire was modified slightly. Ambiguous questions were revised and the questionnaire was shortened considerably. After the necessary surgery, both questionnaires were finally ready.

The student pilot study indicated that it would be best for me to be with the students in class while they completed the questionnaire, which, for simplification purposes, was in English. The pilot study hinted at the possibility that language would be a major constraint. Although students study English throughout their school years, a number of them have difficulty in understanding or communicating in the language. For this reason I believed that it would be useful to be there to translate questions into Maltese if students failed to understand them in English. The pilot study demonstrated that it would take at least an hour to complete the questionnaire. This meant I had to be in class for two forty-minute lesson sessions.

The questionnaire was distributed to two Form 1 classes, two Form 3 classes and two Form 5 classes – a total of 126 students. It was not easy to keep students interested in the questionnaire for an hour at a stretch but the fact that they were missing two lessons in order to do this was a great motivator! What I also found useful was the relationship I had built with the students prior to administering the questionnaire. I must add that, at this stage, students were informed that they could opt out of the exercise if they wished and could spend the lessons in question in the library.

As mentioned earlier, feminist studies include a strong connection between researcher and participants. In line with my pro-feminist stance, before I distributed the student questionnaire, I ensured that the students and I got to know each other better, and particularly that they got to learn about my research. Studying the institution from within proved to be beneficial in this respect, as I was on site all day and therefore could access classes whenever it was possible for me to do so. Consequently, I replaced teachers who were on sick leave in the classes I had targeted and did so at least three times in each class before actually handing out the questionnaires and at least twice after the research process was completed. This rapport bore fruit when I later carried out my interviews with a sample from each class.

Distribution of the teacher questionnaire constituted the final part of the process. I handed these out after the students' questionnaires were completed and all interviews with students carried out. I had already informed some colleagues about my studies. However, the majority still had no idea about what I was working on. Therefore, I attached an informal letter to the questionnaires, describing what I was doing in some detail and specifying a return date. I distributed 55 questionnaires in all: 28 to all female members and 27 to all male members of staff. 35 questionnaires were returned – i.e. 64% (17 by males and 18 by females), a greater percentage than I had originally expected.

The interviews

It was clear from the start that to expect someone to reveal important and personal information without entering into a dialogue was untenable. If interviewees were to share information with me, effective communication required a degree of trust between myself as that interviewer and the students as interviewees. This meant I had to be informal, casual and understanding and could not wear the 'hat' of teacher during the sessions. Rather, my role had to be chiefly one of the facilitator encouraging students to express their views on a wide range of topics and to share their experiences freely. The fact that I was not a teacher in the Secondary section of the school was advantageous, in the sense that students did not view me as a teacher in the strict sense of the word, though they knew I was a teacher in another section of the school. My contact with the students prior to the questionnaire and interview proved to be fruitful too. I was keen to view the interviews as social encounters and not simply as a passive means of gathering information.

Prior to the interviews, I ensured that the location chosen was appropriate. I believed it was important to find a quiet place where we could feel relaxed and where we would not be disturbed. I originally intended to conduct the interviews in my office but there were two problems which led me to seek alternative arrangements. First, the window of my office overlooks a recreation area which would be distracting and, second, my office is adjacent to other teachers' offices and could compromise responses given the sensitive and confidential nature of the research. Consequently, I asked a colleague if I could make use of her office, which is situated in a very quiet part of the school. In order to create an informal and relaxed atmosphere I used four comfortable armchairs and provided snacks and drinks. Playing home, as it were, came into its own – I knew the school environment inside out, hence knew exactly what would be the best venue for the interviews, and the fact that I could approach colleagues for help was an added advantage.

I had originally intended to conduct one-to-one interviews, yet, within a context of ever-increasing numbers of reports of sexual abuse of children, I felt that it would not be wise to pursue these plans. Besides, some researchers also suggest that one-to-one interviews may be too pressurising and difficult for some children (Mauthner 1997). Consequently, I resorted to small group interviews (three students at a time) which I believed would provide a secure enough environment for students to express their opinions and voice their concerns freely if the atmosphere within the group was intimate and relaxed.

Participation in the interviews was voluntary and a great number of students were enthusiastic to participate. The choice of students from the classes concerned was random. Before I conducted the study, the interview schedule was tested with three 15-year-old students. Each interview (6 sessions and 18 students in all) lasted approximately 60–70 minutes.

An important area of discussion within the literature on interviewing in recent years, particularly so in the work of feminist writers, has been the role of power in the interviewer/respondent relationship (Lee 1993). I was fully aware of the imbalances of power that existed between me and the participants. Although it was clear that students had power over what they chose to say and therefore over my data collection, I understood that I had more power over the students by possessing information which would be potentially damaging to them if I were to disclose what they told me about my colleagues. Therefore, in an attempt to achieve as great an equivalence as possible, whenever students became so engrossed in their own experiences that they discussed them at some length, which at times was irrelevant to my purposes, my role was deliberately non-interventional. In other words, I allowed them to exercise some control. Furthermore, when they expressed views which, in other circumstances, would have elicited a swift and sharp rebuke on my part as teacher, I deliberately chose to remain silent and grit my teeth!

On further reflection it dawned on me that I had power not only over the students but over my colleagues as well. Students' responses were tremendously revealing of the nature of teachers' pedagogies, as well as their relationships and behaviour with students and towards one another. Some of the findings did not do credit to a number of colleagues and they would have a lot to answer for were this information to become public. I found this disconcerting and wondered whether possessing such knowledge would affect my friendship or alter the way I regarded them. What was also particularly disturbing was the information I gathered about the way English was being taught by certain individuals. As Head of the English Department, it was my responsibility to take action and speak to the teachers concerned in the hope of redressing matters immediately. However, I knew I could not intervene based on what had been revealed during the course of my research as I was bound by my promise of confidentiality. It would have been highly unethical to do so.

Quite rightly, Pring (2001) remarks that research requires very special sorts of virtues, both moral and intellectual, and it is true to say that ethical considerations played a major role throughout the research process.

Ethical considerations

Ethical issues are inseparable from research. Therefore, just as it was important to know the principles of research methods and adapt them to my own needs, so was it equally important that I be aware of the professional approach to research ethics and consider what the ethical implications of my own research were going to be.

What is nowadays taken as given and essential in research is the notion of 'informed consent' (David et al. 2001). It was immediately apparent to me that I had to communicate the purpose of my study as well as making clear what it was I wanted participants to do. As I have said, I used whole-class sessions in order to introduce myself and the study. Another fundamental principle for ethical acceptability is the principle of privacy and, understandably, the greater the sensitivity of the information, the more safeguards are called for to protect participants.

Two ways in which participants can be protected are Anonymity and Confidentiality. Confidentiality was, in fact, an issue I faced from the outset. Where the teacher questionnaires were concerned I ensured that (i) information about subjects taught and years of teaching experience would not be sought and (ii) the questionnaire would be handed back to me personally in a sealed envelope. As regards questionnaires with students I did not ask for any personal information, such as parents' occupations or social background. The fact that I did not teach any of these students also meant that I could not identify them by their handwriting. Although anonymity could not apply to the interviews, I guaranteed confidentiality. My aim was not to create any disturbance in the working arrangements, the lifestyle or the relationships of the people involved. I had an ethical obligation to protect them and to act responsibly and morally. This is why the confidential and anonymous nature of the research was stressed.

Nonetheless, I felt a tension between telling the truth and withholding or modifying it for fear of the consequences. Even though I used a pseudonym for the school, anybody in Malta knowing me and where I teach would also know the identity of the school. I felt that, in view of the sensitive nature of my findings, this could jeopardise the reputation of the school and its administration. In this respect, Lee (1993) gives strong indications that identification carries with it the risk of sanctions and stigma from various sources.

Therefore, on the one hand, as a researcher, I was determined not to play down certain aspects of my findings when I discussed them and, on the other, as a teacher within the same institution, I knew I had responsibilities to the school and to my colleagues. Consequently, from the start I had to take into account possible ways in which my research findings were going to be used. Following Lee (1993) and Pring (2001), I decided that I would exercise self-censorship by omitting sensitive material from the copies I would circulate locally. However, I could still refer to this information within the school, for example during staff seminars some time in the future though **not** in a report to the Head or Administrators.

Writing and disseminating the results

The research started in January 2002 and was completed in June 2002. The results section of my thesis took me six months to write and edit and I submitted my thesis in January 2003. As an off shoot from the thesis, I wrote two papers: 'Role of Boys' Peer Groups In A Secondary School In Malta' (2004), published in *Journal of Maltese Education Research*, and 'Language: An important signifier of masculinity' (2006), published in *Gender and Education.*

Working with the results of my research

The research I carried out within my school enabled me to become fully aware of strategies that had to be introduced to ensure better 'masculinity training' for the students attending the school. However, at the time, I was not part of the Senior

Management team and there was very little I could do to influence a change of practice where this was deemed necessary. In fact, in the period immediately following my study, I was disappointed, since the Head had never asked me about my research nor enquired about the findings of my study. This was a letdown because I had imagined originally that my study would be put to good use for the benefit of all students at school. I thought I would be invited to deliver a talk during staff development day/s or, at least, discuss the generalised findings with all members of the school management team. Unfortunately, this was not to be. Hence, one major advantage of carrying out research from within had been negated. The school had a wealth of information at its fingertips which it could have utilised, yet it missed the boat.

However, I felt I could still contribute as the Head of the English Department. My first priority at the start of the scholastic year following the analysis of my data was to encourage members of the department to reflect on whether they were sending out messages about masculinity and using pedagogical practices that are not primary motivators for boys. Furthermore, on the basis of my findings, I alerted them to the fact that they, as teachers of English, are at a disadvantage because of the prevalent impression among many boys that speaking English is a 'female' thing to do. Additionally, as a result of my research, I felt that the time had come to review current pedagogies and text books and that process was immediately initiated.

Leaving the field

Although researching from within did enable me to make some use of the results of the research to try to improve things, albeit on a very small scale, there are a number of matters that still weigh on my mind. First and foremost is the extent to which my position as a male, a former student and a teacher in the institution affected the data that I obtained and subsequently influenced my analysis. I am very conscious of the influence that my own experiences at the school as a student have had on my research, specifically influencing my decision to focus on certain activities which troubled me during those years. These include the way sport is practised and the way some male teachers demonstrate a liking for particular kinds of boy, rather than for others. As for my looking into the language problem, that arose from a professional interest in the subject.

Another area of concern was that, however pro-feminist my perspective, and the aims or methods I adopted, however much I tried to establish a good rapport with the students and avoid treating them as 'objects', there was no getting away from the fact that they were the 'subjects' of my research. Despite the 'power' I let them wield during our encounters, I was perturbed by the thought that, unless my research could be utilised as a mouthpiece against injustices in the school, I had ultimately taken advantage of them for my own purposes.

Unfortunately, too, developments that took place in the institution very soon after my research was concluded only served to strengthen this impression.

I am referring here to the promotion of the Assistant Head, frequently referred to disparagingly in interviews, to the position of Head. Interestingly, those students who declared that they were convinced that if the opportunity arose it would be he who would get the job have been proved correct. At first, I was also concerned about the fact that the questions I asked students, both in the questionnaire and during the interview, around their choice of who they deemed ideal to fill the post of Head of School very soon sounded somewhat 'suspect'. Did students believe I had deceived them and that my research had been carried out with an eye to providing information to the school authorities as to who was the best candidate for the job? At the same time I felt that I had also let the students down, considering that my research has not been of much help to them once the person they had expressed such negative opinions about was now their Headmaster! These feelings of guilt would not have arisen had I not carried out my research within my own institution.

Moreover, carrying out research from within created some problems for me living in a small country like Malta, where everyone knows everyone, which I had not envisaged on drawing up my research proposals. One major hindrance is the fact that I cannot divulge all the findings of the study because, once I state I carried out research from within, readers in Malta are automatically alerted to the fact that I am discussing one particular school on the island. I found this to be an obstacle in my decision or otherwise to write for academic purposes. In fact, in my writing for the local journal, I did not specify that my study involved carrying out research from within.

I faced an embarrassing moment last year during a lecture to Masters students at the University of Malta, when I was discussing some of the findings of my study without spelling it out to them that I had carried out inside research. One of the students is a teacher at the college who knew only too well which school I was discussing and to which teachers I was referring. This put a great strain on me, since I knew that I couldn't divulge all my materials, but at the same time was aware that I would have driven my points home more effectively had I been able to provide all the information.

Conclusion

From my own experience, carrying out research from within has many points in its favour. First, one works in an environment one knows well, access may be easy to obtain and colleagues may be very supportive and helpful. Second, if the researcher works full time in an educational institution such as a school, it is practical to carry out research within that institution and less stressful in the sense that the researcher doesn't have to visit other schools during their free time or take time off to do so. Third, it may be rewarding to obtain results from one's own institution and be able to work with these results for the benefit of all.

However, experience has taught me not to be too idealistic. There is no guarantee that researchers will find superiors who are keen on using some or all of the results obtained during the research process. Second, when sensitive information is obtained, such as information on colleagues, it is hard for the researchers' attitude towards those people to remain unchanged. The researchers may also feel rather awkward in their everyday dealings with them, fully aware of the fact that they are in possession of certain information which may not be that pleasant about the person concerned. I experienced this myself in my dealings with certain colleagues after my study. Third, colleagues' attitude towards the researchers may be affected, with their knowing only too well that you as a researcher may have information about them which you may make use of, even though confidentiality is promised at the earliest of stages.

Therefore, when one contemplates one's research methodology, one has to give the matter enough thought and be prepared to face the consequences of one's action. One needs to understand that the outcome of one's decision may not be what one had envisaged prior to the research process.

Research from within can be very rewarding yet disappointing too. It's all a matter of the context one works in and the numerous circumstances one faces, which often only come to light after the research has been completed.

Notes

1 In order to preserve anonymity, this is the pseudonym I used for the school in my thesis.
2 By Form in this study, I mean Year-Group.

References

Anderson, G. (1990) *Fundamentals of Educational Research.* Bristol, The Falmer Press.
Bassey, M. (1992) 'Creating education through research'. *British Educational Research Journal,* 18, 1, pp 3–16.
Bell, J. (1997) *Doing Your Research Project.* Buckingham, Open University Press.
Blaxter, L., Hughes, C. and Tight, M. (1996) *How to Research.* Buckingham, Open University Press.
Brown, A. and Dowling, P. (1998) *Doing Research/Reading Research: A Mode of Interrogation.* London, Falmer Press.
Burgess, R. G. (1985), 'Key informants and the study of a comprehensive school', in Burgess, R.G. (Ed) (1985) *Strategies of Educational Research.* London, Falmer Press.
Carr, W. and Kemmis, S. (1986) *Becoming Critical.* Bristol, The Falmer Press.
David, M., Edwards, R. and Alldred, P. (2001) 'Children and School-Based Research: "informed consent" or "educated consent"?. *British Educational Research Journal,* 27, 3, pp. 347–365.
Deem, R. (1996) 'Theory, User Relevance and Feminist Research in Education', Paper presented at The British Educational Research Association Conference, Lancaster, September.
Drysdale, D. (1985) 'Research and the Education Administrator', in Shipman, M. (ed) (1985) *Educational Research, Policies and Practices.* Lewes, The Falmer Press, pp. 72–80.
Fielding, N.G. and Fielding, J.L. (1986) *Linking Data.* Qualitative Research Methods Series, 4, California, Sage.

Finch, J. (1986) *Research and Policy: The Uses of Qualitative Methods in Social and Educational Research.* London, Falmer Press.

Gilbert, R. and Gilbert, R. (1998) *Masculinity goes to School.* London, Routledge.

Griffiths, M. (1998) *Education Research for Social Justice: Getting off the Fence.* Buckingham, Open University Press.

Hammersley, M. (2000) 'The Relevance of Qualitative Research'. *Oxford Review of Education.* 26, 3 and 4, pp. 393–405.

Hammersley, M. (2002) *Educational Research: Policy Making and Practice.* London, Paul Chapman Publishing.

Haywood, C. and Mac an Ghaill, M. (2002) 'Coming out as a man: methodologies of masculinities', in Haywood, C. and Mac an Ghaill, M. (2002) *Men and Masculinities: Theory, Research and Social Practice.* Buckingham, Open University Press.

Hitchcock, G. and Hughes, D. (1989) *Research and the Teacher: A Qualitative Introduction to School-Based Research.* London, Routledge.

Holtzhausen, S. (2001) 'Triangulation as a powerful tool to strengthen the qualitative research design: The Resource-Based Learning Career Preparation Programme (RBLCPP) as a case study', Paper presented at the Higher Education Close Up Conference, Lancaster University, 16–18 July.

Johnson, D. (1994) *Research Methods in Educational Management.* London, Longman.

Lee, R.M. (1993) *Doing Research on Sensitive Topics.* London, Sage Publications.

Mauthner, M. (1997) 'Methodological aspects of collecting data from children: Lessons from three research projects'. *Children and Society,* 11, pp. 16–28.

May, T. (1993) *Social Research: Issues, Methods and Process.* Buckingham, Open University Press.

Mortimore, P. (1999) *Does Educational Research Matter?* Institute of Education, University of London, Presidential address to the British Educational Research Association Annual Conference, University of Sussex at Brighton, September 2–5.

Peshkin, A. (1988) 'In search of subjectivity'. *Educational Researcher,* 7, pp. 17–21.

Popkewitz, T.S. (1988) 'The Ontario Institute for Studies in Education'. *Curriculum Inquiry,* 18, 4, Ontario, John Wiley and Sons.

Portelli, J.R. (1998) *Working Together: Collaboration in a Secondary School in Malta,* unpublished dissertation for the M.Ed. course, University of Sheffield.

Portelli, J.R. (2004) 'Role of Boys' Peer Groups In A Secondary School In Malta'. *Journal of Maltese Education Research,* 2, 2, December 2004, pp. 1–18.

Portelli, J.R. (2006) 'Language: An important signifier of masculinity in a bilingual context'. *Gender and Education,* 18, 4, July 2006, pp. 413–430.

Pring, R. (2001) 'The Virtues and Vices of an Educational Researcher', Paper presented at the *British Educational Research Association Annual Conference,* University of Leeds, 13–15 September.

Ralph, E.G. (1999) 'Oral-questioning skills of novice teachers: … Any questions?' *Journal of Instructional Psychology,* 26, 4, pp. 286–297.

Reinharz, S. (1992) *Feminist Methods in Social Research.* Oxford, Oxford University Press.

Sikes, P. (2006) 'On dodgy ground? Problematics and ethics in educational research'. *International Journal of Research and Method in Education,* 29, 1, pp. 105–117.

Soltis, J.F. (1990) 'The Ethics of Qualitative Research', in Eisner, E.W. and Peshkin, A. (eds) (1990) *Qualitative Inquiry in Education: The Continuing Debate.* New York, Teachers College Press, pp. 247–257.

Thomson, C. (1998) 'Researching for Myself: The Challenge of Achieving a Distinction between Research and Professional Roles, Responsibilities and activities', Paper presented at the Scottish Educational Research Association Annual Conference, September 24–26, West Park conference centre, Dundee.

Walker, R. (1985) *Doing Research: A Handbook for Teachers,* London, Methuen.

Wellington, J.J. (1996) *Methods and Issues in Educational Research.* Sheffield, University of Sheffield Division of Education.

Chapter 7

Is it all about me?
How Queer!

Mark Vicars

Introduction

This chapter considers my experience of doing research as a gay man with other gay men for my Doctoral study: *Dissenting Fictions: A study of the formative literacy practices of gay men.* My thesis investigated the influence that childhood and adolescent reading practices had on identity formation and I sought to map a relatively uncharted terrain of the socio-sexual contexts in which literacy behaviour is embedded. Throughout my research journey, I struggled to discipline and disentangle my voice from the communities of practice in which I have sought belonging and my positioning in the field as a man, as a friend, as a person aligned with a university doing a Ph.D. troubled the notion of a unified, authoritative stance from which to speak and write.

In this chapter, I reflect on how positionality can be used in social science investigations to contour differently nuanced research practices (Fonow and Cook, 1991; PNG, 1989). I consider how our ways of being with each other facilitated a Queer movement in methodology, where the production of knowledge shifted away from procedures guaranteeing uniformity, standardisation and normalisation into perspectival dispositions that rapidly erased the boundaries between the researcher and the researched.

My worry about entering the domain of fieldwork was fuelled by existing limitations of what I could be and how. To extenuate the dualities of insider/outsider, I drew upon the theoretical framework of Queer theory to interrogate how a way of being, as well as a way of thinking, is a relation to others and started to think about identity as something that gets done in multiple locations. In deciding to Queer the field, I felt better placed to question the dominant idiom, the silent, the unspoken and the normalised. Adopting a Queer stance made

> ... it possible [for me] to see the world differently and so be able to act in different ways ... it [provided me] with the space to ... be different.
>
> (Schratz and Walker, 1995, p. 125)

What, When, Where, How?

Without insider access, it would have proved difficult to find gay men in education willing and prepared to talk openly about their experiences (Squirrel, 1989). Therefore, the research design employed a non-probability snowball sample and I contacted ex-colleagues and someone I had known for some time who recruited friends and ex-lovers. The informants, who took part in the group discussions, eventually comprised of three men who work in education and live in a major city in the north of England and two men who worked abroad. Due to their overseas location, my original design had to be modified, so over the stretch of one summer I had several meetings with these two informants and did one-to-one interviews. The group meetings began in September 2004; we met twice a month at the house of one of the men for a total of sixteen sessions that each lasted, on average, between four to five hours.

At the first meeting, I solicited the men's opinions of conducting the interviews in a group setting. I/we decided to pursue this arrangement as it was felt we might be able to cross-fertilise each other's stories with a collective commentary as we discursively interrogated the wider contexts, social structures and social relations that have had an impact on our private and public lives (see Davies and Gannon, 2006). It was also felt that an open forum 'allow(ed) for the discovery of unanticipated issues' (Frith, 2000, p. 278).

As a starting point I drew guidance from the Biographic Narrative Interpretive Method (Chamberlayne et al., 2000), and asked informants to Tell me the story of their reading practices in relation to their life experiences. At the outset I didn't have any assumptions about the stories that would be told and the first session(s) got off to a clumsy start, hampered by doubts of my efficacy as a novice researcher. I didn't want my presence in the interviews to be solely that of a 'researcher' and sought to position myself 'beside'. I wanted our relationships to happen in a different kind of communicative space and I spoke of how I hoped to 'Queer' the procedural rules that underpin fieldwork identities, construct social relations and govern the practice of the researcher's science. Being 'beside', I believed would offer the potential of dislocating and transforming relations within the field; as Sedgewick (2004) has noted:

> Beside comprises a wide range of desiring, identifying, representing, repelling, paralleling, differentiating, rivalling, leaning, twisting, mimicking, withdrawing, attracting, aggressing, warping and other relations.
>
> (Sedgewick, 2004, p. 8)

I was interested to explore how the self in dialogue with others can position the researcher in important ways (Sparkes, 2002) and I discussed with the men how our ways of being together might provide opportunities for us to discursively re-produce the ethnographic space.

Liminal ... location, location, location

Russell and Kelly (2002) have noted how subjectivity in research information originates with both the researcher(s) and participant(s), each of whom brings individual experiences and pre-existing perspectives into the research event. However, within legitimising institutional discourses 'sexual identity is regarded as part of one's private life, and therefore, according to the prevailing norms of academic culture, not supposed to intrude into one's professional life (Wafer, 1996, p. 262). Such a view has its origins in an ideological system that constructs and legitimises the terms and conditions of how the ethnographer enters the ethnography, however, the premise that sexuality should be absent or concealed in the research encounter has been questioned by Kulick and Willson (1995) and Lewin and Leap (1992). I soon came to realise that our way of being with each other was being cultivated by our willingness to participate in those habits of being through which we had become and are revealed as gay men, what Miller (1998) has termed the 'open secret'. Some of the men talked about how they made visible a queer identity through camp performance, and our conversation spiralled into how the use of campy language is often a way of acting visible within intricate relations with others. As a chosen manner of being in the world, we talked about the utility of using a camp in terms of identity formation, self-definition and as a means of affiliation. We referenced our encounters with Polari[1] and spoke of its utility as a form of knowledge (Hill, 1996), it being social semiotic through which gay men materialised their identities, pre-decriminalisation of homosexuality in the U.K. in 1967.

In my attempt to make queer voice visible within the largely heteronormative framework of hegemonic educational discourse, I decided to represent our 'improper' ways of being and speaking by utilising Polari-inflected names to textualise positionality in the thesis.

Getting stuck in

The discussions became increasingly 'messy affairs' and it would be fair to say that they didn't conform to my expectations of what I thought I would be doing when doing research. At the first session we all brought the host flowers. He, in turn, tried out his latest recipe book and, as we dined on a range of Mediterranean fare, we engaged in scurrilous gossip and 'dished the dirt'.

As the evening progressed, I became increasingly concerned that the conversation had not extended much beyond work place bitching, sex encounters and boyfriend troubles. This was nothing like fieldwork and the uppermost thought in my mind was, 'When would I get to collect the "real" data?' I wanted to get the men talking about their reading practices but the conversation spiralled off into what Barton and Hamilton (1998) have called 'ruling passions':

> When we went to interview people we wanted to find out about reading, writing and literacy practices. Unfortunately, it seemed the people we

interviewed often wanted to talk about something else; each person has a ruling passion ... We talked to them about literacy, it seemed, and they talked to us about their lives.

(Barton and Hamilton, 1998, p. 83)

We talked at some length about being positioned in relation to the straight cultural imaginary and how it produced varying degrees of anxiety about embodying a stigmatised identity. We spoke about how the prevailing narratives surrounding lesbian and gay subjects within the public order tend to normalise stories that habitually work to deposit sexual difference outside of accepted cultural and sexual boundaries, identities and communities. As we flowed in and out of each other's stories we began to meander into intersubjective territories, and Herda (1999) has noted how:

The creation of a text is a collaborative achievement and by virtue of people working together to uncover shared meanings there is opened in front of the text the possibility of a different and presumably a better world. This world is not validated by scientific criteria that measure neutrality, simplicity, or repeatability.

(Herda, 1999, p. 2)

During the drive back home after that first session, I was somewhat perplexed as to what had been going on and to what extent, if any, fieldwork had taken place. Admittedly, it had been a thoroughly enjoyable evening and I felt that it had been successful in grounding our emerging relationships in a context of open, honest and trusting discussion. I had shared some of my own stories of disastrous blind dates and doomed sexual exploits, but I remained uncertain about what could be constituted as data. Playing back the recording of the evening a few days later, I struggled to find anything that I considered as being worthwhile. Could any of this be of any use?

Inauthentic tales – making a dramatic spectacle out of ourselves.

Dramatis personae:
MOTHER – Flamboyant, all singing and dancing host for the occasion.
AUNTY – Mother's ex-lover, a butch(ish) top.
INGENUE – Mother's protégé and work colleague.
NOVICE RESEARCHER – Friend to Mother.

Act One, Scene One

A dinner party, at the table are arranged four 30-something gay men. Tonight is the first time, as a group, they have met face to face. Two of the men are ex-lovers, two are current work colleagues and two are ex-flatmates from University. The conversation reveals that all are teachers and as Mother clears away the dishes from the first course, refreshes drinks, changes the CD to yet another torch song compilation, he announces:

MOTHER: Enough, ENOUGH of work talk!
[He embarks on a different course of conversation and as the talk shifts to 'the dishing of dirt', the previously formal atmosphere is replaced by squeals of delight, a verbal applause at the revelation of the intimate. As more and more scurrilous gossip pours forth, appetites are whetted, another bottle of expensive red wine is opened and Mother embarks on exhaling the outrageous, each snippet punctuated with plumes and swirls of tobacco smoke.]

NOVICE RESEARCHER: Err … well; I was wondering if you had all managed to get a look at the outline of the research that I e-mailed.
AUNTY: Oh we will get to that later, have something more to drink. Tell us about the bathhouses in Bangkok.

[An hour later and after what could only be described as a confessional epic, the flow of conversation started to ebb …]

INGENUE: Do you have any specific questions that you are going to ask us?
MOTHER: Where do you want me to start, I could about myself talk all night.
INGENUE: Well … I enjoyed reading Batman, Spiderman and Superman comics.
AUNTY: That's 'cos you're a closet Muscle Mary fan! All you were interested in was the pictures of rippling thighs and pecs …. Do we all remember the cartoon called *He Man*? He had unfeasibly large thighs, he was absolutely fantastic! I love thighs! If you look at rugby players' thighs they are absolutely gorgeous. You know you couldn't possibly walk with the thighs of *He Man* ….
INGENUE: Oh shut up about thighs. Can we talk about something else?
AUNTY: What about telly? I have used to have a thing for the *Man from Atlantis*, he did this flagellic action that I found very, very erotic. I used to watch it loads and thought it absolutely fantastic! It turned me on in a way that I didn't know I could be turned on.
MOTHER: Oh, and *Thunderbirds*, what about that in terms of getting your rocks off, I mean in terms of cartoon characters. I thought Virgil was the better looking out of all of them in Thunderbirds

Gossip has been acknowledged as important in establishing and maintaining social relations and norms within a group (Blum Kulka, 2000; Coates, 1998) and Hodkinson (2005) has noted in his research on youth cultures how:

An ability to share sub cultural gossip, anecdotes and observations with respondents further enhanced initial rapport, as well as offering an invaluable and effective additional stimulus for conversation during the interviews themselves.

(Hodkinson, 2005, p. 139)

However, gossip is often constructed as an inauthentic discourse that merely repeats what is heard without critically examining the grounds or validity of the subject matter in question. As I became distracted by the increasing exchange of sex gossip, I was reminded of Cameron and Kulick's (2003) comments that: 'it is only when he engages in or talks about sex that an out gay man, say, can claim a gay identity or be perceived as being gay by others' (Cameron and Kulick, 2003 p. xi). It has been proposed that discourses be thought of as 'practices that systematically form the objects of which they speak, (Foucault, 1972, p. 149), and this idea assisted my thinking on how to conceptualise our sex gossip as a form of speech activity that initially operated to define our social relationships. Employing Roscoe's (1996) notion of 'gay culturing', a term that refers 'to the negotiation and formulation of homosexual desire into cultural forms and social identities' (Roscoe, 1996, p. 201) enabled me to grasp the significance of the type of talk being traded in our interactions.

Reflecting on the evening, I gradually realised how our gossiping acted as a type of dialogic interaction that helped to forge an emotional bond and build an interpersonal bridge that facilitated self-disclosure. Listening to accounts of how we stammered into knowing in relation to our sexuality, I realised that a 'grid of intimacy' (Trow, 1981) had emerged that facilitated an almost seamless flow of stories. The absence of an asymmetry of power afforded another kind of space to develop. We shared the asking of questions, commented on each other's stories and supplemented each other's telling with fragments of knowledge that folded in our multiple identities into a spiral narrative, as opposed to a logo centric sequence of events. The men and I worked together to uncover a collective understanding of the role that literacy had played in determining our preferred way of being within interactions with others and self. We talked about how books and movies became the main instruments of our confession. We discussed how we reconstructed texts for our own purposes and how we developed interpretive strategies that successfully displaced what has been called the heterosexual imaginary (Ingraham, 1997), those heterosexual forms of meaning that make it almost impossible to consider being anything but straight. We spoke about elaborating on what a text had given to fashion new stories and as we unearthed the past in the present, we acknowledged our various attempts and struggles with identifying with 'difference as the grounds for identity' (Britzman, 1995, p. 161).

Through the sharing of our life world experiences, we were able to identify how our textual interactions had over time inculcated understandings of self as members of gendered, classed and sexual communities. Through my proximal location as an 'insider', I became, to some degree, better positioned to participate in an internalised language and was thus better placed to collectively explore a range of experiences.

It's not what you do it's the way that you do it!

It's not what you do it's the way that you do it! Individuals inherit a particular space within an interlocking set of social relationships; lacking that space, they are nobody, or at best a stranger or an outcast'.

(MacIntyre, 1981, p. 32)

Act One, Scene Two

[Four weeks later. The men are seated on scatter cushions, Mother is finishing off lighting candles, pouring wine, rearranging cushions and making sure that the scattered bowls of olives and nuts are within easy reach.]

NOVICE RESEARCHER: How do you feel about doing this as a group?

INGENUE: It's not a problem, it's not stopped me talking

MOTHER: I am happy to talk about myself. I am happy to talk in a gay context as well, in terms of my everyday life; I think I live in a very heterosexual world. A lot of my friends are straight and even though I do have pockets of my friends who are gay we don't normally talk about these issues. I mean it's lovely that we can talk this way about being who we are.

AUNTY: I find our evenings very interesting and at the moment it is even more so because at the moment I live with my parents. I tend not to talk about my life with my parents 'cos even though they know that I am gay, it is not part of their life. I suppose I am living in a very heterosexual bubble so to do this … it's a bit like free therapy … You know when you talk with people about things and they go 'Oh yeah, I did that too' … you get a sense that you're not alone … and sometimes you just need reminding that gay people are everywhere. You know what I mean?

(To Novice Researcher)

I see you as a person who is actually in the group but you have to jump out sometimes, I suppose I see you as a subjective observer.

INGENUE: You are doing a Ph.D. but this is not at all clinical or clear cut and you're not being unsympathetic. There is a friendship value to this so I don't feel defensive; I feel that you are … testing the waters.

AUNTY: I think that you are getting a lot more than you anticipated. The brief that you gave us, whilst not narrow; I think has been exceeded …

MOTHER: I think the stories will come if you let us talk, that may mean endless eons of tape but I think the stories will come when we are talking.

Act One, Scene Three

[The men are sat in Mother's front room. The remains of paella and sangria are strewn across the floor and as they stretch out, relax and make themselves even

more comfortable they sink back in to oversized armchairs, stretch out on sofas and start to make fun of the Novice Researcher's antiquated tape-recorder.]

AUNTY: I've enjoyed tonight! It has been good to look back and reflect with a group of like minded people about who we were.

MOTHER: I've enjoyed the commonalities. We have all had common experiences and since the last session I have thought about that quite a lot.

AUNTY: I don't feel it has hindered us doing it this way and that is the best you can get. At the outset I thought that you might have had a set agenda that you had a list of research questions you wanted us to answer. What has happened from letting us talk is that things have come out and I guess that you will be able to pick from that what you need. I think of our conversations as being akin to free verse poetry. If you had started to restrict the stanzas of our speech by the way you formed the question then you are not going to get out of it what I think you want. Whereas, when you let people talk within a loosely based frame, as we are doing, then I think we all get more out of doing this. I think that we have got to continually refer to texts and my text is my experiences. Unless I am allowed to revisit quite a few of them there is no way I am going to bring out the one that I think is the best one. Revisiting my experiential texts is really a way about talking about my life in general.

MOTHER: I think I assumed that this would be quite easy because we have lots of things in common … but (to Aunty), I think your sexuality and personality as a gay man is very different to mine in respect of your experiences of growing up. I don't think that hinders, I think that in many ways it has helped.

The way in which our stories came to be told productively yielded narratives of complexity, diversity and texture and they did so by our being situated, not only as confidants, but as co-generators, co-elaborators and co-interpreters of meaning. The men's willingness to reveal the intimate details of their lives had, I believe, much to do with becoming united in a common rhythm, in a different 'dance of knowing' (Leck, 1994, p. 90). Drawing heavily on 'insider-oriented' knowledge, our discussions became infused with productive relations and inflected with doubled practices. As each of us became a witness to the processes of how as individuals we made sense of ourselves in the world, we drew upon shared frames of meaning to describe our experiences. I began to rethink the manner in which life stories, told in a group setting, could attend to issues of informant agency, advocacy and empowerment.

In the telling of their stories, the men often mixed styles; they were at times amusing, highly dramatic, sometimes sad, often ironic and camp. They refused to be constrained by convention and defied a model of operational logic. As we got lost in play and song, our discussions spiralled out of control, disturbing not only the techne of inquiry but also unsettled sedimented meanings, memories and desires. By evoking our histories together, we gave support, demonstrated care and, in synergy, challenged interpretations. The stories we told of the self knitted together our individual orientations with the needs and structures of society at large. We came to understand how our queerly nuanced narratives could in themselves be read as texts that spoke of the micropractices of power relations (Foucault, 1986). Lopez (1990) has remarked how:

> The stories people tell have a way of taking care of them. If stories come to you, care for them. And learn to give them away where they are needed. Sometimes a person needs a story more than food to stay alive. That is why we put these stories in each other's memory. This is how people care for themselves.
>
> (Lopez, 1990, p. 60)

Sitting in the room I used as a study, surrounded by photographs of friends, and ex-lovers, I began to reflect on the queer tales of coming-out, of bashings, of sex and of finding love in unlikely places. As I recalled the names and places, the incidents and experiences of living with shame and pride, I comprehended once more why, over the years, storytelling has mattered in our lives and as Sedwick (1994) has noted:

> The knowledge is indelible, but not too astonishing, to anyone with a reason to be attuned to the profligate way this culture has of denying and despoiling queer energies and lives … Everyone who survived has stories about how it was done.
>
> (Sedwick, 1994, p. 1)

Through thick and thin

As a gay man doing research with other gay men I spent many months reconsidering what was happening through being together in a friendship group. I increasingly questioned taken for granted assumptions about what can constitute 'data'. As we recalled the sensations elicited from past texts, as they flooded and coursed, transcending the separation between body and brain, we told of the risks that lurked in the most innocent of sentences and how we fell prey to the waiting page. We spoke of becoming hooked on the thrill of finding ourselves in text and of the shame we sometimes felt and how, with each turn of page, it grew stronger. As the words slipped from our mouths, I became increasingly anxious of how our illegitimate narrations would be interpreted. There were many moments of doubt and uncertainty when reflecting on our ways of being; I stumbled and fell towards new horizons of understanding. Reflexively thinking on the ways I behaved with the men involved negotiating the 'Being Here' space of the field and the 'Being There' space of the academy (Geertz, 1988 p. 148). However, being in-between is familiar territory and I came to regard it as a productive location to connect, to make sense and write a way out of our experiences. In many ways, my positioning in the field induced intellectual and emotional uncertainties. However, I came to realise, on leaving the field, how doing insider research had meant working within an 'ideology of doubt' (Richardson, 1997, p. 91) that had provided a productive space from which the 'data' could emerge.

St. Pierre (1997) suggests that post-foundational research aims to produce different knowledge and to produce knowledge differently. I began to think about my presence in the field as a form of transgressive data (Richardson, 1997) and how it would come to contextualise the telling of the stories. I had entered the field with the belief that situatedness is not a hindrance to knowledge but rather its condition and by breaching the legitimate boundaries of the knower/known relationship, questions had been raised about my positioning. Reflecting on the insider/outsider polarity that characterised my relationships with the men, I thought long and hard about why the men were so willing to share intimate details of their lives. Whilst we habitually take for granted that people are able to talk about themselves and their lives, we rarely question what makes us tell (and listen to) life stories and what interlocutors accomplish by that kind of talk. Enunciating a vulnerable self as a researcher and engaging in acts of collaborative storytelling had enabled me to disintegrate the boundaries between the knower and the known. The quality of the interpersonal encounter which Rogers (1962) regarded as the 'most significant element in determining effectiveness' (Rogers, 1962, p. 416) situated me as a companion, as opposed to an external interpreter and facilitated an interpersonal bridge along which could flow the two-way traffic of our lives.

Coming together as a group to explore our queer literacy practices, we found that we had shared many similar types of experiences and I used these and my knowledge of the men as the basis from which to start writing the stories of their lives.

Performing the page

> For those of us who write, it is necessary not only to scrutinize the truth of what we speak, but also the truth of that language by which we speak.
>
> (Lorde, 1984, p. 43)

Rehearsing my entrance onto the page, I was caught between wanting to tell stories but having to find the words first through which to speak. Language had been the substantive material that had bound us to the bulk of our experiences. It had formed the ways through we had been revealed/ hidden to the world. I could no longer pretend that our stories were just stories, they were '… the processes, procedures, and apparatuses whereby truth and knowledge are produced (Tamboukou and Ball, 2003, p. 4).

Brah (1996) has noted 'if practice is productive of power then practice is also the means of challenging power, (Brah, 1996, p. 125) and a central concern of mine in writing was to address the problem of trying to make queer voices visible within the largely heteronormative framework of hegemonic educational discourse. I wanted to erode the 'proper' orthodoxies of ethnographic representation and decided to play with style as a modality for representing the different voices of the men. For each man I used different typefaces and font sizes, I wanted to blend together our voices in the texts and drew upon on poetic devices and a performance syntax to create evocative moments that showed how 'Being marginal and flowing in and out text is … a construction from … being QUEER' (Leck, 1994, p. 90).

Tyler (1986), writing about evocative post-modern ethnography, has commented that texts constructed from out of this paradigm consist of 'fragments of discourse intended to evoke in the minds of both reader and writer an emergent fantasy of a possible world' (Tyler, 1986, p. 125). Writing evocatively meant showing interaction so that the reader might 'participate fully in the emotional process, and not merely observe the resolution' (Ellis, 1997, p. 127). Evocative narratives that engage a feeling, as well as a thinking, self are 'at the boundaries of disciplinary practices' (Sparkes, 2000, p. 21) and by resisting in telling a chronological story of my research I felt better equipped to represent the non-linear relationships and the flow of voices of the field.

I attempted to write out of '*the enactment of hybridity*', to construct a text of belonging that connected 'simultaneously to the world of engaged scholarship and the world of everyday life' (Nayarain, 1993, p. 672). I did so to critically break with the notion of the researcher as having authority and mastery over the research process and the written artefacts produced.

Plato (1974) spoke of how 'We don't know the truth about the past but we can invent a fiction as like it as maybe' (Plato, 1974, p. 138) and Geertz (1973), in *The Interpretation of Cultures*, comments that ethnographies are 'fictions', 'something made, something fashioned' (Geertz, 1973, p. 15). I experimented with writing to resist the structural frameworks that legitimise a mode of being and a method of telling. Richardson's (1993) encouragement 'to doubt any method of knowing or telling that can claim truth' (Richardson, 1993, p. 706) guided me in my efforts to find a modality that could authentically describe and represent our worlds.

I offer the idea that the reconstructed life histories in my thesis were socio-sexual cultural scripts, materialised within a framework of evocative storytelling (Sparkes, 2004), constructed on a canvas prepared by anthropological poetics (Brady, 2000) located within a temporal order of chaotic and epiphanic inducing research moments (Denzin and Lincoln, 2005). In my endeavour to Queer disciplinary epistemologies, I endeavoured to reconceptualise writing as a performative act. If, as it has been suggested, 'writing has nothing to do with signifying. It has to do with surveying, mapping, even realms that are yet to come' (Deleuze and Guattari, 1987, pp. 4–5), then my playful text helped to illustrate the complexity and richness that is afforded by opening up new possibilities of understanding.

However, by drawing on our multiple and overlapping histories, I struggled with the difficulties of enunciation. Throughout our discussions, there occurred a layering of understanding which evoked the copious ways through we have come to know the fabric of our lives. As I moved between socio-cultural identities constituted by relations of power, I was preoccupied with shifting the focus away from closure to opening up and trickily playing with the ritualistic scripts of the privileged and the represented. The stories that emerged could best be described as a blending of fact and fiction, memory and amnesia, the referential and the textual, the historical and the rhetorical. At times, I felt that I was journeying in foreign landscapes. Talburt (1999) has commented how:

> For ethnography to engage queer theories can be a difficult task, particularly when voice, visibility, the self and experience have inherently mediated forms and when knowledge and ignorance do not readily offer evidence of their workings. A difficulty is to discover how epistemologies that rely on seeing and hearing can be brought into dialogue with epistemologies that question what is seen and heard.
>
> (Talburt, 1999, p. 529).

In troubling the text I attempted to represent queer voices as necessary fictions that can parade the unspeakable and think the unthinkable. In my attempt to fracture what Atkinson (2004), regards as the 'deafening silence on sexualities in education' (Atkinson, 2004, pp. 55–56), I dismantled the wall between private and professional experience. There were moments of uncertainty and fatigue in which Other voices urged:

> you must go on, I can't go on, you must go on, and I'll go on, you must say words, as long as there are any, until they find me, until they say me, strange pain, strange sin, you must go on, perhaps it's done already, perhaps they have said me already, perhaps they have carried me to the threshold of my story, before the door that opens on my story, that would surprise me, if it opens, it will be I, it will be the silence, where I am, I don't know, I'll never know, in the silence you don't know.
>
> (Beckett, 1997, p. 418)

I subsequently came to realise how the production of knowledge inevitably bears the imprint of its knower and that 'No textual staging is ever innocent, we are always inscribing values in our writing, it is unavoidable, (Richardson, 1990, p. 12).

Conclusion

> Dowager: Doing this with you, telling you about my life is difficult because it is putting me in a position to truth and I feel that telling anyone about my life is the highest form of trust. It is about believing that one is not going to be betrayed. So when you say 'Tell me about that', I think 'Do I really want to?' However, telling some people is a risk worth taking. Being gay is private, having a private life, except with you, we have a shared common experience and there are times when one has to recognise the context of the telling.

Ethnographic narratives that seek to construct knowledge from the complexity of the unknown must surely involve a questioning of the regimes of truth that naturalise knowledge production. In my research, I employed my positionality to push the limits of ethnography and endeavoured to amplify how the formation of subjectivities and practices of self are discursively constituted in communities of practice and within relations of power. Utilising Queer Theory to '… question the constitution and effects of social and institutional norms' (Talburt, 1999, p. 537), I sought to fracture the mythical subjective/objective divide. Halperin (1995) in *Saint Foucault* notes how:

> Queer is by definition whatever is at odds with the normal, the legitimate, the dominant. There is nothing in particular to which it necessarily refers. It is an identity without essence. 'Queer' then demarcates not a positivity but a positionality vis-à-vis the normative … [Queer] describes a horizon of possibility whose precise extent and heterogeneous scope cannot in principle be delimited in advance.
>
> (Halperin, 1995, p. 62)

Reflecting on how my way of doing research questions emerged from my values, passions and preoccupations, I have subsequently come to understand that '… research is not an innocent or distant academic exercise but an activity that has something at stake and that occurs in a set of political and social conditions' (Smith, 2001, p. 5). If being in the centre gives knowledge of the centre, not of the margins, then it could be said that those who are at the margins have a double knowledge both of the centre and of the margins, thus a hidden dialectic exists. To contribute to a Queer visibility within the field of educational practice and research, I sought to 'decenter centres and disrupt hierarchies (Kamberelis, 2004, p. 167). By thinking of positionality as that which focuses on actions and not actors (Britzman, 1995) as a way of knowing, rather than something to be known (Kopleson, 2002), I endeavoured to trouble normalising expectation practices and pedagogies within educational research. By centring the queer I sought to Queer the centre and realised that the norms through which normativities are reiterated have a history and are recognisable, depending on who is involved and who is speaking.

Note

1. Polari is a vernacular lexicon that was in popular usage from 1930s to 1970s. As a form of 'insider' language, it offered homosexuals a vocabulary from which to speak about and from their identities in an age when to do would have resulted in punitive social consequences. See Baker, P. (2002) *Polari–The Lost Language of Gay Men*. London: Routledge.

References

Atkinson, E. (2004) 'Sexualities and resistance: queer(y)ing identity and discourse in education, in J. Satterthwaite, E. Atkinson and W. Martin (eds), *Educational Counter-Cultures: Confrontations, Images, Visions*. Stoke-on-Trent, Trentham Books.

Barton, D. and Hamilton, M. (1998) *Local Literacies: Reading and Writing in One Community*. London, Routledge.

Beckett, S. (1997) *Trilogy*. London, Kalder.

Blum Kulka, S. (2000) 'Gossipy events at family dinners: Negotiating sociability, presence and the moral order', in J. Coupland (ed), *Small Talk*. London, Longman.

Brady, I. (2000) 'Anthropological Poetics', in N. K. Denzin and Y.S. Lincoln (eds), *The Handbook of Qualitative Research* (2nd ed). Thousand Oaks, CA, Sage.

Brah, A. (1996) *Cartographies of Diaspora*. London, Routledge.

Britzman, D. P. (1995) 'Is There a Queer Pedagogy? Or Stop Reading Straight', *Educational Theory*, 45, 151–165.

Cameron, D. and Kulick, D. (2003) *Language and Sexuality*. Cambridge, Cambridge University Press.

Chamberlayne, P. Bornat, J. and Wengraf, T. (eds) (2000) *The Turn to Biographical Methods in Social Science: Comparative Issues and Examples*. New York, Routledge.

Coates, J. (1998) 'Gossip revisited: Language in all-female groups', in J Coates (ed), *Language and Gender: A Reader*. Oxford, Basil Blackwell.

Davies, B. and Gannon, S. (eds) (2006) *Doing Collective Biography*. Maidenhead, Open University.

Deleuze, G. and Guattari, F. (1987). *A Thousand Plateaus. Capitalism and Schizophrenia*. London, Continuum.

Denzin, N. and Lincoln, Y. (2005) 'Introduction: The Discipline and Practice of Qualitative Research', in N. Denzin and Y. Lincoln (eds), *The Handbook of Qualitative Research*. 3rd ed, Thousand Oaks, Sage.

Ellis, C. (1997) 'Evocative authoethnography', in W. G. Tierney and Y. S. Lincoln (eds), *Representation and the Text: Re-Framing the Narrative Voice*. New York, State University of New York Press.

Fonow, M. and Cook, J. (1991) *Beyond Methodology: Feminist Scholarship as Lived Research*. Bloomington, Indiana University Press.

Foucault, M. (1972) *The Archaeology of Knowledge and the Discourse on Language*. New York, Pantheon.

Foucault, M. (1986) *The History of Sexuality* (trans R. Hurley). New York, Random House.

Frith, H. (2000) 'Focusing on Sex: Using Focus Groups in Sex Research'. *Sexualities*, 3 (3), 275–297.

Geertz, C. (1973) *The Interpretation of Culture*. New York, Basic Books.

Geertz, C. (1988) *Works and Lives: The Anthropologist as Author*. Cambridge, Polity Press.

Halperin, D. (1995) Saint *Foucault: Towards a Gay Hagiography*. Oxford, University Press.

Herda, E. A. (1999) *Research Conversations and Narrative: A Critical Hermeneutic Orientation in Participatory Inquiry*. Preager, Westport, Connecticut.

Hill, R. (1996) 'Learning to transgress: A socio-historical conspectus of the American gay life world as a site of struggle and resistance'. *Studies in the Education of Adults*, 28 (2), 253–279.

Hodkinson, P. (2005) 'Insider Research in the Study of Youth Cultures', *Journal of Youth Studies*, 8 (2), 131–149.

Ingraham, C. (1996) 'The Heterosexual Imaginary: Feminist Sociology and Theories Of Gender', in R. Hennessy and C. Ingraham (eds), *Materialist Feminism: A Reader in Class Difference and Women's Lives*. New York, Routledge.

Kamberelis, G. (2004) 'The Rhizome and the Pack: Liminal Literacy Formations with Political Teeth', in K. Leander and M. Sheehy (eds), *Spatialising literacy research and practice*. New York, Peter Lang.

Kopleson, K. (2002) 'Dis/integrating the gay/queer binary reconstructed identity politics for a performative pedagogy'. *College English,* 65 (1), 17–35.

Kulick, D. and Willson, M. (1995) *Taboo: Sex, identity and Erotic Subjectivity in Anthropological Fieldwork.* London, Routledge.

Leck, G. (1994) 'Queer relations With Educational Research', in A. Gitlin (ed), *Power and Method: Political Activism and Educational Research.* New York and London, Routledge.

Lewin, E. and Leap, W. L. (1992) *Out in the field: Reflections of Lesbian and Gay Anthropologists.* Urbana, University of Illinois Press.

Lopez, B. (1990) *Crow and Weasel.* Farrar, New York, Strauss and Giroux.

Lorde, A. (1984) *Sister Outsider: Essays and Speeches.* Berkeley, California, The Crossing Press.

MacIntyre, A. (1981) *After Virtue. A study in Moral Theory.* Notre Dame, Indiana, University of Notre Dame Press.

Miller, J. (1998) 'Autobiography as Queer Curriculum Practice', in W. Pinar (ed), *Queer Theory in Education.* London, Lawrence Erlbaum Associates Publishers.

Nayarain, K. (1993) 'How Native is a Native Anthropologist?' *American Anthropologist,* 95, 671–686.

Personal Narratives Group (1989) *Interpreting Women's Lives: Feminist Theory and Personal Narrative.* Bloomington, Indiana University Press.

Plato (1974) *The Republic* (trans by D. Lee). London, Penguin.

Richardson, L. (1990) *Writing Strategies: Reaching Diverse Audiences.* London, Sage.

Richardson, L. (1993) 'Poetic Representation, Ethnographic Presentation and Transgressive validity: The Case of the Skipped Line', *Sociological Quarterly,* 34, 695–710.

Richardson, L. (1997) *Fields of Play: Constructing an Academic Life.* New Brunswick, Rutgers University Press.

Rogers, C.R. (1962) 'The interpersonal relationship: The core of guidance'. *Harvard Educational Review,* 32, 416–29.

Roscoe, W. (1996) 'Writing Queer Cultures: An Impossible Possibility?', in E. Lewin and W. Leap (eds), *Out In The Field: Reflections of Lesbian and Gay Anthropologists.* Urbana, University of Illinois Press.

Russell, M.G. and Kelly, N. H. (2002) Research as Interacting Dialogic Processes: Implications for Reflexivity', Forum: *Qualitative Social Research* 3, No. 3 http://www.qualitative-research.net/fqs-texte/3-02/3-02russellkelly-e.htm (accessed 16 January 2005).

Saint Pierre, E. A. (1997) 'Methodology in the Fold and the irruption of Transgressive data'. *Qualitative Studies in Education,* 10 (2), 175–189.

Schratz, M. and Walker, R. (1995) *Research as Social Change.* London, Routledge.

Sedwick, E. K. (1994) *Tendencies.* London, Routledge.

Sedgewick, E. (2004) *Touching Feeling: Affect, Pedagogy, Performativity.* London, Duke University Press.

Smith, L.T. (2001) *Decolonizing Methodologies: Research and Indigenous Peoples.* London and New York, Zed Books Ltd.

Sparkes, A. C. (2000) 'Autoethnography and narratives of self: Reflections on criteria in action'. *Sociology of Sport Journal,* 17 (1), 21–43.

Sparkes, A. (2004) *Telling Tale in Sport and Physical Activity: A Qualitative Journey.* Leeds, Human Kinetics.

Squirrel, G. (1989) 'Teachers and Issues of Sexual Orientation'. *Gender and Education,* 1 (1), 17–35.

Talburt, S. (1999) 'Open Secrets and Problems of Queer Ethnography: Readings from a Religious Studies Classroom'. *Qualitative Studies in Education,* 12 (5), 525–539.

Tamboukou, M. and Ball, S. J. (2003) 'Genealogy and ethnography: Fruitful encounters or Dangerous Liaisons?', in M. Tamboukou and S. Ball (eds), *Dangerous Encounters: Genealogy and Ethnography.* New York, Peter Lang.

Trow, G. W. S. (1981) *Within the Context of No Context.* Boston, Little Brown.

Tyler, S. (1986) 'Postmodern ethnography: From document of the occult to occult document', in J. Clifford and G. Marcus (eds), *Writing culture: The Poetics and Politics of Ethnography.* Berkeley, University of California Press.

Wafer, J. (1996) 'Out of the Closet and into Print: Sexual Identity In the Textual Field', in E. Lewin and W. Leap (eds), *Out In The Field: Reflections of Lesbian and Gay Anthropologists.* Urbana and Chicago, University of Illinois Press.

Chapter 8

Researching educational governance and control

LEA and OFSTED

Peter Dickson

Introduction

Researching from within an organisation in which one is employed has its own unique problems and difficulties. In this personal account of my own experiences of researching within an English Local Education Authority (LEA), I describe some of the problems I encountered and offer my thoughts about undertaking what, in retrospect, was a fairly ambitious study. There are many stories that I could tell and my field notes, documents, research diary and reviews of related literature are extensive. This chapter, however, reflects on some of the personal dilemmas I faced, the problems I experienced and the mistakes I made. I hope what I have to relate will be of interest to, and useful for, others engaged in similar research within their own organisation.

My story concerns the case study research I undertook as part of my Doctoral studies at the University of Sheffield, entitled *Inspecting the LEA*. This involved an investigation of an inspection of a Local Education Authority, the local unit of educational administration, by the central government watchdog, the Office for Standards in Education (OFSTED). The inspection had far-reaching consequences for many of my colleagues (several of whom lost their jobs) and led to the whole-sale re-organisation of the LEA. My study revealed political and other agendas behind the inspection's published findings, and the LEA's perceived shortcomings, which were subject to a very damning public scrutiny.

At the time of my research, I was responsible for the delivery of customer services involving complaints and appeals (against exclusion from school, against failure to secure admission to a particular school and against refusal of financial assistance for travel to school) and also information services. I was not directly 'involved' in the inspection in so far as inspectors did not interview me, but I 'participated' in the inspection as a senior LEA officer; from this perspective, I was an 'insider'. My intention in using my own LEA as the basis for a case study was to gain an in-depth perspective on the lived realities of the inspection process. My view is that inspection constitutes a 'critical incident' in UK educational policy and, while a review of the literature threw up references to numerous studies of school inspections, there was nothing about inspection of LEAs.

I had considered looking at another LEA (or LEAs) but believed that, whilst there would have been clear advantages in using such an approach, it would not have yielded the quality or depth of data I sought. I also believed that it would be difficult to achieve a suitable level of engagement/acceptance/understanding in another LEA. Pragmatically, too, time constraints meant it would be difficult to engage in effective research if I was to visit other sites. Although I believed that using my own LEA for the case study was the most appropriate option for me, I was aware of the potential problem areas this approach would involve, specifically, loss of objectivity, negative effects on my relationships within the organisation and, not least, senior management's view of what I was doing. It is fair to say my awareness of, and readiness for possible difficulties, in no way prepared me for the real ethical and other dilemmas I faced during the course of the research.

Purpose of research

The purpose of my research was to analyse and comment on the complicated procedures and outcomes that constituted the lifecycle of one LEA undergoing inspection, with a view to suggesting some generalisation about the wider impact of such inspections on educational processes as a whole.

I was informed by a belief that it is crucial to try to gain an understanding of the lived experiences of all the subjects within a social context. This included myself as a researcher, and as part of 'being there', observing and participating in the social activity under investigation; I wanted to tell the story of my own awareness of the many levels and many realities within the research process. I believe that understanding social processes cannot be simply reduced to describing social interaction between the various participants involved in the situation being studied and that the ideological structuring imposed on the research context by regulation and governance must be accounted for. All experience is situated and, therefore, the many levels and forms of reflexivity must be observed if we are to account for our own personal reflexivity, theoretical reflexivity, historical reflexivity and so on. Often, however, discussions about research from the personal perspective fail to emphasise the more abstract characteristics of a research context, in particular issues of power, bias and regulation. As the research context in which I undertook my investigation was itself situated within a wider framework of dominant power relations, I believed that I must explore how that research context – the LEA – was subject to specific modes of governance and regulation and this could only be achieved by looking at the complexity and historically determined nature of LEAs and inspection regimes. 'There is no straightforward polarity of academic autonomy and state instrumentalism, as no research is separate from policy' (Ozga, 2000: 76).

Ozga suggests that the real issue is one of the relationship between knowledge and power that is at the core of the practice of research. The interplay between these two is interpreted by the researcher and the balance of power determined according to whether the research is itself policy-controlled research, and is governed by and very much controlled by the preordained requisites of policy makers, or self-controlled research which permits researchers to define their own agendas and report on their own relationship to policy. Policy-controlled research has a more fundamental and, indeed, instrumental role in policy than research which is self-controlled and which by definition has more of a conceptual influence. The reciprocity between research and policy is crucial and I believed that, given my station, I was in a position to create new knowledge with regard to the lived experience of the inspection process. I was not engaged in simply commenting on this particular aspect of educational policy, but rather engaging in a critical discussion within the framework in which this particular aspect of educational policy was being formulated and played out. It was recognition of this, however, that perhaps was my first problem.

The field

OFSTED was created in September 1992, under the Education (Schools) Act of that year, as the Office of Her Majesty's Chief Inspector of Schools. Headed by Her Majesty's Chief Inspector (HMCI), its statement of purpose is to encourage 'improvement through inspection'. It was established to improve standards of achievement and the quality of education by means of regular 'independent' inspections of institutions and other informed advice to government ministers and parents through the public reporting of inspections.

The Education Act, 1997, extended OFSTED's powers of inspection to cover LEAs, and the publication of its *LEA Support for School Improvement: Framework for the Inspection of Local Education Authorities* illustrated the challenges facing LEAs and the background against which their performance was to be gauged. Many of these challenges are outside the scope of LEA operation so they are, therefore, examined, scrutinised and judged according to criteria over which they have little or no direct control. Since the Education Reform Act of 1988 and the introduction of 'Local Management of Schools', increasing delegation of function to schools, combined with increasing delegation of budgets, which at the time of my research amounted to nearly 90%, meant that LEAs retained little effective control and financial influence over the schools for which they were responsible.

In November 1998, the LEA in which I was employed was subjected to an 'ad hoc' mini-inspection that concentrated specifically on its programme for the maintenance of its school buildings stock. The inspection was ordered by the Secretary of State under powers established by Section 38 of the Education Act 1997. Led by the Audit Commission, the inspection comprised an initial overview by two audit Commission inspectors and this was followed by a second phase of four days of interviews and school visits, at which time the Audit Commissioners were joined by three OFSTED inspectors.

The aim of the inspection, the LEA was advised, was to examine its effectiveness with regard to the efficiency of its buildings maintenance for schools and was prompted in part by the closure, for health and safety reasons, of one of the LEA's largest secondary schools in June of the same year, owing to problems with its roof. The closure of the school was instigated by the school's Head Teacher – a Head with local and national political connections – against the advice of the Authority. The inspection determined that the Authority as a whole faced substantial problems with the condition of its school buildings. Visits to other primary and secondary schools, whose OFSTED inspection reports all raised buildings 'issues', followed. OFSTED inspectors subsequently announced that there was clear evidence of an unacceptable level of poor conditions existing within the Council's stock of school buildings. In addition to poor physical state, there was inadequate space and insufficient accommodation and concerns were such that it was suggested that there would need to be closure of some parts of some schools and possibly wholesale school closure in the future.

During the mid-1990s, councils across the UK were faced with severe financial difficulties and the capital resources procurable for school repairs and maintenance were limited due to the reducing availability of borrowing approvals from the central government. Whilst the inspectors acknowledged that restricted capital and revenue resources had an impact on the level of investment available for maintaining and improving school buildings, they severely criticised the Council for allowing its school buildings to fall into disrepair. The inspection report condemned local spending decisions and the discretion the Council had used in its support for other projects, notably social services care for vulnerable people, rather than channeling those admittedly limited resources to education. No reference was made to the fact that successive governments had failed to adequately resource local authorities and that this in itself had resulted in falling revenue reserves. This had then ensured that a backlog of repairs had accumulated.

There is firm evidence that when the Conservative Government in the United Kingdom abolished the Inner London Education Authority, which looked after the interests of the London LEAs and introduced both the Poll Tax and the Standard Spending Assessment to calculate how local authorities would be funded, a movement of resources took place which supported the individual London boroughs at the expense of large metropolitan authorities such as my own. Gibson estimates that something approaching 80% of the £180,000,000 increase in education spending that resulted in these authorities being favoured at the expense of others was the result of political manipulation, a virement of resources that continued throughout the 1990s (Gibson, 1998). Arguably, had the LEA not been deprived of crucial resources, school buildings would have been better maintained and there would possibly have been no need for the initial inspection by OFSTED. Furthermore, one may speculate that had the initial inspection not been so damning there would not have been a clear agenda prior to the announcement of the full inspection.

In the spring of 1999, it was announced that the LEA would be subjected to a full inspection by OFSTED in conjunction with the Audit Commission in the autumn of that year. The LEA, along with three other geographical neighbours, would be inspected in the third round of LEA inspections. Those LEAs which were inspected in the first round of OFSTED inspections were said to have been selected purely on the basis of the performance of pupils at Key Stage 2 (the end of the primary phase) and at Key Stage 4 (the end of the secondary phase) in national standard assessment tests in schools within the LEA. The criterion by which LEAs were 'selected' for scrutiny in the third round of inspections was, however, subject to much speculation.

The particular round of inspections in which my own LEA found attention focused upon it, it was suggested, was due to involvement in a central government initiative entitled *Excellence in Cities.* However, there were arguably more specific reasons for inclusion at this particular juncture. The LEA's Education Development Plan (a plan setting out the LEA's proposals for developing the education of all children in their area, either by raising the standards of education provided for children or by improving the performance of schools), which was submitted in early 1999, was initially rejected by the government as being inadequate and giving serious cause for concerns. This was due to a perceived lack of clarity and a perceived failure to specify procedures for identifying, challenging and supporting schools which had serious weaknesses or were giving cause for concern. This was despite a notable strength of the LEA having been identified as its policy on wide consultation with schools and other agencies about targeting support.

The full inspection report when published reflected that the LEA compared favourably to other metropolitan authorities and similar LEAs in many respects, and that the LEA's work to support school improvement was at the time of the inspection at least 'adequate', 'good' or 'better than satisfactory'. Furthermore, standards were well in line with similar LEAs at the end of both the primary and secondary phases. Such plaudits continued in all eight of the main areas of LEA support for school improvement focused on during the course of the inspection, which were identified as key areas of concern following the publication of the LEA Education Development Plan.

This being the substance and tenor of the final inspection report, it was difficult to reconcile this with the conclusions drawn by OFSTED. In their summary, inspectors reported that on the whole schools were coping well but that their success had little to do with the LEA. The leadership team, elected council members and not least schools themselves, were astonished to learn that, despite its considerable and recognised efforts, the LEA had been branded as 'failing'. The long list of recommendations, running to three pages in the final report, is both critical of the service provided by the LEA and the LEA's senior management. These are somewhat at odds with the main body of the report, which, in itself, would not suggest that fundamental weaknesses were apparent and that a radical re-assessment of the LEA was therefore necessary. It is also questionable whether such perceived weaknesses were in fact evident during the inspection process and would therefore be indicative of the fate that would eventually befall the LEA. My observations, interviews and other information sourcing would suggest that, whilst often harsh criticism would be an expected and indeed given result of the inspection, the full and eventual repercussions for the LEA could not have been predicted.

Entering the field

Access

It may appear somewhat strange drawing attention to access when, strictly speaking, I already had it. When I started my research, I had worked for the Authority for nearly fifteen years. Some two years before the inspection took place, I had already alerted colleagues to the fact that I was undertaking an EdD and would be looking for a suitable topic for my research. I initially approached the Senior Management Team primarily for assistance with my course of study. I was not simply seeking financial assistance but assistance in the widest sense – time out of work on a regular basis and some form of moral or other 'support'. This was flatly refused. The excuse given was that assistance must be prioritised for staff seeking initial or basic qualifications and, as I already possessed advanced academic qualifications, I was not in this category. This extended to study time also. I was further asked why I was undertaking a Doctorate and what I hoped to gain from it. I found the response perverse to say the least. I was nevertheless undeterred and though somewhat perturbed by the reaction – after all, I worked for an education department where standards and attainment were promoted and educational excellence trumpeted – I determined that I would continue my study and consider a suitable research proposal. I kept my head down, so to speak, did my job and studied in my own time.

As time went on I felt that 'as Punch states' 'gaining consent [was] quite inappropriate, because activity [was] already taking place that [could] not be interrupted' (Punch, 1998: 171). As the initial inspection came to a close and the results published, it became apparent that the Authority would be subject to a full inspection, sooner rather than later. Seizing the opportunity to use the full inspection as a topic for my research project, I made it known to Senior Management and other officers that I intended to use the inspection as the basis for a case study research project and discussed this personally with an Assistant Director. I sent a note to education directorate staff explaining my intentions and stating that I would be looking for information from willing volunteers as interview informants. Unfortunately, my requests for information and assistance went largely unanswered and I encountered a further problem in that officers were required to remain silent about the inspection, especially as it neared completion and the inspection report became due for publication. The Assistant Director, who had initially agreed to assist, was limited in what information could be provided but, whilst I cannot say that I was allowed unfettered access to inspectors and official documentation, I was provided with useful information, was kept informed of developments and advised of key dates, times and meetings. I used this as the basis for my research diary and to structure my research plan.

Ethical issues

There are obvious ethical considerations for any piece of sustained research, and considerations of the many dilemmas that are likely to confront the researcher must be inherent to the planning and execution of that research. Researching from within my organisation created a number of additional issues of an ethical nature. First, I felt torn between my sense of self as a researcher, attempting to gather as much information as possible by studying every aspect of interaction between the inspectors and staff. Colleagues offered information that I am sure would not have been offered to an outside researcher. But I am convinced that more senior managers were reluctant to divulge particularly sensitive information to me, as they were aware that it would find its way into my research. Second, as I reported above, managers had been required to remain largely silent about the inspection itself.

Inspecting the LEA was undertaken before the requirements for EdD and other student researchers to follow Ethical Review Procedures and, in a sense, although I had spoken with tutors at the University about my proposals, I could have undertaken virtually anything I wanted to at the time. Whilst I attempted nothing underhand and did not engage in anything dishonest as I consulted and sought 'informed consent' whenever appropriate, I cannot say with any degree of certainty that, on occasion, I did not undertake any form of covert research. I reasoned that, as I was not permitted access to question the OFSTED inspectors themselves nor the managerial consultants commissioned to take forward the recommendations arising out of the inspection report, a pragmatic approach to the research dictated that, as Punch puts it, 'some dissimulation' was necessary in order to 'get at data not obtainable by other means' (Punch, 1998: 172). It would have been useful to be able to interview these people – especially as one of the consultants was a personal tutor from my early undergraduate days, an academic with some definite left-wing leanings turned management guru, whom I am sure would have consented to be interviewed. This would have added a further dimension to the research.

There are many issues to which researchers need to give careful consideration in thinking about the politics and ethics of a proposed research project and these will inevitably come into sharp focus when that piece of research is contemplated, as it were in 'one's own backyard'. There is a great deal of available literature on the subject; however, there is no definitive consensus about what is and what is not permissible, what constitutes an infringement of privacy and what is acceptable on the grounds of adding to the corpus of knowledge about a particular area or subject. Whilst there are ever-increasing regulations and guidelines to attempt to prevent the use of unethical practices, there is little effective control to prevent an individual from employing dubious methods to conduct a particular piece of research. On the contrary, some would argue that sometimes, one *must* engage in suspicious methods in order to expose powerful institutions and organisations such as OFSTED and other quangos. Essentially, as Punch emphasises, the individual researcher must determine his or her own way and, ultimately, it is a matter of 'where you stand will help to determine not only what you will research but also how you research it' (Punch, 1998: 179).

In the field

I am aware that my representation is only one of any number of interpretations of the inspection process and its consequences. I know that I probably overlooked many taken-for-granted assumptions, not least in the interactions between the many officers and officials involved. Moreover, I know that I, as a member of the group under observation, possibly disregarded important data and significant information simply because I too took for granted much of what was happening during the interactions being studied. I did nevertheless determine to remain critically conscious of my own values and the extent to which these influenced what I was seeing. My primary task was to gather as much information as possible, to observe, to uncover 'facts' and to record accurately all data whether they appeared significant or otherwise. I tried to approach my fieldwork with awareness that each and every situation was unique and unlikely to be repeated. I tried to remain as 'objective' as possible, whilst maintaining the view that any sense in which the researcher can be thought of as wholly unbiased and indeed dispassionate about the task in hand is illusory. I had from the outset imposed my own individual identity on the research. I had selected what was to be researched and how that research was to be conducted. My hope was that, by engaging in continual reflection, I would try to ensure that my observations and the interpretation of those observations would not 'degenerate into the mere accumulation of information' (Evans, 1979: 21). I kept a research diary through the course of my research and this enabled personal reflections on the development of the research to be recorded together with day-to-day observations. However, I was concerned to ensure that the very process of information gathering, albeit refined as 'data collection', did indeed 'serve some definite purpose' and could as a result be defined as research (Evans, 1979: 21). I was satisfied that my particular case study could be regarded as what Cohen and Mannion refer to as 'the examination of an instant in action' (Cohen and Mannion, 1994: 171) and as such that it would qualify to be regarded as 'systematic and sustained enquiry', to use Stenhouse's definition of educational research (Stenhouse, 1979).

Methodology

Observation and interaction

Cohen and Mannion note that 'the case study researcher typically observes the characteristics of an individual unit'. 'The purpose of such observation', they continue, 'is to probe deeply and to analyse intensively the multifarious phenomena that constitutes the life cycle of the unit with a view to establishing generalisations about the wider population to which the unit belongs' (Cohen and Mannion, 1994: 106). 'Whatever the problem or the approach, at the heart of case study research', they conclude 'lies a method of observation' (Cohen and Mannion, 1994: 106–107).

I had already determined that participant observation was to be my main source of data gathering. However, I was fully prepared for the level of participation and of observation to change as my research developed and that these would move along a continuum, similar to that suggested by Hammersley and Atkinson. Sometimes I would be a complete participant; sometimes I would be a complete observer moving forwards and backwards during the course of my research, gathering data and information as the situation dictated.

Robson refers to these different forms of observational technique as: *participant observation*, where the researcher is more than a passive observer and participates in the events being studied; *systematic observation*, where the researcher utilises standardised observation; and *simple observation*, where the researcher utilises passive unobtrusive observation; including a range of facial expressions, language and behaviour (Robson, 1993: 159). All these different types of observation are key to the compilation and development of the case record which I built up over a period of time to include interview data, documentary records and other information to provide a framework for my final case study report, which Rudduck defines as 'the product of the field worker's reflective engagement within [the] case record' (Rudduck, 1985: 10). Again, much of the framework was contained in my research diary which I maintained throughout the course of my research.

Interviews

It is impossible to observe everything; therefore, in order to supplement my observational record of the inspection, I interviewed a selection of officers as they emerged from their interviews with members of the OFSTED inspectorate team. I selected a cross-section of Education Directorate staff to interview and asked for their co-operation. Not all responded and some of those who did respond did not agree to participate. The 'selection' I was left with comprised of anyone who agreed to talk about their experiences of the inspection and more particularly their own experience of being interviewed by the OFSTED inspectors. This was a random sample but, nonetheless, was largely representative of gender, age, experience and seniority across the Directorate.

All interviewees gave informed consent and understood that their responses would be used alongside documentary evidence in the writing up of the research. I attempted to assure respondents of the anonymity of interview data but stressed that this would not necessarily mean that others reading the research could not possibly identify them. The interviews took about 30 minutes and all the interviews were conducted at a time when I believed respondents would be keen to talk. The interviews took place as informants left interviews with either OFSTED inspectors or later members of the consultancy team. Interviews were spontaneous, but nevertheless their execution involved a great deal of planning. The interviews were unstructured and were undertaken in an open situation, at an informant's workstation or in the Department's library and on one occasion in the kitchen, locations I considered would promote a greater degree of flexibility and freedom. Although unstructured, I guided all the interviews and I retained a high degree of control. As Moser and Kalton (1971) emphasise, although interviews are themselves conversations, the interviewer has taken the initiative and is in control, even during unstructured interviews. Interviews are reported as recorded conversations and contribute to the reporting of information gathered during the research process and therefore differ from everyday discourse.

During the interviews themselves, some degree of participant observation was also possible and I again moved along Hammersley and Atkinson's continuum with respondents, often referring me to documents or other information to which I had not previously had access. All interviews were transcribed verbatim and in so doing I tried to convey something of the mood of officers during this very difficult process. The interviews were supplemented with an analysis of virtually any relevant documents that I could lay my hands on such as e-mails, minutes of meetings, Council minutes, reports, newsletters and media coverage. Many of these were in the public domain, some were not and I happened upon them by chance, many arriving on my desk marked 'Confidential', the source often being unknown. All of these usually opened up other areas of investigation.

Throughout the course of my research and observations, it was the more informal types of interaction that threw up interesting data and information. For example, some officers who had not consented to be formally interviewed assisted (sometimes unwittingly) in providing information and personal insights into the inspection process and these again added new dimensions to my research, either by confirming or by adding a different perspective to what I had been able to understand from other sources. One could argue that in such circumstances it would have been appropriate to negotiate or re-negotiate consent to use the information given in the writing up of my research; however, once I was engaged in interviewing my informants and immersed in data collection, it would not have been appropriate for me to re-negotiate the terms of that data collection. I am here drawn to what Punch argues in that 'whilst not arguing that the field-worker should abandon all ethical consideration once he or she has gotten in, but rather that informed consent is unworkable in some sorts of observational research' (Punch, 1998: 171).

The research took just over two years to complete. As I noted earlier, my request for assistance with study leave had been declined and I undertook most of my research alongside my day job and wrote up many of my observations, interviews and other field notes in the evenings or at weekends. During this time, I never really left the research field. Whilst at work I was continually on site and, afraid I might miss some crucial piece of information, never really withdrew from active research. When the time came to start writing up the research and completing my thesis, I had real difficulty in determining when the research had actually been completed as I wasn't able to leave the field in any real sense. There was always some other document or other to consult and scrutinise, one more piece of 'evidence' to examine. If I had not been researching from within, then I am sure that matters would have been easier and more straightforward to deal with, as I could have left the field and continued to observe from outside as did others.

In the hiatus that followed the departure of the OFSTED inspectors, it was clear that many staff had a bad feeling about the eventual outcome of the inspection. The mood across the Education Directorate and, indeed, it is fair to say across the Council generally, was perceptively heavy. My observations continued and I carried on making copious field notes, ensuring that my research diary was maintained on a weekly if not daily basis. I attempted to resume interviews with my respondents but most were unwilling to make further comment. Two respondents who did allow further remarks and observations to be noted, each spoke of a perceived though intangible 'hidden agenda'.

As time went on, the repercussions of the inspection itself widened like the ripples emanating from a pebble thrown into the water. More and more of my colleagues left the Council (or were pushed), and within little more than 6 months a new senior management team took up their posts and a new structure was implemented in the Directorate. A new Chief Executive was recruited to run the Council, a new Cabinet structure developed and there was a change of leadership.

Leaving the field

Writing and disseminating the research

The writing of *Inspecting the LEA* was difficult, to say the least. I had a huge amount of data from observations, my research diary, interviews and other field-work notes, in addition to official publications, minutes of meetings and so on. I had to organise this 'story' into not only some form of workable, structured and systematic account of the inspection but also one that was accessible. I then had to be able to demonstrate how my narrative account of the inspection could satisfy the rigours of the requirements for a doctoral thesis. Finally, the overall structure of my research report and my thesis emerged into an account that focused on the origins of OFSTED and the development of LEA inspection, the changing fortunes of the purpose and role of LEAs in the UK, linking this to the in-depth study of the inspection of my own LEA and its local consequences.

Careful consideration was given to the presentation of the research and I had to make a very difficult decision when writing up the research with regard to the naming of the LEA that had formed the basis of my case study. To attempt to have concealed the identity would have, I reasoned, been fruitless. However, whilst the identity of the LEA was itself not disclosed, I concealed the individual identities of senior officers, inspectors, consultants and those I interviewed without changing details I considered pertinent to the research. I was aware that publication of *Inspecting the LEA* could potentially cause me problems both at work and elsewhere, and therefore I made the difficult decision that access to my research be withheld for a period of five years following submission. The problem of how to then disseminate my 'findings' was made much more difficult.

Nevertheless I wanted to talk about my experiences in undertaking case study research from within my own organisation and I therefore initially presented papers which formed the basis of *Inspecting the LEA* at a number of postgraduate student conferences. I presented a paper entitled *Case Study Research in Education from, Within* at a research students' conference at the University of Cambridge in June 2001 and a paper entitled *Researching LEA Inspection* at the Policy and Professionalism Research Centre at the University of Sheffield in April 2003. These papers were well received and opportunities for presenting other papers were discussed but until I was asked to prepare a chapter for this publication I have to say that I was pre-occupied with fulltime work as an education officer, having changed employment and having been promoted twice since the completion of *Inspecting the LEA* and the birth of my two children in March 2000 and subsequently in January 2003.

Colleagues who read *Inspecting the LEA* commented that it was a somewhat depressing but realistic account of the inspection and its aftermath. No one remarked that they had been able to identify themselves, however, I am convinced that all respondents had they wished to could have identified both themselves and others even though all were disguised and none were directly named. Some commented that there was a defensiveness that permeated the research, which could have arisen from its nature as research from within the organisation. It was felt that I portrayed the LEA as being defensive particularly in relation to OFSTED and central government in general and that I was myself also defensive in my comments about OFSTED.

Conclusion

Researching one's own organisation is not for the faint-hearted. The sense of isolation is probably more heightened than it is for other types of research. There were intensities of emotion, which I experienced in trying to write an account of what I perceived to be happening in the field, whilst also acknowledging the emotional impact of those events on colleagues in the field. I was also trying to analyse reflexively the differences between the values of the 'self' (my values) and those of others. On one level I was attempting to see beyond the emotions generated at times of crisis in order to facilitate an analysis of the everyday social relations between participants embroiled in the inspection, whilst on another level I was trying to deal with the personal impact of these emotions on others and myself. Whilst my supervisor appreciated those problems, I am not sure I was able to fully articulate these to others and therefore others, including peers on the EdD course, did not wholly appreciate the depths of these emotions and the problems that they produced for me. Researchers contemplating research from within their own institution or organisation obviously need to consider issues that face every researcher, such as access, ethics, and methodology and so on, but there are other important additional considerations. Researchers should also think carefully about possible reactions to the research, specifically from others within the organisation, including managers and colleagues. There may well be reactions such as 'I don't recognise that as being the organisation I work for' or 'That's not how I see it'. And, although in my particular case this was lessened as I had decided to withhold access to my research, there is the question of reactions to the publication of the research and the researcher's own perceived response to this. Questions concerning the validity, reliability and credibility of the research could be quite disconcerting and the researcher's own responses to such questions could determine how well or otherwise the research community receives the work. I take comfort, however, in Delamont's observation that 'it is impossible to do research that is value free and that does not take a position' (Delamont, 2002: 39). I hope that, whilst the open narrative style of my autoethnographic research offered a significant contribution to education case study research and something of the personal, reflected in the writing up of the research which revealed my own 'vulnerability and subjectivity openly in the text' (Ellis and Bochner, 2000: 747); this added to rather than distracted from the finished product. I also hope that I raised some important methodological issues and that these issues will have encouraged other researchers to explore the many positives that can be gained from researching within their own organisation.

Bibliography and references

Cohen, M. and Mannion, M. (1994) *Research Methods in Education.* 3rd ed. London: Routledge.

Delamont, S. (2002). *Fieldwork in Educational Settings: Methods, Pitfalls and Perspectives.* 2nd ed. Roultledge-Falmer.

Ellis, C. and Bochner. C. P. (2000) *Autoethnography, personal narrative, reflexivity: researcher as subjectity,* in Denzin, N. K. and Lincoln Y.S. (eds.) Handbook of Qualitative Research. London: Sage.

Evans, K. M. (1979). Bristol *Planning Small Scale Research.* Revised edition. Windsor: NFER.

Gibson, J. (1998). Political Manipulation or Feedback in English Local Authorities' Standard Spending Assessments? The Case of the Abolition of the Inner London Education Authority. *Public Administration,* 76, 4, pp. 629–647.

Moser, C. A. and Kalton G. (1971). *Survey Methods in Social Investigation.* London: Heinemann.

Ozga, J. (2000). *Policy Research in Educational Settings: Contested Terrain.* Buckingham: Open University Press.

Punch, M. (1998). Politics and Ethics in Qualitative Research, in Denzin, N. and Lincoln, Y. (eds.) *The Landscape of Qualitative Research: Theories and Issues.* Thousand Oaks, California: Sage, pp. 156–184.

Robson, C. (1993) *Real World Research: A Resource for Social Scientists and Practitioner Researchers.* Oxford: Blackwell.

Rudduck, J. (1985) A Case for Case Records? A discussion of some aspects of Lawrence Stenhouse's work in case study methodology, in Burgess, R. G. (ed.) *Strategies of Educational Research: Qualitative Methods.* Lewes: Falmer Press.

Stenhouse, L. (1979) The problem of standards in illuminative research. *Scottish Educational Review*, 11, 2, pp. 8–20.

Section 4

Inside research in universities

Chapter 9

Insider research in schools and universities

The case of the professional doctorate

Pat Drake and Linda Heath

Introduction

Professional doctorate students usually study part time whilst working full time in a profession and/or workplace, with their workplace generating the focus of their study. This means that such students may be particularly compromised by the insider nature of their research, and in managing their location as 'insiders', they may necessarily change position, sometimes frequently, along axes with respect to both their research and their professional practice. Humphrey (2007) makes the torque implied by insider–outsider status explicit by drawing attention to the hyphen. She suggests that researchers can lose their sense of self if they are pulled one way or the other by being seen alternately as an insider or as an outsider (depending on whether they are colleague and/or researcher).

Potts (in this volume) draws attention to the complexities that ensue when university lecturers explore their own practice. In this chapter, we draw upon a small study in two universities in order to illuminate some of the challenges experienced by students taking Doctorates in Education who are attempting to develop a critical research-based perspective on the workplace.

Background

The notion of a professional doctorate is not new, and can be traced back to the mission of universities in the UK in the 18th century. At that time, the main concern of the university was with the development of the professions, but reforms of the 19th century challenged this conception and instead developed a degree based on the search for universal 'truth' through research, which became the model for the Doctor of Philosophy degree (Scott *et al.*, 2004).

Bourner *et al.* (2001) suggest that the recent re-emergence and growth of the professional doctorate in the UK reflects, in part, the pace of change in the professions and in society more generally. The need for new, up-to-date knowledge of professional practice creates the need for new means of creating knowledge and theories (Bourner *et al.*, 2001: 42), and, in the face of government dissatisfaction that 'traditional PhDs were not well matched to careers outside academia or an industrial research laboratory' (OST 1993: 2; see also The Dearing Report,

1997; QAA, 2007), the development of professional doctorates may be seen as part of reshaping knowledge to include new paradigms for doctoral research (Usher, 2000).

This presents problems for universities since they are under some pressure to develop more professionally relevant programmes, whilst at the same time maintaining the 'gold standard' of traditional doctoral study (see Barnett, 2000).

Practice and knowledge production

In Education departments in UK universities, the discourse of researching one's own practice is central to professional and academic work with students. Many students are postgraduates who are, furthermore, often practising professionals, e.g. teachers or social workers (Heath, 2006), looking for means of investigating their practice. The professional doctorate is the most recent exemplification of research training for these practitioners, and it is frequently also undertaken by university teachers who have moved from the professions into the academy.

With the intention of improving practice, there is an expectation that professionals will engage with critical reflection (Schon, 1983, 1987), demonstrate experiential learning (Boud and Walker, 1990; Eraut, 1994), develop transferable skills and gain higher qualifications in order to make a significant contribution of knowledge of practice through research (Becher, 1989; Bourner et al., 2001). From this perspective, at the centre of the professional doctorate is the notion of critical reflection which links experiential learning with tacit knowledge (Eraut, 1994; Claxton, 1998). The recognition that knowledge-production takes place outside the academy as well as inside it (Brennan, 1995) underpins this view.

For adult learners on a professional doctorate programme, the relationship between concepts, ideas and theories and the relevance and application of these in their professional lives is a central concept (Eraut, 1994). Thus, the challenge of a professional doctorate is to integrate learning and knowing at the highest academic level with the intention of bridging the theory-professional knowledge gap. However, professional doctorate students may see their doctorates as quite separate from their workplace, for whilst they are required to critically reflect on practice during the life of the doctorate, they may be unable to bring about any real changes because of localised and national constraints.

Insiders are located within a shared way of looking at the world (Scott et al., 2004). They identify the rules and characteristics of a community of practice, centring on dependency relationships with other members of the community and a shared way of going about things. Within these communities, there is a rapid flow of information and implied knowledge of what other members know. It is therefore not difficult to envisage the problems that a professional doctorate student may encounter in positioning themselves simultaneously as an insider and outsider, raising 'suspicion' from colleagues in terms, not only of the way they go about doing their research, but also regarding the length of time they may keep findings from peers, and the fear of the consequences of being identified with 'negative' or 'uncomfortable' findings. For example, a teacher identifying through research what they perceive to be unsound practice may be accused, by managers and peers, of being unprofessional or uncollegiate. They may experience resistance to any suggested change (Scott *et al.*, 2004) and even feel unable to share their views.

Doing education research as an insider

Education research is riven with debate as to the relative merits of different approaches to it. For example, the benefits or otherwise of randomised controlled trials versus small-scale qualitative research (e.g. McClure, 2004; Oakley, 2000, 2003; Torrance, 2004; Sebba, 2006) are hotly discussed. These binaries focus attention on how research findings are obtained, on whether they can be applied and on how they relate to the means of producing them (e.g. Dunne *et al.*, 2005). Professional doctorate students, however, face other issues too, some of which we wish to consider here.

In professional settings, 'research' is a very seductive word, conveying as it does the use of considered and thoughtful intelligence to analysing problems and seeking a means of addressing them. Professional doctorate students must engage with methodological issues, are granted access to research discourse in academia *and* also have to find a means of addressing problems in their day to day work.

It is ironic that, whilst research is in tension with teaching for faculty in departments of education (see Sikes in this volume), the professional doctorate requires that candidates manage precisely this tension between research and practice in the micro-context of problem solving at work.

Insider researchers often choose their project as a result of several years of experience of working with the issues. Thus, they often have assumptions and ideas about what they expect to find out and, on the basis of experience as a practitioner, they actually have a theoretical stance before beginning their project. Research in the workplace is likely to be small scale, involving few people. This closeness may seem to compromise the researcher's ability to critically engage with information, and so they need to devise means of stimulating reflexivity whenever possible, as an important aspect of 'self-triangulation' of their interpretations of their data. Professional doctorate students may be searching for methodologies that enable them to be simultaneously a practitioner and a researcher, unlike the methodological discourses that sustain a distinction between the 'investigator' and the 'respondents', the 'researcher' and 'practice', respondents and reality, 'because it is their constructions of reality that the inquirer seeks to reconstruct' (Lincoln and Guba, 1985: 41). This search will engage them with complex interacting methodologies, provoke a re-examination of concepts of rigour and validity and lead towards post-modern ideas of research as a means of critical reflection (see, for example, Lincoln and Guba, 2005).

Our methodology

This research arose from our own Education Doctorate studies undertaken at different universities (Heath, 2005, 2006; Drake, 2006). We found that we had each independently suggested in our theses that, in addition to generic methodological and data collecting problems that many doctoral students experience, we found specific issues related to researching one's own practice which we wanted to explore further.

We interviewed 13 students undertaking Education Doctorates at two universities, one a pre-1992 'old' university and the other a post-1992 'new' university. EdD students from the old university consisted of headteachers and teachers in primary and secondary schools, FE colleges and higher education; EdD students from the new university were lecturers, senior lecturers and principal lecturers from a range of faculties within that institution. Table 9.1 illustrates the participants in this study and identifies whether they had changed jobs during the life of the doctorate, and whether or not they had completed their studies.

Interviews took place at the respective universities and at a time convenient to participants. One telephone interview was recorded and one student preferred to talk at home, away from both his workplace and the university.

Difficulties in conducting a research study in one's workplace, the subject for this chapter, beset us as well methodologically, for we are both university lecturers and we work on the doctoral programme at one of the universities.

We believed that since people may understand the world in very different ways, according to their beliefs and experiences, it was important to attempt to comprehend issues from the perspective of the individuals most closely involved (Birley and Moreland, 1998; Maykut and Morehouse, 1994; Denzin and Lincoln, 1994),

Table 9.1 Participants in the study

Name	Job and sector	Changed jobs	Completed
Alan	University lecturer	No	No
Colin	Senior University lecturer/practitioner	No	Yes
David	Principal University lecturer	No	No
Elizabeth	Primary freelance consultant	No	No
Florence	Principal University lecturer	No	No
George	Primary Headteacher	No	Yes
Jane	Senior University lecturer	Yes	No
Jonathan	Secondary Headteacher	Yes	Yes
Louisa	Principal University lecturer	Yes	No
Marian	University lecturer	No	No
Pam	Secondary school teacher	Yes	Yes
Sarah	Teacher/Post-Compulsory manager	Yes	No
Simon	Secondary school teacher	No	Yes

acknowledging the importance of their perspectives as a means of understanding their world (Rogers, 1983). However, it is also our world. As tutors and EdD graduates we were, by definition, insiders in this study.

Our 'insider knowledge' helped us understand the particular language and conventions often referred to by the participants, provided us with an understanding of the variety of settings in HE in which this practice took place and gave a 'feel for the game and the hidden rules' (Bourdieu, 1988: 27). At the same time we needed to attempt to challenge any assumptions resulting from our 'insider knowledge', instead searching for new and underlying meanings experienced by the participants (Woolfe and Dryden, 1996).

We selected interviewing based on active listening (Rogers, 1983) and rapid interpretation (Eraut, 1994) as the most appropriate method for revealing participants' perceptions, emotions, experiences and feelings (Denscombe, 1998).

> ... qualitative data are sexy. They are a source of well-grounded, rich descriptions and explanations of processes in identifiable local contexts ... they have a quality of 'undeniability' ... words have a concrete, vivid, meaningful flavour that often proves convincing to a reader.
>
> (Miles and Huberman, 1994: 1)

'Rapid interpretation' is a form of constant monitoring as an interview progresses and depends on the ability of the interviewer to notice and select information rapidly at the time of the encounter' (Eraut, 1994: 109). Having noticed and selected information, the process further depends on the ability of the interviewer to probe, challenge or remain silent and give the interviewee time to reflect on their thinking.

Initially, we pasted on the virtual learning site for one of the universities our concern to understand the issues experienced by professional doctorate students undertaking insider research in their own organisations, and invited responses. The responses were encouraging and so we invited a wider group of people on the professional doctoral programmes at both universities to participate further. We chose loosely structured interviews (as a means of potentially keeping our roles as unobtrusive as possible), allowing the direction of the interview to be driven by the participants' agenda, within the overall framework of our enquiry.

This style of working was possible because of our easy access to the participants; and we must live with the consequences of this, as must they. Preserving confidentiality within the group is challenging, and needs continual renegotiation and so not only do we change names but also disciplines to maintain participants' anonymity. We also sent a draft of this chapter to the participants for their agreement, as well as interview transcripts which were to be checked for accuracy.

Our approach adhered to the notion of a trail of discovery in the spirit of grounded theory rather than as grounded theory narrowly defined (see Strauss and Corbin, 1998). We recognise clear difficulties in our position through our own collegiality and realise that we were, probably at least to some extent, told what the participants thought we wanted to know.

In the next three sections we explore participants' experiences under the following headings:

- Relationships and boundaries
- Being critical and workplace mission
- Managing research and writing

Relationships and boundaries

Working with colleagues whilst doing research means that professional doctorate students have to adopt complex positions in relation to people connected to their project. They may be supervised by, or be supervising colleagues, whilst working with them as members of a team. Denicolo (2004) highlights the generalisable difficulties associated with any doctoral supervision and some additional issues involved when supervising colleagues. She warns that such relationships tend to produce 'safe' but not highly creative research as a result of students feeling more vulnerable than they perceive others to be. 'Safe' scholarly work is thought to be less risky than innovation in subject area and/or in research methodologies.

Currently, the professional doctorate is seen as a route for lecturer–practitioners in higher education to gain research qualifications and experience, and this group is likely to comprise a significant minority on any programme. This means that complicated supervisory and assessment relationships are highly likely to impact this group of students. It also means that the employing institution may well have a vested interest in the students' success on the programme, and the norms and prevailing institutional mission will shape the research undertaken by the student. For students working outside higher education, the issue is likely to be cast in terms of the researcher working with colleagues for whom they have some responsibility.

We found that participants in our study found ways of negotiating and re-negotiating relationships with their colleagues, with a number of additional layers of complexity for professional doctorate students investigating their own practice, as opposed to researching practice outside their direct workplace. However, there are obvious potential difficulties for students who have had previous difficult relationships with particular members of staff.

> *Florence*: '... my second marker was X ... I know he doesn't like me ... but I felt this was very spiteful and I wondered what the hidden agenda was ...

The possibility of 'hidden agendas' was also raised when more than one student found themselves made redundant during their doctorate, once fieldwork was completed in the workplace:

> *Sarah*: ... the new principal had very different ideas, he didn't value research ... he really didn't want it at the college I think. So that's when I was

made redundant ... there is a niggle ... as to whether it was part of the issue that we were identified as people to go. Difficult to tell'.

If the student's data pertains to particular individuals at work this can also cause complications, both in terms of what the students then 'know' about the colleague's work, and what it is possible to take further. Several participants in our study remarked on the challenges of dealing with data that related to colleagues, commenting on the need for maintaining confidentiality and the impossibility of publishing, for example:

> *Alan*: I have had students who've said 'the other tutor taught me and it wasn't very good' ... I have a professional relationship with my colleague I need to maintain ... for a start I could never publish because he would be easily identifiable.

The potential embarrassment for students knowing that their work is to be assessed by colleagues is also expressed:

> *Louisa*: And the other thing that got to me was that I felt they were all looking at my essay ... because I know that's how we moderate ... we get a bag of doughnuts and all the essays and a big cup of coffee ... and I could see this room of people saying things like 'oh God, you wouldn't expect her to write like that.

Students were careful about separating their professional activities from their insider research, especially when they could see the potential for exploitation of junior members of staff. This had an effect on all stages of the research process, from formulating the shape of the project, through designing the study and writing up. One secondary school teacher who was the head of a department told us that as he believed that research in any situation impacts on the environment, he had to think very carefully about 'who I was going to talk to'. He said:

> ... I made up my mind very early on that I was determined not to talk to anybody who was more junior than I was (*Simon*).

However, the status and responsibility of the professional doctorate student in the employing institution means that this is not always possible, as the student feels some responsibility to act on the 'findings'. For instance, a head teacher explained that for an early professional doctorate assignment he had investigated performance in mathematics in the school. Having been told by the school students that maths was boring, he felt the need to pass this back to the mathematics teachers. This was difficult:

> *Jonathan*: they had to discuss how they were going to deal with it and for some of them it was quite upsetting. That was a massive tension.

The above example raises the issue of obtaining data from people whom one teaches, be these school students or students in higher education. EdD students often want to engage their students in their research, but necessarily wonder about the extent to which students' participation is connected to desires for other benefits, for instance high marks. Pam puts this very clearly:

> Oh yes, very much did I need to worry about the fact that I was their teacher affected whether they took part, whether they responded to me in the teaching sessions, things like that. There was chocolate, there were incentives ... now whether they came because I was their teacher or whether they saw it as an opportunity to miss some lessons I don't know.

For some professional doctorate students, there are two or three layers of status to negotiate with colleagues. One relates to the position of a lecturer-practitioner, another relates to education research and the values ascribed to it by colleagues; and the third aspect is the perceived (by others) status of the professional doctorate. Colin, a scientist, was asked 'why don't you do a "proper" doctorate?', which he believed was a direct result of the prevailing research environment in which he was working, which privileged both scientific research and the traditional PhD. Another, Jane, found that negotiating relationships with colleagues related to status issues and the perception of 'knowing her place'. She referred to hierarchical administration–like the mentality of the civil service–and, surprisingly, in view of the fact that she worked in a research-active university, she felt:

> you were seen as somebody who was stepping above their station in life, to express these opinions about things that you weren't allowed to know anything about, or have an opinion about.

We found that there was a sense in which some students had a feeling that whilst colleagues expressed support for their research, there was also an element of suspicion of the research, its intentions and whether or not they might be identified through it, referred to by one participant as 'a sort of schizophrenic experience'. This was also the case where a student had undertaken research outside his own institution, but within his community of practice in the same subject area and where he felt he had been perceived as a 'spy' from a rival institution:

> *David*: ... there was one contact who was very suspicious about what I was doing ... I felt that they felt I was some sort of 'spy' trying to get some inside information to use for our own benefit.

Being critical and workplace mission

Doing a doctorate means developing a critical position with respect to the research and the research setting. This is part of the argument presented in the thesis and, for social science doctorates, is often the means of assessing the 'originality' of the work and its 'contribution to knowledge'.

However, as Walford declares, 'doctoral work is a contribution to knowledge, not just a contribution to the student's self-knowledge' (1998, p. 4). Potentially, this puts the professional doctorate thesis in a place that requires the author to tread a fine line. Adhering to prevailing academic norms and values of the university needs careful navigation with respect to the norms and values of the workplace setting, for the author must be critical of the practices revealed through their study, whilst potentially continuing to engage with them.

In practice, insider researchers are members of an organisation with a particular culture, ethos and workplace mission. As explained above, insider researchers often have to handle interpersonal relationships very sensitively to avoid problems in future dealings with colleagues. Indeed, for the professional doctorate student undertaking insider research within their own department, it was what came after the doctorate that was of equal concern, particularly in terms of the security of their own jobs and their continuing personal and professional relationships with colleagues:

> *Jane*: there's issues of trust there that have to be negotiated as well … when you're actually getting deeper into processes with people … that's fine for writing up an abstract assignment, but in your real job, you then have to think 'what am I going to do about this?

For lecturer-practitioners the tensions become more complex, as these students frequently begin their professional doctorate research in the practice that they have moved away from to become university teachers. Thus, critical aspects of the practice arising from the research may arouse suspicion and doubt on the part of the participants, potentially compromising their co-operation as Colin explained:

> I think they were suspicious of my research because in some respects it made them confront difficult areas

There is no doubt that professional doctorate students recognise that their access to a research setting is privileged, enabling them to contact colleagues either within their own organisation or outside it that they might otherwise not have been able to reach. For some, this was a positive:

> *George:* that gave me a licence to go to see other schools. You think you can just ring up and pop over and go, but you can't, but if you've got research in a way that gives you access … I got an even better understanding of the schools in the situation, I could really begin to use the findings from the interviews in a way that began to fuse the research ideas together.

But for others, it had negative connotations. Students questioned whether as 'insiders' they could achieve any meaningful degree of critical distance from their workplace, or their colleagues. Since these are areas in which professional doctorate students are expected to negotiate successfully, initial discussions suggest that privileged access sets up challenges in itself.

The culture of research within an organisation may be a key element in the success of the professional student. Students felt themselves to be both supported and encouraged when there was a strong institutional culture of research-based practice. This placed lecturer-practitioners in general in a relatively secure position, although these students may decide, having researched their immediate practice for early assignments, to locate the main study for the thesis in the community of practice rather than in their actual workplace. However, students in other settings were vulnerable to changes in their employers' attitudes to research, and changes compromised the students' work. For instance, Sarah began her doctorate in circumstances that encouraged investigative practice, but this changed with the arrival of a new senior manager:

> *Sarah*: there was an ethos of research and they could see the value of it, so I was given quite a lot of free reign …

> … he (the new manager) really found it very difficult to allow us to do anything with it, and he didn't want it at the college at all, I think.

One of the most difficult things for the insider researchers in our study was the challenge of aligning their own situational, tacit, process and conceptual knowledge (Eraut, 1994) with their expressed desire to be 'neutral' researchers. Participants struggled to keep their own views out of interviews, especially when these were out of step with what the interviewee said or appeared to believe. People undergoing doctoral study recognised the improbability of achieving a 'clean' research methodology, explaining that in small-scale research you end up 'talking to your mates' (Simon). Trying to combine knowledge from being part of the team with critical distance compromises even action research. Indeed, one participant questioned whether insider research could ever produce 'reliable and valid' research, and those who had completed the doctorate, including one of us (Drake, 2006), had devoted significant space in the thesis for exploring this particular issue. One person had been challenged by the examiners at the viva to 'go and put himself in the thesis', and in so doing was forced to recognise that the process of doing action research had changed him as well as the situation he was exploring.

Our participants felt that the gratitude that they felt for colleagues agreeing to participate could potentially compromise their work by, for instance, being reluctant to challenge views people expressed and recognising that people who they've known for a long time may 'have said nice things to help my research' (David). Doctoral students are generally encouraged to publish their research findings, but for insider researchers this can be problematic. Whilst researchers

t were indeed
aid:

w they write
ouraging col-
ritten for the
ponsibility to

xpose recognisably poor practice in the
e also a likelihood that participants in
engaging critically with the eventual

ing to only those people who love you …
l, what about this?' and 'what about that?'
'its really good, well done' …

her difficult situations, such as not being
meetings, or even off the record, from
ant said, 'you can't just un-hear it'. For

ies they had
hrey (2007)
eve that the
suspect that
ers of staff,
hey may be
with their
y alongside

ers at that time would reveal one face in a
it of it and say … 'I don't believe that, it's

ilemma of developing a critical research
ution and to her colleagues who were the

n I realised
o identities

access is very privileged but it's one of
very much, the duty to the institution, to

in her uni-
er supervi-
ractitioner
ed, and an
reflexivity
embers of
dertaking
had great
, even on
l problem

professional doctorates are required not only
o knowledge but also to make an original
tice. Currently in the UK this varies from
h suggests:

ctice is that you would be viva'd on 'what's
research now? … how is this going to influence

(Heath, 2006: 34)

you' …
an hour

t participants thought that undertaking profes-
EdD had an impact, affecting the way people
there was less evidence to suggest wider influ-

position,
ng with

. that you're going to come along and actually
do something about it … and of course that
aker at a fairly senior level …

And in our study, the people who were able to claim some imp⋯
senior decision makers, such as Jonathan, a headteacher who⋯

> I'm a lot tougher with colleagues about what they write and⋯
> and the messages they give … one of the things I think I'm en⋯
> leagues to do more research, sharing a lot of information I've⋯
> doctorate with colleagues. So I do feel that out of it comes a r⋯
> work with others.

Managing research and writing

Professional doctorate students frequently acknowledged the diffic⋯
in positioning themselves as a practitioner and as a researcher. Hu⋯
talks of examining the hyphen in practitioner–researcher, but we b⋯
movement from one identity to another is more fluid than this. W⋯
since professional doctorate students are often quite senior men⋯
already experienced at manipulating personal and professional live⋯
in a stronger position to be able to combine practitioner-researc⋯
existing activities. However, identity as a researcher may not sit ea⋯
practice.

> *Pam*: I had a professional identity which I thought was fixed. ⋯
> that over here it was something completely different and the⋯
> didn't fit with each other at all

Whilst undertaking her doctorate, Pat Drake was in a senior positi⋯
versity, being head of school, and consequently the line manager ⋯
sor and her internal examiner. This position as simultaneously seni⋯
and junior researcher needed careful navigation by everyone inv⋯
approach to her project that placed research as an occasion for criti⋯
rather than providing straightforward findings or truths. Senior⋯
staff in our discussions corroborated tensions in this regard. Thos⋯
their studies alongside junior colleagues stated that their colleag⋯
difficulty in seeing them as anything other than their 'line mana⋯
study days and in researcher action learning sets role conflict was a⋯
for these students:

> *Louisa*: people would say 'oh I'm glad I've seen you, I must⋯
> they'd say it would only take 5 minutes but of course it would⋯
> … I used to take sandwiches and go and hide in the end

Managing time to study whilst holding down a full-time manage⋯
maintaining close family and extended family relationships,

unexpected interruptions to study such as a change in job responsibilities or more problematically (and less predictably) managing health problems, all present significant difficulties for professional doctorate students:

> ... for me ... life became a juggling act. Most of the time I managed to keep three balls in the air (work, family, and self) but now and again it fell apart because of particular demands like illness and the family and promotion at work.
>
> (Salmon, 1992:103).

Amongst lecturer–practitioners in our study, the support for research they were given by their departments varied, with one student being given a block of time to complete her write-up, another a regular half day a week whilst a third had no time at all. This seeming inequality (apparent in this sample simply by virtue of the people interviewed) in one university appeared in the other in a different guise. Whilst there is an expectation for full-time academic staff to do research, this is not necessarily translated to the equivalent for part-time staff nor to those in administrative positions. Amongst the teachers in the group, only one, Pam, talked about the time she was given by her employer – i.e. three days for field-work. This time, once negotiated on the calendar, became non-negotiable, despite her being ill on one of the days, because the arrangements involved in providing a room, cover and alternative work, and extracting school students from their scheduled lessons, were too complex to unravel once established.

In our study, people who had completed their doctorates recognised that managing time successfully did not just happen by chance. Writing was done at weekends, in school holidays and to strict, self-imposed deadlines. Both headteachers were funded by the DfES for four years. George had no intention of taking any longer on the research, and although completing the process of writing, submission and the viva took a further year, he achieved his self-imposed target of 'wanting to finish before my daughter started university so I wasn't paying two sets of fees'. Jonathan moved jobs once the thesis fieldwork was completed, deliberately choosing to work 'where I could actually have the time to do the work on the doctorate', explicitly distancing himself from the site of the data gathering:

> *Jonathan*: I think once I'd completed the data collection I wasn't too concerned about remaining in the same school. I was happy to move on. In some senses it was a real sense of distancing myself from the institution and I think it was better not having been in a school. I just tended to block the time off and isolate myself off away from everything.

Pam also changed jobs after her fieldwork, and, like Jonathan, this prevented her from going back to check her data with the school students who had provided it. Unlike Jonathan, Pam regretted this, but saw it as an inevitable limitation, and part of her compromise between duty to her employer and duty to her research methodology.

Some of the strengths and limitations of being an insider researcher have begun to be explored in this section. We conclude by identifying what we see as the three main issues which emerge from our study – the student's need to deal with multiple integrities, with the prevailing political macro- and micro-climates, and our need to re-examine research methodologies for professional doctorate students.

Discussion and conclusion

Professional doctorate students have access to research discourse in academia whilst being motivated to find a means of addressing problems in their day to day work. This premise underpins the degree, but raises questions as to what a professional doctorate actually is and does. Does the degree differ from a traditional PhD by virtue of the research project undertaken, or is it the experience of the students on the programme that distinguishes it? Is the degree characterised by the choices made by those deciding to do it, i.e. does the fact of the doctorate being termed 'professional' arise as a consequence of the student's decision to undertake that type of programme, to investigate practice, to engage with a taught component and to work with a group of contemporaries? These questions are currently under discussion, vide recent UK consultation about the doctoral degree (QAA, 2007).

In recognising that professional doctoral students develop multiple identities with respect to work, research and practice, we must also recognise that they also develop what might be termed 'multiple integrities' as well. Professional doctorate degrees target 'senior professionals' (Heath, 2005), and such individuals have loyalties to their workplace, regardless of what the research uncovers, as well as deepening awareness of what research integrity must entail, especially in the case of small-scale projects. This quest for research integrity necessitates an exploration of validity as a concept, and in a project in one's own workplace, this exploration involves recognising both that the research is not replicable and the need to place oneself as an active participant in the study. We found, although numbers are far too small to generalise, various means of dealing with this problem, including in-depth consideration of research as narrative enquiry (Drake, 2006), changing jobs after undertaking fieldwork or having realised the challenges of having one's colleagues as research participants, deciding to conduct the major project outside their immediate workplace.

People at work in education institutions of all kinds operate in intensely political climates. Dominant ideologies allow for little dissent, and create hegemonies for practice that can be analysed in terms of the distribution of power through networks and maintaining dominance through surveillance (see, for example, Foucault in Gutting (1994)). Current concerns regarding curriculum, quality management, inspection and research productivity can all be read in this light.

In researching one's own workplace one is necessarily positioned by prevailing political ideologies, as are one's research respondents, colleagues and friends. Thus, people's behaviour is driven by political stratagem, and so the research can never be 'clean', 'neutral', 'objective'. So it is unsurprising that when students realise that, as insider researchers, neutrality is not achievable, there is some dismay and puzzlement. We also suspect that the higher a professional doctorate student is placed in their employing organisation, the better positioned they are to place research significantly on their agenda, and find time to do it, without compromising their practice.

Professional doctorate research is often located in an action research paradigm. In this chapter we have only been able to present a very small selection from what our participants shared with us and so we have chosen to draw attention to the complexities of action research at the doctoral level, and what this means for individuals on the professional doctorate programme in education. We would argue that at the doctoral level the issues are sufficiently complex to warrant further exploration of methodologies, and that there needs to be more consideration on the part of those organising and supervising professional doctorates in terms of the multiple integrities that the successful professional doctorate student must sustain.

Bibiolography

Barnett, R. (2000) *Realizing the University in an Age of Supercomplexity.* Buckingham, SRHE and OUP.

Bourner, T., Bowden, R. and Laing, S. (2001) 'Professional Doctorates in England', *Studies in Higher Education,* 26, 1, pp. 65–83.

Boud, D. and Walker, D. (1990) *Reflection: Turning Experience into Learning.* London, Kogan Page.

Becher, T. (1989) *Academic Tribes and Territories: Intellectual Enquiry and the Culture of Disciplines.* Milton Keynes, SRHE and OUP.

Birley, G. and Moreland, N. (1998) *A Practical Guide to Academic Research.* London, Kogan Page.

Bourdieu, P. (1988) *Homo Academicus.* Cambridge, Polity Press.

Brennan, M. (1995) 'Education Doctorates: Reconstructing professional partnerships around research?', *Australian Universities Review,* 38, 2, pp. 20–22.

Claxton, G. L. (1998) 'Knowing without knowing why', *The Psychologist,* May 1998, pp. 217–220.

Dearing, R. (1997) *National Committee of Enquiry into Higher Education: Higher Education for a Learning Society.* London, HMSO.

Drake, P. (2006) *Working for Learning: A Case of Mathematics for Teaching,* Thesis in partial fulfilment for the Doctor of Education degree, University of Sussex, unpublished.

Denicolo, P. (2004) *Doctoral supervision of colleagues: peeling off the veneer of satisfaction and competence,* Studies in Higher Education, 29, 6, pp. 693–707.

Denscombe, M. (1998) *The Good Research Guide.* Buckingham, OUP.

Denzin, N. K. and Lincoln, Y. S. (1994) *Handbook of Qualitative Research.* Thousand Oaks, CA, Sage.

Dunne, M., Pryor, J. and Yates, P. (2005) *Becoming a Researcher.* Maidenhead, Open University Press.

Eraut, M. (1994) *Developing Professional Knowledge and Competence.* London, Falmer Press.

Gutting, G. (1994) (ed.) *The Cambridge Companion Guide to Foucault.* London, CUP.

Heath, L. (2005) *Supervision of Professional Doctorates: Education Doctorates in English Universities,* Thesis in partial fulfilment for the degree of Doctor of Education, University of Brighton, unpublished.

Heath, L. (2006) *Supervision of Professional Doctorates: Education Doctorates in English Universities,* Higher Education Review, Spring 2006, 38, 2, pp. 21–41.

Humphrey, C. (2007) *Insider-Outsider: Activating the Hyphen,* Action Research 5, 1, pp. 11–26.

Lincoln, Y. and Guba, E. (1985) *Naturalistic Enquiry.* Newbury Park, CA, Sage.

McClure, M. (2004) 'Clarity bordering on stupidity': Where's the quality in systematic review?' Paper presented to the British Educational Research Association Annual Conference, Manchester, September 2004.

Maykut, P. and Morehouse, R. (1994) *Beginning Qualitative Research: A Philosophical and Practical Guide.* London, The Falmer Press.

Miles, M. B. and Huberman, A. M. (1994) *Qualitative Data Analysis.* Thousand Oaks, CA, Sage.

Oakley, A. (2000) *Experiments in Knowing.* Cambridge, Polity Press.

Oakley, A. (2003) Research evidence, knowledge management and educational practice: early lessons from a systematic approach. *London Review of Education,* 1, pp. 121–133.

Office of Science and Technology (OST) (1993) *Realising our Potential: A Strategy for Science, Engineering and Technology.* London, HMSO.

Quality Assurance Agency (QAA) (2007) *Discussion paper about doctoral programmes,* http://www.qaa.ac.uk/academic, accessed 25 June 2007.

Rogers, C. (1983) *Freedom to Learn for the 80s.* Columbus, Charles E. Merrill Publishing Company.

Schon, D. (1983) *The Reflective Practitioner.* San Franscisco, Jossey-Bass.

Schon, D. (1987) *Educating the Reflective Practitioner.* San Francisco, CA, Jossey-Bass.

Scott, D., Brown, A., Lunt, I. and Thorne, L. (2004) *Professional Doctorates: Integrating Professional and Academic Knowledge.* Maidenhead, OUP and SHRE.

Sebba, J. (2006) Systematic Reviewing: Myths, Challenges and Possibilities. UCET 2 February 2006, University of London.

Salmon, P. (1992) *Achieving a PhD: Ten Students' Experience.* Stoke-on-Trent, Trentham Books.

Strauss, A. and Corbin, J. (1998) *Basics of Qualitative Research: Techniques and Procedures for Developing Grounded Theory.* London, Sage.

Torrance, H. (2004) 'Systematic Reviewing-the "call centre" version of research synthesis. Time for a more flexible approach'. Invited presentation to ESRC/RCBN seminar on Systematic Reviewing, 24 June 2004, University of Sheffield.

Usher, R. (2000) 'Imposing structure: enabling play: New knowledge production in the 'real world' university', in C. Symes and J. McIntyre (eds) *Working Knowledge: The New Vocationalism and Higher Education*. Buckingham, SRHE and OUP.

Walford, G. (ed.) (1998) *Doing Research about Education*. London and Philadelphia. Falmer Press.

Woolfe, R. and Dryden, W. (1996) *The Handbook of Counselling Psychology*. London, Sage.

Chapter 10

Researching research cultures

The case of new universities

Pat Sikes

Introduction

This chapter tells a tale of insider/outsider – or outsider/insider – positioning. The story arises out of ongoing, collaborative, autoethnographic, critical, action research involving myself and thirty-five lecturers working in the Graduate School of Arts and Education[1] (GSAE) within the Faculty of Education at a 'post-1992'[2] university in the UK. I'll call the institution New University.

The project was originally conceived of as a strategy that would contribute to the School's Continuing Professional Development (CPD) programme. As such, the key aim has been to support those who, whilst experienced HE teachers, are new to the sort of research and writing demanded of academics by the Research Assessment Exercise (RAE)[3] (Sikes, 2006). In addition, the undertaking has also been approached and framed as a research project focussing on 'developing a research culture in a new university'.

Since the work began in 2002, I have been going into New University as both an employee/consultant (insider/outsider), with the formal title of Visiting Reader, and an independent researcher from another (i.e. my own, home) institution (out-sider). I've worked alongside GSAE colleagues, individually and in groups, through all the stages of various research projects and related initiatives. I've led research-based tutorials and seminars and presented my own research papers. I've given lectures and conducted workshops on such topics as research as philo-sophical endeavour, ethical considerations, approaches to re-presentation and writing for publication. At the same time, I have been collecting information relating to the development of a research culture, via interviews, conversations, discussions, written communications and documents, as well as recording and reflecting on my own perceptions and experiences of my involvement. This is the data that I will be drawing on here. In addition, through word of mouth about my work at New, I was invited to spend a period as Visiting Scholar at an Australasian university contributing to similar research culture development and the experiences I had there also inform what I have to say.

Although it may sound somewhat grandiose, I see these research projects to be in the critical action tradition, as discussed by Bourgois (2002) and Foley and

Valenzuela (2005) since my unequivocal objective has been to 'make a difference'. This intention adds a further complication to what is already an especially messy situation when it comes to my location as an insider/outsider (Guba and Lincoln, 2005, pp. 201–202). Having said that my view is that much, if not all, research inevitably situates researchers in ambivalent positional relationships with respect to various aspects of their work. As I see it, it isn't only a question of doing research in one's own 'backyard'. For me, investigating topics in which one has a personal interest (e.g. Oakley, 1979; Sikes, 1997) can also be considered a variant of insider research. But, to return to my specific situation at New: I felt, and could be seen to be, depending on who was doing the seeing and when they were doing it, simultaneously outside and inside the institution; outside and inside the CPD project; outside and inside research that GSAE colleagues undertook as a consequence of the CPD initiative; and outside and inside the 'developing a research culture' research. Seeking a metaphor to describe this complexity I thought of onion skin layers, Russian dolls, *mis en abyme*[4] (Stronach and MacLure, 1997, p. 126), rhizomes (Deleuze and Guattari, 1988), folds (Deleuze, 1993) and pleats (Richardson, 1997), to name but a few. None of these seems adequate, although Donald Schon's (1983) 'swamps of practice' resonates with my sense of the muddiness that I feel is involved here! It would be interesting to know what images and allegories the story that I'm telling evoke for readers, who, by virtue of their engagement with the text, can themselves be considered to have an insider outsider take on the matter.

Entering the field

My involvement with New University initially came about as the result of a mix of circumstances implicating, amongst other things, personal contacts and relationships, misunderstandings about who had said and meant what, the imperative of the RAE and the geographical distance between New and my home. Suffice it to say that I was invited to apply for, and was offered, a high-ranking position at the university. For various administrative and personal reasons, I didn't take the job but both me and senior staff in the GSAE wanted us to work together regardless. Consequently, we came up with the idea that I be appointed as a Visiting Reader, and would spend a number of days each year as a consultant to New University. This satisfied me, the GSAE and my home institution. My remit in the role was to develop a research culture; how I went about doing that was up to me.

During the four months before my contract formally came into effect (in September 2002), I made enquiries about the sorts of research and writing experience individual members of staff had. I found that, although a couple of people had doctorates and a handful held Masters degrees involving a research-based thesis, the majority had never done any research beyond that necessary for their first degree or professional qualification. These folk had been hired for their expertise as teachers. Teaching was what they were good at and what they knew, but now the rules had changed and they had to become active researchers too.

But that wasn't all; they had to become researchers whose work was published in peer reviewed journals. Even for those who welcomed the chance to develop identities as researchers and writers (Hartley, 2002; Lee and Boud, 2003; Morley, 2003; Sikes, 2006) these were threatening circumstances, circumstances that I was about to become personally associated and identified with as I embarked on my task.

Thus, right from the start there were insider-outsider aspects to my role, in that I was brought in from outside to work inside the School. That it was senior insiders who had formally asked me to come in and join them adds yet another dimension. However, it is important to note that I have never felt that I was being brought in as a sledgehammer, a Trojan horse or in order to do anyone's dirty work. New has a long tradition of visitors who work in a collaborative fashion with home staff and I was just the latest in the line. Moreover, when I had originally been interviewed for the post, which I didn't take, I had been the chosen candidate of the majority of staff. They knew my work, they liked my style and I had their vote of confidence.

Bearing all this in mind, and considering the focus and nature of the work that I was to do in the GSAE, my own professional need to research and publish, my interest in autoethnography, and my previous experiences of supporting teacher action research, I decided that working alongside people, demonstrating, embodying and demystifying research practice could be a way forward. So, exploiting the potential the situation offered, I drew up a plan that was also a research proposal that firmly cast me in an insider-outsider role.

Being in the field

Initial encounters

My first meeting with the entire assembled GSAE was to take place immediately before the start of the summer vacation. It is practice in the School to hold an end of year event incorporating presentations of work undertaken during the past academic session and setting out agendas for the future. In July 2002, I had a place on the bill.

I knew that for me to have any chance of success it was imperative I conveyed a strong sense of my sincerity, independence and commitment to working collaboratively. There was no artifice in this. I was sincere, independent and committed. Furthermore, by this time, I felt that I, personally, had invested quite a lot, both in terms of needing to achieve some degree of success in developing research in the GSAE and with regard to my own research agenda. Because of this, I felt that I was very much an insider. If my plan was not accepted I was going to have to go back to the drawing board and would also have to cope with the emotions of personal rejection which, even at this early stage, would not be easy. I agree with Amanda Coffey when she writes, 'having no emotional connection to the research endeavour, setting or people is indicative of a poorly executed project' (1999, p. 159). To my mind, emotional connection can be considered a form of insiderness and acknowledging that this is the case is a characteristic of the sort of research

I would wish to be associated with and identified in terms of (see Denzin and Lincoln, 2005, for an overview). However, the proposal, which, with some trepidation, I distributed, was as follows.

Strengthening the research base in the GSAE: a reflexive action approach

NB

This paper should be regarded as a 'thinking in progress' document. The ideas contained in it are ideas offered for consideration and discussion; they are not definite statements of intent.

Remit

The proposed research would take an autoethnographic, reflexive, action research approach to the task of strengthening and developing the research base of, and research activity within, the Graduate School.

Aims

Key aims are:
- to involve staff in innovative, collaborative research;
- to provide support for those new to research;
- to capitalise on research opportunities offered by the CPD contexts in which colleagues work;
- to strengthen research based teaching through experience and example;
- to attract external funding for the research;
- to improve the rating achieved at the next RAE (provided previous criteria continue to apply) through publications arising from the research.

Rationale

The 'Strategy for Education Research in New University'[5] states that:

> Members of GSAE ... are committed to undertaking education research and scholarly activity that enriches their teaching, promotes course development and constitutes an important aspect of their staff development. The Faculty ... recognises the importance of such research for all its staff as a means by which they add to their understanding and enhance their practice as well as being for some a means of developing their careers as researchers.
>
> (Blenkinsop[5], 2002, p. 3)

This statement is underpinned by the notion that educational research is not just research about education but rather should be research with an educational purpose.

Educational research is applied research, applied in that it explicitly helps us to better understanding and, thereby, is capable of informing, developing and improving our practice.

Working with practitioners (as members of the GSAE do) offers privileged opportunities to set up a research-based dialogue founded on real concerns, grounded understandings, reflective insights and shared commitments to improving practice.

The proposed research could be a way of developing a collaborative project that

- models the sort of interactive relationship between teaching and research that is the foundation of New University's CPD programme;
- enables people to continue to do the teaching and research that interests them and that they are already involved in;
- provides a nurturing and supportive environment for those who lack experience and/or confidence in research;
- could be a way of helping more members of staff to publish their work in 'quality' outputs.

The research

The focus of the study would be on the process of strengthening the research base within the Graduate School. One way of describing that process would be as 'meta-research', in that it is research that investigates aspects of the various research activities colleagues are already engaged in. What would actually be entailed would be for staff themselves to decide, but possibilities include drawing up and monitoring personal and team research and writing plans, research and work in progress seminars, writing groups, conferences, working with students on assessed workplace-based research assignments, brainstorming research possibilities, developing collaborative projects and providing support for individual research projects. The intention is that staff would become intimately involved and would take 'ownership' of planning, executing, evaluating, writing about and disseminating findings.

Methodology

Again, the precise methodology/ies that are adopted would depend on the research design staff develop. However, it would seem to be appropriate to conceive of the research as an autoethnographic action research project – with the 'auto' referring to both individuals' perceptions and experiences of their various involvements and to an overall collective/institutional perspective.

The full range of research methods could be employed – for instance auto/biographical approaches (e.g. journals and other forms of personal writing, life history, narrative), observation of various kinds, interviews, questionnaires, (quantitative) monitoring – yielding an extremely rich data base. It is anticipated that analysis would be, essentially, interpretative.

Timescale

The project would probably need to run for a minimum of two years. Year One would be mainly concerned with devising and setting up systems and structures and beginning to collect reflective data. Year Two should begin to see some outcomes – in terms of research conducted or commenced, papers, etc. being accepted for publication. As this would be 'action research', evaluation and reflection would be ongoing and built in to the overall design.

Personnel

Ideally, all members of the Graduate School would be involved in some way but this may not be realisable.

References

Blenkinsop, X.[5] (2002) 'A Strategy For Education Research in New University' Unpublished Internal Document

I began the presentation by outlining my background, career and professional interests, then talked through the proposal, and finished by inviting questions and asking whether colleagues were 'up for it'. I emphasised that I saw myself as working alongside, and for, them. I stressed that I was there, fundamentally, to offer support of whatever relevant kind, and made it clear that I would not be feeding back any information which might be used for appraisal purposes. Had I accepted the original post, I would have been involved in evaluating staff performance but in my present capacity I was independent of that sort of thing. I talked about the way in which I would be seeing the research as my own, as well as 'ours' and stressed the collaborative nature of the venture.

Initial questions mainly concerned logistics, i.e. when and how often I'd be at New and how people could contact me between visits. This moved to discussion around the (then) Vice Chancellor's aspirations to raise the research status and profile of the university and the implications that such ambitions had for individuals already burdened with heavy teaching and administrative timetables. There was also some talk about resisting the push, but this was desultory because the general opinion appeared to be that research had to be a part of all university teachers' work. The chief barrier was identified as finding the time and space and support individuals felt they needed. I made it unequivocally clear that I saw providing support as my responsibility and emphasised my opinion that becoming research active and productive was achievable and also that it should be, primarily, something people did for their own, rather than for institutional, ends and satisfactions.

We then broke for coffee and during the interlude the majority of staff confirmed that they 'wanted to play' and were looking forwards to the new academic year and the chance to get going. A number of folk also shared ideas about research projects they'd like to get off the ground and, consequently, I left that day with a list of individual appointments for my first stint at New University in September.

My positioning

As I have mentioned, my involvement with New is ongoing. At the time of writing, in 2007, our relationship has endured for five years and I am contracted to the institution until the end of the academic year 2009, with an option to renew. Does this mean that I have gone 'native'? Am I more insider than outsider – or *vice versa* – in an institutional sense at least? What are the implications of where I am positioned, in terms of my role relating to CPD, my autoethnographic research on developing a research culture and my relationships with colleagues/research respondents? This is not something that can be answered in a straightforward way and I intend to address the questions by outlining what I/we did and are doing. Before then, it seems worth taking a step back and considering what I mean by 'insider', 'outsider' and 'native'.

The whole notion of insider/outsider research comes originally from anthropology. Anthropologists were amongst the first to conduct fieldwork in communities that they were not indigenous members of, their aim being to uncover the cultures, rules and customs by which these communities operated. It's fieldwork in social settings which seeks to investigate how and why things happen as they do that is the key thing here, whether that be fieldwork undertaken by anthropologists, ethnographers, educators, authors contributing to this text, or whoever. It is useful to keep these origins in mind when considering how I was positioned and what we/I did. George McCall's account of the fieldwork tradition provides a further viewpoint.

The researcher's perspective on native society could easily range from that of an ordinary member (later termed an 'emic' perspective) to that of a complete stranger (later termed an 'etic' perspective). The great risk of holding tightly to the member perspective is that of 'going native', and retaining a strict stranger perspective is that of 'ethnocentrism'. The necessity of transcending those opposing perspectives was established very early (in the development of anthropology); the fieldworker must remain open to native views while simultaneously seeking an academic understanding. A balance must be attained between description and explanation, between the idiographic and the nomothetic. Such a transcendent perspective is especially vital in view of fieldwork's commitment to examine not only the objective behaviours of natives but also the subjective, meaningful aspect of those behaviours. The fieldworker's participation in many native activities is a direct source of knowledge about the subjective aspects, while simultaneous observation about those activities is a source of knowledge about the objective aspects, hence the double consciousness that is distinctive of participant observers.

> Almost always, some native activities are found to be accessible even to outsiders, while certain other activities are not so initially, but can become accessible as trust and rapport are achieved. Because some activities occur

only rarely, they are directly accessible only to that participant observer who stays around for a long period of time. Early trials soon showed that a fieldworker should stay at least a year

(MacCall, 2006, p. 8)

McCall's description is concerned primarily with research *per se*. My involvement at New University was, however, a hybrid of research, action and teaching. In terms of the complete member, insider (emic) complete stranger outsider (etic) continuum, it seemed to me that I could be variously positioned depending upon exactly what was being considered. For instance, I knew something about and had subjective knowledge and experience of the culture of HE institutions generally, but, initially at least, I knew little about specific customs and practices at New. As time went on, this obviously changed. Then, in order to both do the job of developing a research culture and get on with my own research, I needed to be able to attain a degree of what MacCall terms 'academic understanding'. Similarly, achieving trust and rapport was essential and as the years have passed and as my field notes and reflections reveal, the benefits accruing from mutual confidence have been considerable as colleagues have increased in their research assurance and my own understandings have developed.

As an inside outsider, outside insider, I am well placed to reflect on plans, developments and changes which have consequences for staff. For example, during the time I have been working with the GSAE, colleagues have experienced internal reviews, restructuring of teaching teams, staffing changes and reorganisation of lines of management, as well as major refurbishment of buildings and relocation. Such things have less importance for me but I can see how they affect those whose working conditions are impacted by them. Such knowledge feeds into and informs both the research culture development work and my own research.

What we / I did

The proposal that I presented put forwards various ways by which research could be supported, developed and enacted, and from September 2002 these suggestions began to be realised. Thus began a programme that involved research consultations with groups; mentoring of individuals; seminars, workshops and lectures; and collaborative research and writing projects. These activities continue to be the focus of my involvement at New University and I will consider each in turn before moving on to discuss my own autoethnographic research project, although because everything that I have done at New feeds into that, distinctions are somewhat artificial.

Research consultations with groups

Staff in the GSAE belong to teaching teams, each of which is responsible for a particular area, such as delivering a modular masters programme, teaching the

Postgraduate Certificate of Education and Training, or running courses for the accreditation of Teaching Assistants. Whilst some people work in more than one team, everyone has a primary allegiance. Teams and programmes offer a good starting point for developing collaborative research projects and my role here has been to sit down with colleagues and talk about and brainstorm possibilities, which have turned out to include: action research projects designed to explore content, teaching strategies and modes of assessment; investigations of students' perceptions and needs, using, in some instances, assignments in order to collect data; and, studies of the experiences of certain groups of students, e.g. male teaching assistants. In addition to what it has done to develop practice, this work has resulted in a number of papers in peer-reviewed academic journals[6], articles in professional publications, two books, published by major houses, and various conference presentations.

My involvement here is, essentially, that of a consultant outsider whose knowledge and experience are tapped and used. As time has gone on and I have learnt more about the individuals concerned and the workings of the school, my suggestions regarding research have been influenced by what I know and, maybe too, by what I assume I know. Also, what people chose to reveal and what they ask of me are similarly coloured by their growing knowledge and consequent assumptions. This highlights a phenomenon which must always play a part in any social research enterprise, since researchers always come into social settings accompanied by some social knowledge, their own and that of others, which may affect the research that ultimately happens. In my case, my particular insider/outsider status emphasises the situation.

Mentoring of individuals

I made it known that I was prepared to act, on a one-to-one basis, as a mentor or critical friend or whatever people wanted me to be with regard to their personal research involvement. It was up to individuals to approach me and I made it clear that I would not be telling anyone else anything about any meetings. The sorts of assistance I have provided here include: discussing research proposals, reading papers and dissertations prior to submission and advising what to do about reviewers' comments when papers submitted to journals have been returned.

Until I began my consultancy and research at New University, I didn't know anyone at the GSAE. As a result of working with colleagues and, in particular, following seeing individuals about their work, I have come to make some very close friends with whom I now spend time on a social basis. Lots of people have written about relationships in the research field (e.g. Behar, 1993; Oakley, 1981; Wolcott, 2002) and about the impact these can have on various aspects of the research process. In short, they affect insider outsider positioning in a variety of ways that are, variously, 'positive', 'negative' or 'positive and negative'. Once again, my view is that this is inevitable when it's a question of social beings taking part in social situations.

Seminars, workshops and lectures

With relatively few exceptions, back in 2002, the GSAE staff had little research experience. I decided to tackle this by holding workshops and lectures dealing with topics relating to methodologies, specific methods and techniques of data collection and analysis, ethical considerations, writing, dissemination and so on. These sessions were opened to the School of Education as a whole and to any doctoral or masters students who wished to attend. As I wrote with regard to the group consultation work, as I have got to know and have become better known, my insider–outsider positioning has shifted, enabling me, I believe, to more specifically meet and target needs.

In order to provide a safe and supportive environment in which people could share the research they were doing, I instituted research seminars at which any one could present work in progress, early drafts or completed papers. On a number of occasions I have given presentations about my autoethnographic, 'developing a research community' work. In terms of my outsider-insider position, this has been a strange experience. On the one hand, I am talking as an outsider from another institution and, on the other, I have been talking about 'us', i.e. those of us in the room, engaging in the sorts of activities we are in the room to do. A form of *mis en abyme* in action perhaps, and one which casts a new light on respondent validation!

Collaborative research and writing projects

As a person who is fundamentally curious (if not nosy – see Goodson and Sikes, 2001, p. 1) and enthusiastic about research, it didn't take much for casual conversations about possible projects to turn into collaborative ventures. Consequently, I have been involved in my own, independent, outsider right, in two research projects and in joint writing with three other colleagues. To date this has resulted in six major conference presentations, three publications in peer-reviewed journals, with other projects currently ongoing[6]. I would not have been in a position to know and work with these people had I not been an insider and it was the case that, in collaborating, I was also furthering research culture development, although, in these instances, this was not the primary intention of my involvement.

My own autoethnographic research

Autoethnography is an approach, which seriously takes C. Wright Mill's (1959) injunction to employ the 'sociological imagination' to connect the personal and subjective with the public and political. As Carolyn Ellis puts it,

> 'What is autoethnography?' you might ask. My brief answer: research, writing, story, and method that connect the autobiographical and personal to the cultural, social and political. Autoethnographic forms feature concrete

action, emotion, embodiment, self-consciousness, and introspection portrayed in dialogue, scenes, characterization and plot.

(2004, p. xix)

In taking an autoethnographical stance, my concern has been to interrogate my own experiences of attempting to develop a research culture. I agree with Melanie Walker and Elaine Unterhalter that 'in excavating (my) own subjectivity, the point is not to produce research as therapy or stories for their own sake, but a disciplined and reflexive understanding of the known and the knower' (2004, p. 290). My view is that the approach has much to offer to me, personally, in terms of helping me to gain a privileged understanding of the process I was involved in and also that the insights provided might be of interest to others engaged in similar research development work. Since university status and funding are presently dependent upon research performance there is clearly a public and political element, if not imperative, involved here. Indeed, the fact that the overseas university wanted me to visit them and share my experiences suggests that this is a fair assessment.

Given that its focus is on the researcher themselves, autoethnography could be considered to be insider research *par excellence*. That this is the case has laid it wide open to accusations of being 'vanity ethnography' (Maynard, 1993, p. 329) and a vehicle for 'privileging the white middle-class woman or man's need for self-display above all else' (Apple, 1996, p. xiv). In some instances the charges, undoubtedly, stick. I would argue that they simply do not apply here, primarily because the work has not been all about me. As I wrote in the original proposal put before the GSAE, I saw what we were to be engaged in as 'meta-research', and that 'it would seem to be appropriate to conceive of it as an auto-ethnographic action research project – with the 'auto' referring to both individuals' perceptions and experiences of their various involvements AND to an overall collective/institutional perspective' (Sikes, 2002). In my view, the way in which all of us could simultaneously be considered to be insiders and outsiders was important to both individual success – whether my own in terms of research culture development and the progress of my autoethnographic project or GSAE colleagues' with respect to them becoming research active – and the success of the venture in raising the School's research profile overall.

I have always been completely open about the various aspects of my work at New University. Everyone has always been clear that I was treating my involvement as a research project. I have no evidence to suggest that this has affected how people have behaved or influenced what they have been prepared to talk about and share with me. I have always stressed that I perceive what we have been doing as collaborative; thus we have, all of us, been engaging in research of various kinds, including research focusing on developing a research project. I do believe, and staff members have independently voiced the same view, that the undertaking has been more successful with me in the position as an outside-insider than it would have been had I been in a full-time post at New. This is because, as previously noted,

I am not in any supervisory or evaluative position with regard to individuals. I am there to work with and for them in a manner that would not be possible if I was a member of the permanent professoriate. In some respects, this can be seen as putting us all in a win win situation. I win with regard to my research and they win in that they can use me as an independent resource and confidant.

Other chapters in this book have included sections on 'leaving the field', 'writing', and, 'disseminating the results', but these headings are not appropriate for the story I've been telling. The 'developing a research culture project' was conceived of, and has been realised as, an holistic, unique and evolving enterprise. It is not amenable to being organised in terms of prefabricated and standardised structures. For a start, it continues and I have not 'left the field'.

And then, 'writing' has been an integral part of the research, right from the very beginning. In fact I find it hard to imagine any research that I might be involved in where this would not be the case, for I share Laurel Richardson's (2000) view that writing is a method of inquiry that shapes thinking, furthers understanding and influences the overall shape of each and every research project. So I have written plans, proposals, field notes, memos, emails, lectures, notes to remind me what to say in presentations, and newsletters updating on developments as well as much, much more, and all of these writings have played a part in the overall whole. Then there have been the joint and individual publications and conference papers arising from the work. These have had the effect of taking the insider out to a wider world at the same time as they can be seen to have achieved one of the aims of the project: namely, making a difference by encouraging the staff to write and be published.

For some of the insider researchers contributing to this volume, writings in general and publications in particular have been problematic because they have revealed sensitive or controversial information or judgemental assessments. This was not an issue in my case because of the nature and focus of the project and as a result of the collaborative way in which I and GSAE colleagues have worked together. When I was working on the paper 'Working in a New University: In the Shadow of the RAE?' (Sikes, 2006) I did ask colleagues to read, offer critical comment and, if it was felt to be appropriate, veto submission and, ultimately publication.[7] This was different from other writing I had been involved in as part of the project, in that it was written solely by myself and took an essentially outsider perspective. In the event, the changes that were made were minor and concerned some factual inaccuracies. I shall, obviously, have to put the present piece up for the same sort of scrutiny.

Writing is, of course, dissemination, thus this too has been on-going throughout the life of the project. Much dissemination has been 'inside', in that it has been communication between colleagues within the GSAE and between them and me. I mentioned that my visit to the Australasian university came about because of word of mouth. Staff from that institution heard about me when a colleague from the GSAE, whilst at a conference dealing with her specialist area, spoke about what we were doing at New. This highlights the way in which dissemination happens by informal as well as formal means and cannot, therefore, be controlled. This can be a particularly difficult issue in those cases where insider research does deal with sensitive matters because, even with assurances of confidentiality and anonymity, word can sometimes be spread.

Finally

By virtue of the particular insider-outsider position from which I have been writing, this chapter has offered a slightly different take on insider research than have some of the others. All social research is complex and each instance reflects a unique set of circumstances, as well as involving the perceptions and realities of however many individuals are involved. In writing about research I have long been convinced of the importance of telling it as it was, whilst acknowledging that, ultimately, the version of reality that is recounted will usually be that of the person doing the writing. Omitting to one's own work, interpretations, words and representations is, in my opinion, an ethical and a moral failing. And yet, distance and 'objectivity' continue, in some places, to have currency as standards towards which researchers should strive. Having said this, I do not wish for one moment to appear to be suggesting that researchers should not seek to be principled and rigorous. However, as Egon Guba and Yvonna Lincoln remind us (2005, p. 206), there are different variants of research rigour and maybe insider researchers need to think carefully about what rigorous practice means in their situations and settings. It is unlikely to be sufficient or appropriate simply to adopt conventional approaches. I'm in agreement with Norman Denzin and Yvonna Lincoln when they say, 'objective reality can never be captured. We know a thing only through its representations' (2005, p. 5). Insider research highlights this in that every participant in a situation is likely to make their own particular representation. Thus, whilst staff at New University will, on reading this chapter, know it is their/our institution I am writing about, their account of what has been happening would be different coming, as it would, from their unique perspective and experience base. That this is a truism does not make it any less worth saying, particularly when it is a truism that will apply to any account of insider research. My insider-outsider positioning at New University was and is special and it has allowed me both to experience and to tell a very particular story. But then, isn't that always the case.

Notes

1. Despite its name, the main work of the School is providing professional training and certification for lecturers in institutions of Further Education, accrediting Teaching Assistants and running continuing professional development courses of various kinds in schools, colleges and local education authorities. The School also runs a modular masters degree programme, but many of the modules are taken as one offs.
2. In the UK, 'post-1992' universities are those establishments of higher education which, following legislation in 1992, changed their designation, usually from polytechnic or college to 'university'. They are also sometimes referred to as 'new' universities.

3. The RAE is the process by which all UK university departments have been assessed in terms of their research excellence. Each department receives a grade based on quality of staff members' publications, funding from prestigious research bodies and other esteem indicators. Top-rated departments receive monies from the Higher Education Funding Council and are more likely to attract high quality staff and students. The USA, Australia, Hong Kong and New Zealand have their equivalents (Greenwood and Levin, 2005; Middleton 2005; Rogers, 2005).

4. *Mis en abyme* is the effect created by artists who represent a scene in a room containing a mirror, in which the scene in the room is reflected in the mirror, in which the scene in the room is reflected ... *ad infinitum.*

5. Pseudonyms have been used.

6. I am not going to give references for or substantive details about any of the publications that have arisen out of this work because that would enable New University to be identified.

7. The editor of the journal to which the paper was submitted sent it to two reviewers, one of whom was X. Blenkinsop, a member of staff at New. On receipt, X replied that s/he was unable to comment because, although the author's name had been removed, s/he knew them and, furthermore, worked in the institution and was involved in the research the paper described. The editor, knowing where I worked but not the identity of New, responded that X must be mistaken but sent the paper to another reviewer. X told me about this and we had a laugh about the coincidence. A week later I had a social email from Anthony Potts, my friend and the co-editor of this volume, in which he commented that he had just reviewed a paper describing some 'poor buggers' in a new university who had extremely heavy teaching loads and the requirements of the RAE to contend with too. I replied that I thought he must have reviewed my paper. Tony said that he hadn't recognised it as my work but when I sent him a copy he acknowledged that it was indeed one and the same piece. This little story in itself tells us something about insider-outsider positioning with regard to the international academic community.

References

Apple, M. (Ed) (1996) *Cultural Politics and Education.* New York, Teachers' College Press.

Behar, R. (1993) *Translated Woman: Crossing the Border With Esperanza's Story.* Boston, Beacon.

Bourgois, P. (2002) 'Ethnographers Trouble the Reproduction of Academic Habitus', *International Journal of Qualitative Studies in Education,* 15, 4, pp. 417–420.

Coffey, A. (1999) *The Ethnographic Self: Fieldwork and the Representation Of Identity.* London, Sage.

Deleuze, G. (1993) *The Fold: Leibniz and the Baroque.* London, Athlone.

Deleuze, G. and Guattari, F. (1988) *A Thousand Plateaus.* London, Athlone.

Denzin, N. and Lincoln, Y. (2005) 'Introduction: The Discipline and Practice of Qualitative research', in Denzin, N. and Lincoln, Y. (eds) (2005) *The Sage Handbook of Qualitative Research.* 3rd ed. Thousand Oaks, Sage, pp. 1–32.

Ellis, C. (2004) *The Ethnographic!: A Methodological Novel About Autoethnography.* Walnut Creek, AltaMira.

Foley, D. and Valenzuela, A. (2005) 'Critical Ethnography: The Politics of Collaboration', in Denzin, N. and Lincoln, Y. (eds) *The Handbook of Qualitative Research:* 3rd ed. Thousand Oaks, Sage, pp. 217–234.

Goodson, I. and Sikes, P. (2001) *Life History Research in Educational Settings: Learning From Lives.* Buckingham, Open University Press

Greenwood, D. and Levin, M. (2005) 'Reform of the Social Sciences and Universities though Action Research', in Denzin, N. and Lincoln, Y. (eds) *The Handbook of Qualitative Research*: 3rd ed. Thousand Oaks, Sage, pp. 43–64.

Guba, E. and Lincoln, Y. (2005) 'Paradigmatic Controversies, Contradictions and Emerging confluences', in Denzin, N. and Lincoln, Y. (eds) *The Handbook of Qualitative Research*: 3rd ed. Thousand Oaks, Sage, pp. 191–215.

Hartley, S. (2002) 'The impact of research selectivity on academic work and identity in UK Universities', *Studies in Higher Education*, 27, 2, pp. 187–205.

Lee, A. and Boud, D. (2003) 'Writing Groups, Change and Academic Identity: Research development as Local Practice', *Studies in Higher Education*, 28, 2, pp. 187–200.

MacCall, G. (2006) 'The Fieldwork tradition', in Hobbs, D. and Wright, R. (eds) *The Sage Handbook of Fieldwork*. London, Sage, pp. 3–21.

Maynard, M. (1993) 'Feminism and the possibilities of a postmodern research practice', *British Journal of Sociology of Education*, 14, 3, pp. 327–331.

Middleton, S. (2005) 'Disciplining the Subject: The Impact of the PBRF on Education Academics'. Paper presented at BERA Conference, Glamorgan, September.

Mills, C.W. (1959) *The Sociological Imagination*. Penguin, Harmondsworth.

Morley, L. (2003) *Quality and Power in Higher Education*. Maidenhead, Open University Press and SRHE.

Oakley, A. (1979) *From Here to Maternity: Becoming a Mother*. Penguin, Harmondsworth.

Oakley, A. (1981) 'Interviewing Women: A Contradiction in Terms', in Roberts, H. (ed) *Doing Feminist Research*. London, Routledge, pp. 30–61.

Richardson, L. (1997) *Fields of Play: Constructing an Academic Life*. New Brunswick, Ruttgers University Press.

Richardson, L. (2000) 'Writing: A Method of Inquiry', in Denzin, N. and Lincoln, Y. (eds) *The Handbook of Qualitative Research*, 2nd Ed. Thousand Oaks, Sage, pp. 923–948.

Rogers, A. (2005) 'Colleagues Down Under'. *autLOOK*, January, 233, p. 8.

Schon, D. (1983) *The Reflective Practitioner*. London, Temple Smith.

Sikes, P. (1997) *Parents Who Teach: Stories From Home and From School*. London, Cassell.

Sikes, P. (2002) 'Strengthening the Research Base in the GSAE: A Reflexive, Action Approach'. Unpublished Paper.

Sikes, P. (2006) 'Working in a New University: In the Shadow of the RAE?', *Studies in Higher Education*, 31, 5, 555–568.

Stronach, I. and MacLure, M. (1997) *Educational Research Undone: The Postmodern Embrace*. Buckingham, Open University Press.

Walker, M. and Unterhalter, E. (2004) 'Knowledge, Narrative Work and National Reconciliation: Storied Reflections On the South African Truth and Reconciliation Commission', *Discourse*, 25, 2, pp. 279–297.

Wolcott, H. (2002) *Sneaky Kid and its Aftermath*. Walnut Creek, AltaMira.

Chapter 11

Researching academic staff

The case of colleges and new universities

Anthony Potts

Introduction

This chapter examines the research that appeared in my book *College Academics* (1997*)*. The book is an insider study from two perspectives: that of an academic studying other academics and of an academic studying the institution that he worked in. The chapter also makes reference to my ongoing insider research, tentatively called *Beyond the Ivy League*, and to my book, *Civic Leaders and the University* (2003).

College Academics, Beyond the Ivy League, Civic Leaders and the University

College Academics is a study of the occupational socialisation of academic staff at an Australian college of advanced education. It examines how staff learnt the skills, attitudes and values that helped them adapt to their occupational world. *College Academics* utilises socialisation theory from the Chicago School of symbolic interactionism. The research methods used were participant observation, interviewing and document analysis. *Beyond the Ivy League* is a current study of academic staff in new universities. *Civic Leaders and the University* examined Australian politicians' perspectives on universities.

Entering the field

Access

College Academics was prompted by the comments of Clark (Halsey, 1992) that academics study everything but themselves and that, consequently, little is known about the academic profession. The research site for *College Academics* was partly chosen because of time and other limitations. *Beyond the Ivy League* originated with a comment by Gary Rhoades, editor of *Higher Education*, that 20 years after the research on which it was based was conducted, *College Academics* should be revisited and updated. A stimulus for the study was to test Gary's notions and my opposing ones on academic career choice in new universities.

Civic Leaders and the University was prompted by the alleged disparity between what universities and their immediate local communities respectively desired from each other.

My experiences of gaining access to the research sites for the three studies illustrate changing research and institutional climates. For all studies, being a member of the institution and occupational group investigated was no guarantee of access. I needed to obtain the co-operation of as many groups as possible within the institutions, and not offend or neglect or become identified with any particular one in order to maximise my chances of gaining full co-operation (Kahn and Mann, 1952, p. 5).

The original research proposal for *College Academics* was initially discussed with the Acting Director of my institution, who gave it his full support. However, more importantly the research had to gain the approval and acceptance of the academic staff members who were to be the respondents in the study. The issues confronted were well stated by Kahn and Mann (1952, p. 7), who noted:

> It is not enough ... to use the ready-made authority structure, and to try and gain acceptance with those at the lower levels by having those at the top of the organisation communicate the purpose of the study to the rest of the structure.

Overt support from the Acting Director for my research would have undermined its acceptance by academic staff who may have viewed it as part of the administration and, consequently, treated it with suspicion.

Acceptance of the research for *College Academics* was fostered in a number of ways. First, my institution's study leave committee, which approved the research, had as one of its members the president of the academic staff association. The fact that he supported the proposed research helped to give it legitimacy in the eyes of others. Furthermore, I was a member of an institutional committee concerned with staff evaluation (a more threatening subject) and had good relations with people which, again, helped foster positive attitudes towards the research. The majority of staff selected for interview were generally interested in the research and continually inquired as to its progress and this interest was used to keep access to staff open. I was particularly careful to stress that the project was independent of the institution's administration and was chiefly concerned with academic staff perspectives. The latter was especially important in gaining access to respondents.

Advantage was taken of the fact that my college and its staff had been the subject of research by other researchers. It was reasoned that, because staff had been respondents in these investigations, my task in gaining access was easier than it might otherwise have been. With hindsight, whether this was the case is debatable.

It was necessary to gain unfettered access to the institutions being studied and their staff in order to obtain 'honest' and comprehensive information on the perspectives of the academic staff. It also meant it was more likely that relevant research findings could be used to effect improvements in the institutions (Kahn and Mann, 1952, p. 8).

The research proposals for *Civic Leaders and the University* and *Beyond the Ivy League* came up against the changes effected by the establishment of human research ethics committees in Australian universities, new government privacy laws and changes in institutional climate at the university where I was employed. Research proposals for each project had to be approved by the human ethics committee in my own and the other institution I proposed to study. Persons to be interviewed had to give informed consent. These processes caused considerable problems, stresses and delays. Long gone were the days that marked the research for *College Academics* when unfettered access to my institution and its staff was easily obtained.

That proposals for both studies were rigorously scrutinised and that informed consent had to be obtained resulted in great difficulty obtaining academic staff and politicians prepared to be interviewed. Furthermore, it was exceedingly difficult to access information at my own institution. Requests for information often went unanswered. Because large amounts of planning and finance have been expended in making universities competitive they are reluctant to divulge information and are certainly anxious not to publicise areas of underperformance (Anderson, Johnson and Milligan, 1999, p. 27).

The research approval processes contributed to me ending up with half of the academic staff (and even less the number of politicians) I initially intended to interview and with a sample, which bore little resemblance to the one originally planned. It may also have been the case that academics are so busy now that they have little time to be the respondents in research. Furthermore, academic life is so ruthless and competitive (Brett, 2000, pp. 144–155) that academics may simply be less likely to assist colleagues, even those they work with and know.

Ethical issues

College Academics occurred before the advent of university human research ethics committees. Almost anything could have been done at the time, even though this wasn't the case, and ethical considerations were given proper consideration. As a researcher from the inside ethical issues were faced in terms of my loyalties both as a researcher and as a member of the institution and group studied. Academic staff volunteered information to me that they would not have offered to outsider researchers. The opposite also occurred where some academics were reluctant to divulge information in spite of the fact that they had previously discussed such information with me as a friend and colleague.

No covert research was attempted for *College Academics*. With new institutional regulations covert-type research would never have been approved for *Beyond the Ivy League*. The academics studied for *College Academics* were told of the nature of the research and what it entailed. All respondents understood that each non-schedule standardised interview would be tape-recorded, transcribed and would possibly be quoted verbatim. They were informed that interview material would be used, along with document analysis, in the writing up of the research. Academics were also warned that, while anonymity and confidentiality would be offered, this would not necessarily mean that others could not accurately guess their identities.

Academic staff were informed that their permission to participate for the particular specified research ends would not be assumed to imply permission for something different. I also discussed how the findings were likely to be used. This made it even more important to ensure the validity of the research. When considering the ethical issues associated with the research for *College Academics*, I was particularly conscious of what Adelman, Jenkins and Kemmis (1976, p. 144) referred to as a research contract, which was often called a 'victims' charter. This particular phrase had the effect of making me afford due respect to those without whom my research would be impossible.

Being in and leaving the field

Participant observation

Participant observation meant the adoption of the perspectives of the academic staff researched 'by sharing their day-to-day experiences' (Denzin, 1978, p. 182). I attempted to capture their lives through their symbolic world. The use of participant observation was appropriate for the studies because it involved:

> A commitment ... to basic principles of symbolic interactionism and to the naturalistic method [because] to scientifically comprehend the world of interacting individuals, [researchers] must adopt the perspective of those studied – thereby avoiding the fallacy of objectivism
>
> (Denzin, 1978, p. 173).

For *College Academics*, according to Denzin's typology (1978, pp. 186–190), my role was the participant as an observer since my identity was publicly known. Interviews, document analysis, direct observation, participation, the use of informants and introspection were all utilised. In using participant observation for *College Academics* Denzin's (1978: 202), eight steps were used as a guide. Consequently:

1. I decided to investigate the occupational socialisation of academic staff using symbolic interactionist theory. The literature review provided key concepts such as perspectives and commitment.
2. I decided to research my own institutional colleagues.
3. Institutional permission to undertake the study was granted by the Acting Director of the college. Respondents were selected by a stratified random sample with proportional representation based upon the departmental size.

They were contacted by a letter seeking permission to interview them. Observations and document analysis commenced.

4. The college and its academic staff were located in their historical contexts. Key concepts such as perspectives and commitment were further refined.

5. Interviewing commenced. Interviews were transcribed, read, checked and annotated. Early theories, for example, on occupational choice and occupational socialisation were proposed. Negative instances of phenomena were sought.

6. More general categories were developed such as 'Getting the job and on the job perspectives'.

7. Interview data, observations and document analysis were brought together. For example, academics claimed in the interviews that they had unlimited freedom in their professional lives but the institutional record did not fully support this claim. Four key respondents were re-interviewed and confronted with this discrepancy. Responses were compared across the four faculties.

8. Writing up of the results commenced. However, observations and review of the literature continued.

The research for *College Academics* had, as its core, non-schedule standardised interviews with academic staff of the rank of a lecturer and above. That is, each respondent was asked the same questions but not necessarily in the same order. Sixty people were approached out of a total of 120 full-time tenured academic staff at the college. Fifty-three consented to participate in the study. While this manner of selecting respondents was somewhat unusual in qualitative research, it found support in the work of Hammersley (1985, p. 253). The sample offered the prospect of greater generalisation of the findings across the institution as a whole. While staff selected for the research were chosen from the respective Faculties of Arts, Science, Business and Education, the book omits reference to academics in the Faculty of Education. Overwhelmed with data at the time, in an act of desperation the School of Education was omitted. Consequently, *College Academics* has as its centrepiece interviews with thirty-three academic staff only. In retrospect, it is a pity that these School of Education Staff were not included. However, they feature in other publications.

Coupled with the above interviews, nonstandardised interviews were conducted with these thirty-three academic staff, plus other academic, administrative and support staff. Generally, anyone who was willing to talk about the research was interviewed. These interviews supplemented the non-schedule standardised interviews and extended the information available in them. Key academic staff, that is key respondents in each of the faculties of the college and in key departments of the college's administration, also assisted in providing information and insights. They did this by confirming and extending what the randomly selected academic staff had discussed in their interviews.

Interviewing was supplemented with analysis of college minutes, reports, newsletters, and theses concerned with the college, student publications and the local city newspaper. Where possible, written documents were used to check the accuracy of interviews and to open up further lines of investigation. Documents covering crucial time periods were more intensively consulted compared to less important time periods.

In the course of the research, interaction with academics in the Faculties of Arts, Business and Education, respectively, occurred at a deeper level than it did for those in the Faculty of Science. Informal interaction was mainly with academics in the Faculty of Arts and the Faculty of Education. This was largely because I already knew people in certain areas better than in others. At one stage I had lectured in both the Faculty of Education and the Faculty of Arts. However, there was frequent interaction and contact with key informants in the Faculty of Business and with key administrative staff.

The study took eight years in all. It should have been completed earlier, but the lengthy period avoided the problem of 'blitzkrieg ethnography' (Rist, 1980). The time period allowed longitudinal observation of academics and this assisted in exploring their perspectives. Being on site for such a period of time, it was easy for academics' perspectives to be scrutinised. It is doubtful if respondents could have continuously presented a false self for such a period. Academic staff never knew exactly when I would appear to pursue further items of interest. However, being continuously on site did pose difficulties, such as never being able to completely withdraw from the research setting. The problem of leaving the field was made more acute because I could not leave the field in the normal sense. Furthermore, there was always something else to read, someone else to talk to, one more piece of evidence to examine. If I had not been researching from the inside, these difficulties would have been more easily dealt with as exiting the site would have meant they were left behind.

Interviewing

Interviewing was appropriate because it was obviously impossible to observe everything (Patton, 1980, p. 198). Non-scheduled standardised and nonstandardised interviews were used. Each of the randomly selected academic staff for both studies and all the local politicians participated in a non-schedule standardised interview and some also participated in a nonstandardised interview. Key informants were given a nonstandardised interview. Structured or non-schedule standardised interviewing, which was conducted after rapport with respondents, had been firmly established and insight into the meaning and context of questions had been achieved, allowing for a high degree of reliability and validity (Hansen, 1979, p. 55).

The non-schedule standardised interview allowed (Denzin, 1978. p. 115):

1. the meanings of the questions asked to be standardised because questions were phrased in terms that could be understood by respondents.
2. me to approach respondents' worlds from their perspective, acknowledging that they defined their worlds in unique ways.

3. for the fact that no fixed series of questions would be satisfactory for all
    interviewed. Some raised issues of importance, which were not in the inter-
    view schedule or covered a number of issues all at once.

The non-schedule standardised interview took into account the criticisms of
researchers such as Cicourel (Hansen, 1979, p. 54), who argue that the supposedly
increased reliability of the schedule standardised interview is spurious, because
the person being questioned may not interpret the questions the way the interviewer intended. The nonstandardised interview, 'a mainstay of participant observation' (Patton, 1980, p. 203), was used in exploring respondents' perspectives
through the use of key informants. These interviews enabled me to crosscheck
and extend information provided in the non-schedule standardised interviews
undertaken with the random sample of academics and politicians.

In the studies on academics especially, interviewing and participant observation
were used as dual methods because:

> A good interviewer is by necessity also a participant observer. That is, the
> interviewer is participating in the life experience of a given respondent and
> is observing that person's report of himself, or herself, during the interview-
> conversation
>
> (Denzin, 1978, p. 129).

As well as theoretical reasons for using interviews in the research for *College
Academics*, there were also practical ones. In the planning stages of the fieldwork
a number of staff at the college expressed the opinion that they hoped there would
be no questionnaires to complete, as they would be most reluctant to do so.
Having recently completed questionnaires for research centred on the college
they doubted their value. These academics, however, stated that they were happy
to be interviewed. Support for interviewing as a method was provided by
Hamalian (1975, p. 102) who found that academics willingly participated in long
discussions and were pleasant subjects for open-ended interview-type research,
whilst being reluctant to fill in questionnaires.

In the interviews for the three studies being discussed here, a crucial issue was
how did I know if academics and politicians interviewed were truthful (Dean and
Whyte, 1958)? Accordingly, I considered issues which could have influenced academics' and politicians' reporting of their situations. Were there any ulterior
motives which influenced their perspectives, did some issues prohibit them freely
talking, did some of them wish to please me or did some other idiosyncratic factors influence their responses (Dean and Whyte, 1958, p. 36)? For example, at the
time of the research for *College Academics*, engineering staff felt vulnerable over
the security of their employment. This may have influenced their responses.
Rather than ignore this as a source of influence, I discussed it with staff.

In addition, another academic interviewed for *College Academics* was the subject
of college disciplinary procedures and a state government ombudsman's report.

This person raised the issue, brandishing a copy of the report in front of me during an interview. I then discussed with this academic himself and with others how this report might have influenced their responses.

Sources of distortion had to be accounted for if they were not to seriously affect the credibility of information obtained in the interviews conducted for all three studies (Dean and Whyte, 1958, pp. 35–36). One technique I used, in addition to observation, document analysis and cross-checking of academics' replies, was to keep index cards for each person interviewed. These contained biographical details and notes on the conduct, mood and tone of the interview. These cards, for example, showed that one man interviewed for *College Academics* had experienced a severe altercation with his dean of faculty immediately prior to his interview. Sensing this had influenced his responses, I discussed whether it had in fact done so – but at a time and place suitably distanced from the first interview! Academics' teaching hours were easily verified by printed timetables on their office doors. Their research, publications and conference attendances could be easily checked in official college publications. Because staff were aware of this and of my position in the college, they would have been more inclined to present accurate information.

Possible further sources of distortion in firsthand reports of academics and politicians were also considered. The reliability of the 'informants' mental set' and how it might have influenced the perception and interpretation of events (Dean and Whyte, 1958, p. 37) was considered. This was achieved by comparing the accounts given by various academics and politicians and comparing verbal and written accounts of events where possible (Dean and Whyte, 1958, p. 37). Where discrepancies occurred, academics were re-interviewed and asked for further clarification. When the discrepancy was common, as it was in one case, a key informant in each of the four faculties was re-interviewed at length. This particular case centred on the fact that every academic interviewed reported that they had almost unlimited freedom in their role at the college. However, the written record conflicted with this assertion. Consequently, four key academic staff were re-interviewed and confronted with the discrepancy. They produced what they believed were even better examples of academic staff members' freedom at the college.

In assessing the validity of the interviews in the research for *College Academics* and *Beyond the Ivy League*, four issues were considered, namely: my role as researcher, the relationship between me and the academics I was researching, the situation and, finally, the act of observation (Denzin, 1978). To what extent did my position as an academic researching my colleagues in the same institution we both were employed at affect the validity of my findings? To what extent did my own perspectives on teaching and research and other key areas of academic life and work affect the framing of questions asked of my fellows? To what extent did the relationship between me and my fellow academics influence the validity of the findings? Did this vary between those academics selected as part of the random sample of those interviewed and those who were key informants, between academic staff whom I knew well and those less well known to me, between those higher and lower in academic rank to me? Also considered was whether those in more frequent contact with me provided more valid data than those in less frequent contact.

Also considered was the possibility that interviewees changed their beliefs and even developed new ones simply because they were interviewed (Denzin, 1978, p. 127). Did those interviewed provide me with what they thought I wished to hear? Alternatively, did I convey to the academics and politicians I interviewed what I wished them to reply to my questions (Denzin, 1978, p. 128).

Interviews in all three studies ranged from 45 minutes to over three hours. Most averaged one hour. Interviews were conducted in academics' or politicians' offices, my office, academics' or politicians' homes or venues, such as the city council chambers. During the interview, participant observation was often possible. Some academics brought to the interview extensive samples of their college work in the form of photographs and slides. Academics' and politicians' homes and offices also displayed many of the things that they mentioned in interviews, such as art and book collections, work-related antiques, awards, testamurs and certificates. In the case of academics, contact with students could also be ascertained. Indeed, one academic stated that he spent no time giving individual assistance to students. However, during the interview he was interrupted by six different students and gave each of them extensive assistance. This disparity was explored in the interview.

All non-schedule standardised interviews for all three studies were transcribed. Academics and politicians were offered the opportunity to read the transcripts. Only one academic took advantage of the opportunity. He noted that on reading the transcript, he sounded very negative. Another requested a copy of his interview tape to keep.

Going native or being native to begin with

That the research for all three studies was undertaken by me as a member of the same occupational group (in the case of two of the studies) and the same institution as those being studied would be seen as a flaw by some. When *College Academics* was in its planning stages, one academic wrote a strident letter to me warning of the utter folly of such research and urging me to abandon it! However, I was aware of the more measured concerns expressed about researching from the inside. Consequently, the difficulties in studying my own group and institution were noted, but I believed that they could be overcome and be overshadowed by the benefits that would accrue.

Researching from the inside allowed me to quickly isolate key informers, who discussed private knowledge with me because they saw me as personally and equally involved in their world. I knew the language of these academics and their institution with its particular jargon and localised meanings, and I had empathy with them and their organisation. Thus subjectivism and personal involvement, rather than being seen as particular methodological problems, were used to further my understanding of the academics researched and their institutional contexts.

For *College Academics* especially, it was easy to locate information that outside researchers would have had difficulty finding and that the institution may have preferred remained hidden. Coupled with this, the staff researched for *College Academics* were easily and almost continuously accessible. Those willing to participate in the research could be observed over a very long period. It was easy to crosscheck interview material with other sources of data and more difficult for respondents to omit data or to present inaccurate information because there was a greater possibility that I, as one of them, would discover such omissions. What was surprising was the extremely personal and sensitive material that academics offered to me as a researcher. For example, one elaborated how he had been suspended over an incident involving a female student at another institution and how this incident ultimately meant him coming to the college. Not many of the staff seemed nervous about being interviewed, with the possible exception being female staff, who had some concern that, being so few in number, they could be easily identified in any published study.

While undertaking the research for the *College Academics*, I was never denied material by anyone in authority at the college and did not experience any difficulty gaining access to sources. Researching from the inside also meant that I found material that outside researchers might never have. For example, material in the archives concerning staffing issues that outside researchers would have been denied access to, was available to me. Much of it I did not directly use as it was confidential but it provided a useful perspective for interpreting other data.

My unrestricted access was due to my research identity as a 'lone wolf researcher' (Punch, 1994, p. 87). Not externally funded I melted away into the field, in contrast to the 'hired hand' that would be highly visible, tied to contractual obligations and expected to deliver a report in a certain time frame (Punch, 1994, p. 87). But it was not all incident free. Two incidents that occurred during the research for *College Academics* remain in my mind.

The first concerns an unpleasant altercation that I had with one academic that I wanted to interview. After his repeated failure to keep appointments I accidentally met him on campus and politely asked what had happened. He launched into an attack on me, noting how he did not want anything to do with my research. Recoiling from his verbal onslaught and realising that he had the potential to do my project much harm, an apology for any misunderstanding was quickly despatched. I later learnt that he had lodged a complaint about me with his head of department. Fortunately, this person had been interviewed and tried to pacify him. Here my status researching from the inside was a disadvantage. If an external researcher, perhaps I would not have been as upset by this incident.

The second incident is a warning to those researching from the inside that their past investigations may haunt them. Interviewing a very helpful academic, I asked whether there were any particular disappointments in his career. He replied that there were two major ones. The first was the lack of promotion opportunities and the second was that a motion of no confidence had been moved in him when he was president of the academic staff association. He added 'and you would remember that well'. I did when he mentioned it, as I had been the person who seconded the motion. I have never felt so embarrassed in my life. I was amazed at his Christian powers of forgiveness, as I appeared to have had excellent relations with him after the incident, but at the time of the interview it unsettled me.

A small minority of academics interviewed for *College Academics* were rude and offensive. They made disparaging remarks about my colleagues and about educational research. The only thing to do here was to silently suffer. Once they had unburdened themselves of these ideas they were willing to be interviewed at length and were friendly and helpful.

My portrayal of these academics and their institutions was of course only one of a number that could be constructed. It is likely that matters of importance and taken-for-granted assumptions about these academics and where they worked were overlooked by me researching them from the inside. Furthermore, being a member of the occupational and institutional group being studied may have meant that I missed recording certain data or matters of significance because I too readily took certain things for granted. I did, however, attempt to remain sufficiently questioning of what I saw and heard so as to preserve the credibility of the research. Many at the institution studied for *College Academics* argued that I was too questioning and too critical. Their stance was not reflected when the research was finally published.

Writing, disseminating and reactions to the study

Writing

The writing of *College Academics* was hard work. I was constantly aware of someone who said that writing was easy – a person just sits at his or her desk and waits till they sweat blood out of their forehead! My own feelings of professional isolation did not assist for I had almost no one locally to talk to about the academic side of my work. However, this forced me to write. Endless discussions and tearoom debate with others may have helped or, alternatively, they may simply have become another form of avoidance behaviour substituting for the hard task of writing.

During the writing of *College Academics* I became particularly aware of Berger's (1963, p. 12) observation that normal academic life 'is a jungle of bitter warfare between faculty factions, none of which can be relied upon for an objective judgement of members of either his [sic] or an opposing group'. A number of things helped me to persevere. Most important of these was the reading of Punch's (1994) study on the politics of research. Within his account a number of instances in particular gave me determination to continue. Punch's (1994, p. 87) account of Whyte's trouble in publishing what turned out to be his classic 1943 book *Street Corner Society*, having it reviewed and seriously accepted and how its fluctuating sales have reflected the rise and fall of various fads and fashions of sociology, was especially motivating.

For *College Academics* there was a mass of transcript, archival and other field-note data. After sorting this into some sort of manageable structure a way of ordering it was found. After coding it the various questions and pieces of data were linked by means of a narrative story line. After this was done, a coherent and readable narrative emerged. This took many months of trying to piece all the data into some overall structure. Having done this I thought the hard part was over. I now at least had an account that hung together. How wrong I was.

The next phase was much more difficult. My descriptive account of these academics' lives had now to be explained in terms of a symbolic interactionist theoretical framework. Claims that *College Academics* is positivistic *and too readily uses prearranged categories* ignore the sheer agony of seeing if symbolic interactionism could in fact explain the narrative that had been constructed. It took many months before the narrative story and the theoretical framework coalesced into a unified whole. Finally, the overall outline of the book emerged, with chapters that focused on occupational choice, institutional and occupational socialisation, perspectives on teaching, research and commitment.

Disseminating the results and reactions to the study

Initially, papers out of the research data, which became *College Academics*, were given at a number of international conferences. These conference presentations encouraged me to proceed with turning my research data into a book. The support that I received at these international meetings from supportive and friendly peers was crucial in my decision.

Reviews of *College Academics* exceeded expectations. Favourable reviews were written by Stortz (1998), Davies (1998), Tight (1999) and Burns (1999). Burns (2000) in a follow-up email for example, commented further:

> I thought it was a fascinating study, the more appreciated because you weren't trying to be theoretically smart-arse and trendy but rather to apply appropriate theory/methodology (symbolic interactionism). In fact, I found it so interesting I quoted your major findings in my valedictory seminar at Bundoora in Dec. 1998 and am strongly recommending it as an exemplary study to a doctoral student I'm supervising at Deakin who is looking at how to change the culture of engineering education in Australia.

It was realised that the publication of *College Academics* could cause me problems. While I had open access for the research, key college personnel had severely reprimanded one staff member for making unauthorised claims about the college in the press. Ultimately, the state government ombudsman became involved in the case and the staff member was demoted. When writing *Civic Leaders and the University*, all staff of my institution were told by email not to refer publicly to a certain report that the institution had commissioned. One staff member wrote a scathing critique of the same report – but this too was for restricted circulation only.

While carrying out the research for *Beyond the Ivy League*, all staff were informed by email to have nothing to do with one of our colleagues who had been expelled from the campus following alleged financial irregularities. Staff were ignorant of what was happening till the matter was reported in the local media. Similarly, while undertaking the research for *Beyond the Ivy League*, all staff were instructed by the chief executive officer of the campus I worked on to remove a particular picture from the university's annual calendar following a complaint that it featured offensive material.

Perhaps, unsurprisingly then, self-censorship did occur in *College Academics* and *Civic Leaders and the University*. For example, the Director of the college had conducted a strong and partially successful campaign to preserve college engineering courses in the face of government attempts to close them. It was suggested by me to the college's resident cartoonist (a graphic artist who worked in the media department of the college and who also drew cartoons for the city newspaper) that he draw a cartoon of the Director getting off a plane waving his umbrella and in the other hand a piece of paper and proclaiming 'Engineering in Our Time'. The cartoonist somewhat reluctantly drew the said cartoon and submitted it to the college newsletter, which the Director edited. The cartoon never appeared and was never seen again. Initially it was planned to use this in *College Academics* as an example of how the institutional view was carefully controlled by key personnel in the college. Discussion of this with a number of college staff drew varied reactions, ranging from amusement to outrage. An academic friend and mentor at another university wrote, my plan to include the example showed a complete lack of objectivity and suggested that in no case should this example be included. Ultimately, the example was omitted. In hindsight it should have been included. It was a good example of my original point and looking back I was over cautious.

At the same time as *College Academics* was published an outside writer (Wallace, 1997) was commissioned to produce a corporate history of the institution I worked in. The author and others informed me that the final version was heavily censored with contentious issues omitted. My initial suspicions were confirmed. *College Academics* had the potential to make my life difficult. Lest it be thought that these kinds of pressures only apply at 'ordinary institutions', notice should be taken of Roberts' (1998, p. 101) account of his taking up the Vice Chancellorship at Southampton University in the United Kingdom. On arrival he went to the official history of the university for information, but noted that it became bland and uninformative the closer it got to the present time. More interestingly, he found in an interleaved version, in a locked drawer in the vice-chancellor's office, passages interpolated by the author on more recent events, which he considered too risky to commit to the printed page (Roberts, 1998, p. 101).

College Academics did cause me some tense moments where I worked. During a staff seminar, one of the staff who had been interviewed for the book came up to me and said in an aggressive manner 'I expect you are making large amounts from your book. How about giving royalties to those that you interviewed?'

He continued 'You would never get ethics permission to do such a study now'. He was quite agitated and I tried to pacify him. I later discovered that he had allegedly identified himself in the book and did not like what he saw. Why I do not know. The supposed portrayal was in fact complimentary. In any event he must have realised that there was always a possibility that, even when disguised or not directly named, individuals might still be recognised. However, I did fear that he had the potential to make my life awkward.

Some staff commented that *College Academics* was too positive. These comments reflect the issue that Theobald (1977) noted when she asked how well does a book on an organisation capture its essence. *College Academics* was not a typical institutional history but the tone of the book was important. One of the people that made such comments was now a senior academic in another university. On re-reading my field notes and transcripts it became clear that he had enjoyed a very small teaching load and very favourable terms and conditions while employed at the college. However, his extremely ambitious character perhaps helps to explain his sense that my portrayal was overly generous. *College Academics* is not a particularly positive account. Much of its story is one of lost opportunities, lack of foresight, lack of motivation and application by some staff. Not all saw the story of the book as positive. For many it was a depressing tale.

Conclusion

Researching your own college or university and your own occupation may be an acquired taste. A researcher either likes, or comes to like the process, or does not. While some enjoy writing, many more report they enjoy having written. Researching your own college or university may well be like that. There are parts of the actual research and writing process which are rewarding and enjoyable, but the real satisfaction comes when the study is completed and published and favourable reviews appear.

Researchers who study their own college or university and occupation need to consider very carefully at the outset of their research a range of important issues, which can spell success or disaster for their endeavours. Even the most successful study of a college or university from the inside will not be without its problems, which can be very stressful indeed. Researchers who study their own college or university or occupation should carefully consider such issues as access to the institution and its staff, ethical issues (especially steering the project through university ethics committees and the role privacy regulations play in limiting information available), university or college ethos and disciplinary and national research cultures, the research methods and techniques used, being continually on site, withdrawal from the site, their role and history in the college or university (remembering that their past history in the institution may prove an aid or an impediment to their study), writing up the study and publicising the results. They should carefully consider the likely reactions from a range of audiences when the study is finally finished and is publicly available. Will they cope with the reactions of various groups and in particular from the college or university and its members to what they have written? The latter particularly applies if they are still working in the same institution they have written about. Importantly, will how they presume to cope affect the validity and reliability and overall credibility of what they write?

References

Adelman, C., Jenkins, D. and Kemmis, S. (1976) 'Rethinking case study: Notes from the Second Cambridge Conference'. *Cambridge Journal of Education*, 6, 3, pp. 139–150.

Anderson, D., Johnson, R. and Milligan, B. (1999) *Strategic Planning in Australian Universities*. Canberra, Department of Employment, Training and Youth Affairs.

Berger, P. (1963) *Invitation to Sociology*. Harmondsworth, Pelican.

Brett, J. (2000) 'Competition and Collegiality', in Coady, T. (ed) *Why Universities Matter*. Sydney, Allen and Unwin, pp. 144–155.

Burns, R. (1999) 'Review of College Academics'. *Comparative Education,* 35, 3, pp. 355–356.

Burns, R. (2000) Personal Communication.

Davies, R. (1998) 'Review of College Academics'. *History of Education Review*, 27, 2, pp. 70–71.

Dean, J. P. and Whyte, W. F. (1958) 'How do you know if the informant is telling the truth?' *Human Organization*, 17, 2, pp. 34–38.

Denzin, N. K. (1978) *The Research Act: A Theoretical Introduction to Sociological Methods*. New York, McGraw Hill.

Halsey, A. H. (1992) *Decline of Donnish Dominion: The British Academic Profession in the Twentieth Century*. Oxford, Clarendon Press.

Hamalian, A. (1975) 'The 'Good Professors': A subculture of professors in the United States and England'. *Higher Education Bulletin*, 4, 1, pp. 91–103.

Hammersley, M. (1985) 'From ethnography to theory: A programme and paradigm in the sociology of education'. *Sociology*, 19, 2, pp. 244–259.

Hansen, J. F. (1979) *Sociocultural Perspectives on Human Learning*. New Jersey, Prentice Hall.

Kahn, R. and Mann, F. (1952) 'Developing research partnerships'. *Journal of Social Issues*, 8, 3, pp. 4–40.

Patton, M. Q. (1980) *Qualitative Evaluation Methods*. London, Sage.

Potts, A. (2003) *Civic Leaders and the University — State and Municipal Politicians' Perspectives on Higher Education in Australia*. Bern, Peter Lang.

Potts, A. (1997) *College Academics*. Charlestown, William Michael Press.

Punch, M. (1994) 'Politics and ethics in qualitative research', in Denzin, N. K. and Lincoln, Y. S. (eds) *Handbook of Qualitative Research*. London, Sage, pp. 83–97.

Rist, R. (1980) 'Blitzkrieg ethnography'. *Educational Researcher*, 9, 2, pp. 8–10.

Roberts, J. M. (1998) 'Recollections of a pre-revolution'. *Oxford Review of Education*, 24, 1, pp. 99–110.

Stortz, P. (1998) 'New perspectives on the professoriate down under'. *CAUT ACPPN Bulletin*, 45, 8, October, p. 7.

Theobald, M. (1977) 'Problems in writing school histories', *Anzhes Journal*, 6, 1, Autumn, pp. 22–28.

Tight, M. (1999a) Personal communication.

Tight, M. (1999b) 'Review of: College Academics'. *Studies in Higher Education*, 24, 1, March, pp. 127–128.

Wallace, R. (1997) *Inkpots to Internet—Celebrating 125 Years of Tertiary Education in Bendigo*. Bendigo, La Trobe University, Bendigo and Bendigo Regional Institute of Tafe.

Section 5

Conclusion

Chapter 12

Closing thoughts

Pat Sikes and Anthony Potts

What have we got?

The preceding chapters have discussed instances of researching education from the inside. Most of the examples reported took a sociological or anthropological perspective and used a qualitative research methodology. Contributions covered insider educational research in the history of education, on schools and school systems, and on universities and institutions of higher education.

The various chapters well illustrate the changed and changing attitudes to insider research. While once its use was rarely contemplated, today the genre is widely employed, constituting almost an educational movement in its own right. We have moved a long way from the days when such research was looked upon with disdain.

In summary, what the contributors in this volume illustrate are some of the possibilities and potentialities that accompany insider research. Despite some pitfalls, which the contributors deal with frankly and sensitively, inside researchers readily know the language of those being studied along with its particular jargon and meanings, are more likely to empathise with those they study because of in-depth understanding of them, are less likely to foster distrust and hostility amongst those they study, are often more willing to discuss private knowledge with those who are personally part of their world, are often more likely to understand the events under investigation and are less likely to be afflicted by outsiders' arrogance where researchers fail to understand what they observe. Inside researchers find that those they study are often more likely to volunteer information to them than they would to outsiders.

While insider research provides clear advantages, it can simultaneously raise important ethical issues. Inside researchers may find that those under study forget the researcher and his or her role and engage in normal everyday behaviours. However, this then entails balancing the desire for rapport with an obligation to adequately protect those being studied privately. Inside researchers face ethical dilemmas in terms of their loyalties both as a researcher and as an insider of the organisation or group. For inside researchers, studying another person's world creates problems for them because they can come to think not as researchers but adopt the perspective of those they are studying. The inside researcher can end up over identifying with those under study and losing the ability to act as a researcher. Furthermore, insider researchers will soon discover that it is impossible to collect the perspectives of all those being studied and to empathise with all viewpoints or to produce a report which treats all equally.

Where are we now and what does it mean?

In the final chapter of the third edition of *The Sage Handbook of Qualitative Research*, the editors, Norman Denzin and Yvonna Lincoln, offer their thoughts on the current and future shape and state of social science research in general and of qualitative inquiry in particular (Denzin and Lincoln, 2005, pp. 1115–1126). A central theme running through all of the issues they touch on is that of power and an associated ethical awareness and responsibility backed up by legal and legislative mandate. For instance, they refer to methodological contestation and the conflicts and tensions between advocates of different paradigms about what research can do with regard to interpreting, re-presenting and making claims to tell truths about the social world. They point to the ways in which methodologies and methods are often associated with particular political and ethical positions and how these methodologies and methods can, consequently, be harnessed with a view to advancing particular political agenda. They talk about 'speaking truth to power' and, echoing C Wright Mills' (Mills, 1959), call for the 'reconnection of social science to social purpose' (Denzin and Lincoln, 2005, p. 1117). Referring specifically to the United States, but with international relevance, they discuss the 'decolonization of the academy' (Denzin and Lincoln, 2005, pp. 1121–1123) and the ways in which traditional hegemonies that have characterised academia, and which have legitimated both particular approaches to the getting and creation of knowledge and those knowledges themselves, have been challenged. They write that 'political battles that are normally fought in legislative circles, leaving the social scientists untouched and unmoved, have shifted directly into the arenas of educational, social and behavioural sciences' (Denzin and Lincoln, 2005, p. 1122). The establishment of human research ethics committees at the university level in the United Kingdom, America, Australia and Canada amply illustrates this point.

It seems to us that the various chapters that make up *Researching Education From The Inside: Investigations from Within* clearly exemplify and embody some of the ethical and power-related issues and concerns that Denzin and Lincoln raise and that, perhaps, inside insider research is acutely sensitive to and is affected by. However, having said this, our view is that, to some extent, all contemporary research is so influenced, whether or not all researchers recognise and acknowledge this to be the case. Our stance is that explicit recognition and acknowledgement is preferable to ignorance or even denial and that, consequently, would be inside researchers need to be unequivocally clear about just what it is they are getting into when they embark upon an insider project. Certainly for them, as it was for our contributors, power, politics and hard ethical choices will be there in some form and especially so, given that we are adopting a broad definition and are using 'political' to refer to all social relationships which involve interaction, whether between individuals or within groupings. On this view power and ethics inevitably come in to the frame because, in social settings, it is rare for all participants to be absolutely and totally equally positioned in terms of the personal, social and institutional power, authority and status they possess at any particular time. This was as true for Mark Vicars, who persuaded his friends to become his informants, as it was for Peter Dickson, who was an employee in the LEA that was the focus of his investigation. It is often said that knowledge, any knowledge, is power. Inside researchers inevitably accrue power through what they find out. This can make the other members of the group or institution within which the research is located vulnerable in some way or other and these members are often acutely aware that this is the case. Thus, ethical conduct becomes critical in order to protect all parties. And yet, to say this simplifies matters. Consider, for example, John Portelli's situation. When, in the course of his research, John found out that members of his department weren't doing their job properly, the research ethics code that he was working for demanded that he maintain confidentiality in order to protect informants. Doing so, however, meant that he could not easily and quickly protect the students who were being damaged by poor teaching. Similarly, Anthony Potts was so amazed at some of the material provided by his respondents, who were also work colleagues when he did his first study, that he omitted mention of it. Twenty years later he now talks about it.

So, inside insider research can challenge traditional and simplistic understandings of what constitutes research ethics. Rather than using 'off the peg' ethical codes of practice, inside researchers would do well to heed Richard Pring's caution that each research situation generates its own ethical questions and issues that demand their own, unique and contextual answers (Pring, 2000). Going beyond the concern with ethics we would say that inside researchers need to treat every aspect of their research as specific and, rather than following recipes and formula for doing research, they need to develop their own personal approaches. As all of our contributors have noted, inside researchers are well placed to do this. However, this aside, inside researchers will find that their research agendas and protocols are given rigorous assessment by university human research ethics committees and they may also find that, as an offshoot of this, the people they wish to study are so put off by what they learn about the proposed research that they do not become involved at all. This was what Anthony Potts believed happened in his more recent study of academic staff.

Inside insider research is potentially radical. It has the possibility of challenging taken for granted assumptions of all kinds, whether about the groups or institutions on which the insider gaze is turned, or with regard to understandings about what constitute 'proper' legitimate research. Insider research can be used to effect developmental change: it can make things better. Largely because of this potential it should not be embarked upon lightly, or be seen as a convenient solution to the problem of finding a space for research in an already overcrowded life.

Our contributors have shown some of the strengths and some of the weaknesses and we, and they, offer this book in the spirit of sharing experience.

References

Denzin, N. and Lincoln, Y. (2005) Epilogue: The Eighth and Ninth Moments–Qualitative Research in/and the Fractured Future, in Denzin, N. and Lincoln, Y. (eds) *The Sage Handbook of Qualitative Research*. Thousand Oaks, Sage, pp. 1115–1126.

Mills, C.W. (1959) *The Sociological Imagination*. New York, Oxford University Press.

Pring, R. (2000) *Philosophy of Educational Research*. London, Continuum.

Index

Page references followed by t indicate a table

time: concept of 29; management of
138-9, 149, 167
Tucker and Codding 70
Tyerman, C. 57-9
Tyler, S. 105

UK 178; gender and achievement 4-5;
growing popularity of insider
research 3-4; LEA, study of a
111-23; new universities, research
cultures 144-57; practitioner
research 1960s 24; professional
doctorate study 127-41; school
histories 53-5, 57-9; school
leadership programmes 73; school
leadership standards 66; university
histories 60-1
universities 24-5; academic
supervisors 40-1, 42-3; histories 9,
59-61, 171; leadership preparation
programmes 65-6, 71-1 see also
academic staff, researching;
professional doctorate, study;
universities, new
universities, new, research cultures
144-57; autoethnographic research
144, 150, 151, 153-6; collaboration
153, 155; entering the field 145-6;
group consultations 151-2; initial
encounters 146-7; mentoring of
individuals 152; questions 149;
reflexive action approach 147-56;
teaching research skills 153; writing
157-8 see also academic staff,
researching
University of Auckland 60
University of Bhutan, Royal 70
University of Calgary 70
University of Chicago 6

University of Keele 60
University of Liverpool 60
University of London, Institute of
Education 61
University of Malta 91
University of Newcastle upon Tyne 60
University of St. Francis Xavier, Nova
Scotia 70
University of Sheffield 60-1, 80, 84,
111, 122
University of Southampton 60, 171
University of Strathclyde 61
Unterhalter, E. 154
USA see North America

values 17-19, 37, 82-3, 120; value free
research 19, 20, 35, 82, 121
validity see credability
Vendler, Z. 29

Waitzkin, H. 16-17, 18
Walford, G. 135
Walker, M. 154
Walker, L. 55
Weber, M. 30
Wellington, J. J. 82
Whitehead, J. 25-6, 27
Whitehead and McNiff 25
Whitelaw, A. 52
Wolcott, H. F. 66-7
'Working in a New University: In the
Shadow of the RAE' 155, 157
world war 20
writing 75-7, 89; academic staff,
researching 163, 169-70, LEA
inspection study 121-2; new
universities study 155-6; perspective
of gay identity 104-6; time
management and 139